TROUBLED WATER

TROUBLED WATER

RACE, MUTINY, AND BRAVERY
ON THE USS *KITTY HAWK*

GREGORY A. FREEMAN

palgrave
macmillan

First published in 2009 by
PALGRAVE MACMILLAN™
175 Fifth Avenue, New York, N.Y. 10010 and Houndmills, Basingstoke,
Hampshire, England RG21 6XS. Companies and representatives throughout
the world.

PALGRAVE MACMILLAN is the global academic imprint of the Palgrave
Macmillan division of St. Martin's Press, LLC and of Palgrave Macmillan Ltd.
Macmillan® is a registered trademark in the United States, United Kingdom and
other countries. Palgrave is a registered trademark in the European Union and
other countries.

ISBN: 978-0-230-61361-4

Library of Congress Cataloging-in-Publication Data
Freeman, Gregory A.
    Troubled water : race, mutiny, and bravery on the USS Kitty Hawk / by
Gregory A. Freeman.
        p.   cm.
    Includes bibliographical references and index.
    ISBN 978-0-230-61361-4
    1. Kitty Hawk (Aircraft carrier)   2. African American sailors—History—
20th century   3. United States. Navy—African Americans—History—20th
century.   4. United States. Navy—Biography.   5. Mutiny—History—20th
century.   6. Race riots—History—20th century.   7. Vietnam War,
1961–1975—Naval operations, American.   8. United States—History, Naval—
20th century.   9. Race discrimination—United States—History—20th century.
10. United States—Race relations—History—20th century.   I. Title.
VA65.K5F74   2009
959.704'345—dc22

                                                              2009022970

A catalogue record of the book is available from the British Library.

Design by Letra Libre Inc.

First edition: September 2009
10   9   8   7   6   5   4   3   2   1
Printed in the United States of America.

*This book is dedicated to the thousands of
men and women who served on the
USS* Kitty Hawk *in her forty-seven years
of service to the United States.*

CONTENTS

Eight pages of photographs appear between pages 122 and 123.

ACKNOWLEDGMENTS

Thank you to everyone who contributed to this project by corresponding with and granting interviews to a writer who approached you out of the blue and asked you to share your stories, including memories that were sometimes difficult and painful to recount. In particular, I thank Marland Townsend, Ben Cloud, Robert Keel, John Travers, Perry Pettus, Terry Avinger, Tom Dysart, Chris Mason, Garland Young, G. Kirk Allen, and John Callahan. This book would not have been possible without your cooperation, and I trust you will find it is an honorable telling of an important event in your lives.

Drew Mosley was responsible for obtaining a key document in my research. Thank you for your assistance. I also thank the staff and research assistants at the Library of Congress and the National Archives.

Every writer needs a good agent, and I have the best in Mel Berger. Thank you for all you do, Mel. And every writer depends on an astute editor like Jake Klisivitch at Palgrave Macmillan to make his work the best it can be. Thank you, Jake.

I thank Caroline and Nicholas for making every day important to me.

AUTHOR'S NOTE

This is a work of nonfiction. All dialogue, thoughts, and emotions are based on either historical records or the subjects' statements to the author and others. See the notes section for further explanation of the origin of some material.

INTRODUCTION

An aircraft carrier at sea is about the size and population of a small city, it is often said, and the similarities go beyond just the numbers. These cities at sea can face some of the same difficulties as a community back home, and in 1972, the USS *Kitty Hawk* was going through the same social upheaval that was troubling the rest of America. Racial tensions were high, and disaffected young black men were struggling to get by in a society that claimed to welcome them with open arms but in fact regularly threw up roadblocks and then expressed shock that the men couldn't get around them. Those frustrated young men sometimes lashed out in ways that were ill-advised and ultimately counterproductive, often influenced by opportunists who used the cries of social injustice as a cover for crimes. Authority figures struggled to determine how much to negotiate and how much to respond with force.

In 1972, this was America, and in 1972, this was the *Kitty Hawk*.

The long-simmering racial tensions on board were prompted by some of the same everyday discrimination that black men faced back home, the occasional insult from a white sailor or officer, and the institutional procedures that, intentional or not, often thwarted the black sailors' efforts to move up in the ranks and succeed in the Navy. Add to that the unpopular war in Vietnam, economic difficulties back home that prompted many decidedly nonmilitary types to join the

Navy, and one of the longest deployments in the history of American warships, and this crew was ripe for trouble.

The *Kitty Hawk* was the first in a class of three supercarriers and the second Navy ship named after the North Carolina town where the Wright brothers flew their first airplane. Built by the New York Shipbuilding Corporation at Camden, New Jersey, the keel was laid on December 27, 1956, and the ship was commissioned on April 29, 1961. The 82,000-ton carrier departed her home port of San Diego on her first deployment in 1962 and continued to serve the United States until she was decommissioned in January 2009. In those forty-seven years, approximately 92,000 people served on the ship. The *Kitty Hawk* and a variety of Carrier Air Wings completed eighteen deployments in support of operations including Vietnam, the Iranian hostage crisis, Operation Restore Hope in Somalia, and air strikes against Iraq. The ship saw extensive action as a key player in Operation Linebacker, the bombing campaign against North Vietnam that began on May 10, 1972. During the five and a half months of that operation, Navy planes were responsible for more than 60 percent of the total sorties in North Vietnam. The July-to-September quarter was the most intense, with 12,865 naval sorties flown, about a quarter of them at night. In addition to the *Kitty Hawk,* the carriers *Constellation, Coral Sea, Hancock, Midway, Saratoga, Oriskany,* and *America* also participated in the operation. Three or four of the carriers were kept on Yankee Station, the strategic point off the coast of South Vietnam where Navy operations were based, throughout the offensive.

By any measure, the *Kitty Hawk* was a shining star in the U.S. Navy fleet throughout her storied career. But the ship also was the site of one of the most difficult moments in recent Navy history, a crisis that could have been far worse if not for the actions of the ship's two top officers—but also a crisis that might have been minimized if those officers had responded differently.

The *Kitty Hawk* hit troubled water during its long stay in Vietnam for Operation Linebacker. By October 1972, the Vietnam War had dragged on for seven years, and President Richard Nixon was counting on the bombing campaign to stall the advance of North Vietnamese forces and make possible an honorable U.S. exit from the war. Key to that bombing campaign was the *Kitty Hawk,* one of the world's most powerful aircraft carriers. She was among the most important and most highly visible parts of the American war effort. The carrier's deployment had been extraordinarily stressful to the crew from the very start, when she departed San Diego in February 1972, a week earlier than planned and with very little notice. They then went into a combat zone and had to perform at top speed and full capacity most of the time. The workload on a carrier is always heavy, but on this deployment, many of the *Kitty Hawk* crew worked cycles of eight hours on and four hours off, every day—for an astounding 247 days. Some men in the engineering department, one of the busiest, received only six days off during the entire cruise.

The sailors longed to go home, and they were repeatedly teased with the prospect of ending their tour and heading back to San Diego. Captain Marland Townsend, a highly respected and experienced Navy officer, was sympathetic but determined to carry out his orders. Several times the crew believed they were heading home, but then the plans were changed at the last minute. Each time this happened, the men became more restless and every tension was magnified. The stresses were especially difficult for some of the young black sailors, many of whom were recruited under a new Navy initiative designed to increase the ranks and open up more positions to men who might previously have been turned down. To do this, the Navy eased the requirements for test scores, intelligence, and criminal histories— a change that resulted in significantly more recruits for the Navy. But many were inner-city youths whose attitudes and worldviews were formed by their experiences on the streets of Chicago, New York, and Los Angeles, where some had been in violent gangs, and who felt more allegiance to the radical black power leaders of the day than they did to anyone wearing a uniform. They joined the Navy because it was a job and because it kept them from being drafted into the jungles of Vietnam.

When these headstrong young men found themselves on an aircraft carrier halfway around the world, assigned to menial tasks and subjected to some of the same insults and degradations that happen to any sailor, they couldn't help but assume it was because of their color. Numbering only 295 among a total crew of about 5,000, the black sailors on the *Kitty Hawk* were a minority in every sense.

The white sailors working alongside them, and the mostly all-white officers who supervised them, were for the most part ignorant about these issues, more concerned with the enormous tasks before them and assuming that the black sailors saw life on the *Kitty Hawk* the same as any white sailor. They were terribly mistaken.

What happened on the *Kitty Hawk* in October 1972 was a pivotal point in race relations for the Navy. Most people have no idea how close it came to becoming so much more.

TROUBLED WATER IS NOT the story the Navy would tell about the incident on the *Kitty Hawk*. The race riot is no secret; with so many people involved and the media coverage at the time, it would have been impossible to completely hide the incident even if Navy brass were so inclined. Instead, the Navy dealt with the *Kitty Hawk* incident quickly and decisively, then allowed it to fade from memory. The Navy was content to let the unpleasant, some would say embarrassing, episode molder in the little-seen files of the Pentagon, never actively denying that the riot took place but always downplaying its significance and scope if the subject arose—and it arose very infrequently. The reason for downplaying the incident is clear: This was an ugly episode involving brutal, vicious attacks on innocent young men who were in the care of the U.S. Navy, and it all hinged on the ever-sensitive, always inflammatory subject of race. Whether the Navy held any responsibility for what happened on the *Kitty Hawk,* and the extent of that responsibility, can be debated to this day, but it is clear that for more than thirty years, the Navy considered the *Kitty Hawk* incident a dark episode that must be described in carefully chosen words, when forced to discuss it at all.

References to the *Kitty Hawk* riot are scarce in any official Navy publication or Internet site. For most of the time since the incident, little information was available beyond a few lines noting a "disturbance" on the ship. More light was shed on the event in 2007, when the *Kitty Hawk* riot was described in the book *Black Sailor, White Navy: Racial Unrest in the Fleet During the Vietnam War Era* by historian John Darrell Sherwood of the U.S. Naval Historical Center, but restraint and caution is evident in that official version of the story. Sherwood's book is a valuable, well-documented analysis of the extensive racial strife that plagued the Navy during the turbulent years of the Vietnam War. In the course of documenting various race-related problems of the era, he provides a factual outline of what happened on the *Kitty Hawk*. That alone represents progress in the Navy's willingness to discuss this incident openly. Sherwood provides useful insight into how the bigger picture of race relations in the Navy played a role in the *Kitty Hawk* incident, but his account of the actual violence downplays the scope of what happened on the carrier. The disturbance was terrible for those involved, Sherwood says, but the incident involved only a small number of crew members.

From the first days of researching this story, I perceived that the prevailing attitude in the Navy was along the lines of "yes, it happened, but it really wasn't that big a deal." This struck me as disingenuous. For the average person who knows little of the details or has heard only that there was a brief disturbance on the ship, that summary can seem legitimate. But once you know the facts of what happened on the *Kitty Hawk*, it is clear that this was a significant episode in the history of the Navy and the country. And for those involved—far more than just the handful suggested by the Navy—the riot on the *Kitty Hawk* had lasting effects. For some, it changed their lives forever.

I first came to the story of the *Kitty Hawk* as an offshoot of my work on a book about another carrier, the *Forrestal.* Reading more about the history of aircraft carriers, I came across references to the sit-down strike on the carrier *Constellation* on November 3, 1972, a strike that is well documented by the Navy. As intriguing and significant as that strike was, it was a peaceful protest. Many accounts described it as the worst incident of racial strife in the Navy during that period, so I was surprised to find sketchy, brief mentions of a race riot on the *Kitty Hawk* that included a series of violent attacks and even a possible attempt to seize control of the ship by force. If that had happened on the *Kitty Hawk,* how could the *Constellation* incident be considered the worst of the racial disturbances in the era?

The answer, I concluded, lay in the fact that the *Constellation* strike, while serious, was nonviolent, so that story could be told without having to acknowledge some ugliness within the ranks of the Navy. Even if the men of the *Constellation* were insubordinate, and even if their philosophy and their tactics were misguided, they didn't hurt anyone. They used the nonviolent form of protest that had gained respect in Middle America. *That* story can be told far more easily than one in which men from the ranks went on a vicious rampage against their fellow sailors.

Throughout my research, the Navy followed a pattern of not denying any facts about the *Kitty Hawk* incident but also not making any effort to shine a light on what happened. Most of the original documents related to the investigations after the riot, the Navy told me, have been destroyed. When I contacted members of the crew who were aboard during the riot, the full extent of the violence and its effect on those involved became clear. Thirty-five years after the incident, the night of October 12, 1972, was still with them, and they vividly remembered the terror, the uncertainty, the confusion. For them, the riot was not a minor event, not something trivial to be swept under the rug, not just a brief disturbance.

And many of these veterans disagreed vehemently with the Navy position—and with that of the two senior officers on the *Kitty Hawk*—about one of the most contentious words in this story: mutiny. The word has grave meaning within the Navy, signifying a rebellion of the first order, a complete failure of the command structure. It is a word that is not tossed around lightly or applied easily to a set of facts. The Navy and the officers involved have strong motivation to avoid the word, to find a way to say that no matter how serious an insurrection, it did not constitute a mutiny. To declare a mutiny is to admit that you have lost control of your ship, and no officer wants to accept defeat by his own men.

The Navy says there has never been a mutiny on a U.S. warship. The captain and executive officer of the *Kitty Hawk* maintain they were not facing a mutiny, though it is clear from testimony soon after the riot that they feared the incident could take a turn in that direction if they did not stop the violence. The crew of the *Kitty Hawk*, however, have nothing to lose by embracing the word. From their perspective, from the viewpoint of the sailor trapped in a work space belowdecks and fearing the next attack by an angry mob of fellow sailors, this was a mutiny or at least a mutiny attempt. They do not have to parse the word to preserve their careers or the Navy's historical record. They know what they saw, what they experienced on the carrier, and many of them will tell you that they lived through a mutinous attempt to take over one of the world's most powerful warships.

Troubled Water is the story of those men and the two officers who led them through to calmer seas.

PRINCIPAL CHARACTERS

MARLAND TOWNSEND. Captain of the *Kitty Hawk*. At the pinnacle of a stellar career, the white officer commands one of the most active, battle-proven aircraft carriers in the U.S. fleet.

BEN CLOUD. Executive officer (XO) of the *Kitty Hawk*. Second in command. A black senior officer, Cloud is a rarity on a Navy ship in 1972 but is highly qualified.

NICHOLAS F. CARLUCCI. The commanding officer of the seventy-man Marine detachment on board the *Kitty Hawk*. Carlucci is a true Marine who believes in doing things by the book.

CHARLES M. JOHNSON. The lead criminal investigator on the *Kitty Hawk,* Johnson works closely with XO Cloud in matters concerning crew discipline.

PERRY PETTUS. A black sailor who is mostly satisfied with his *Kitty Hawk* experience until the day the rioting begins.

TERRY AVINGER. A black sailor who grew up poor on the streets of Philadelphia. Initially enthusiastic about joining the Navy, he becomes disgruntled while serving on the *Kitty Hawk*.

ROBERT KEEL. The son of a career Navy officer, Keel is a white sailor who works in damage control, making him privy to some inside information.

JOHN TRAVERS. An electronics technician on the *Kitty Hawk,* this California native had spent little time with black people before joining the Navy and is somewhat naive about race relations.

CHAPTER ONE

SEAL THE HATCH

October 12, 1972
Gulf of Tonkin, off the Coast of South Vietnam

The low, rumbling sound outside the berthing compartment got the attention of twenty-three-year-old Robert Keel, who was trying to relax with his buddies on a Thursday evening, about 11:15 P.M. Their days on the USS *Kitty Hawk* were always long and hard. They were exhausted by the time their shifts ended and they crashed on their simple metal racks in the berthing compartment under the aft mess deck, the thin mattresses offering only a bit of relief for tired backs. They tried to rest, despite the uncertainty of just how much danger they might be in.

Normally Keel wouldn't have paid any attention to the noise. An aircraft carrier is a raucous place at all times, and the berthing areas where men slept and spent their personal time were no exception. A man might have a steam pressure pipe running across the ceiling six inches from his face when he lay on the top bunk, and when high-pressure steam shot through on the way to the flight deck catapults, it made a noise that only the most dog-tired sailor could sleep through.

So a low rumble in the passageway outside wouldn't normally elicit any concern. But this wasn't a normal day on the *Kitty Hawk.*

"Maybe it's just a fight," one of the men said, sounding as if he were trying to convince himself. With 5,000 young men locked in a tin can in the middle of the ocean, fights were inevitable. Another scrap between some hotheads was no reason for alarm. There had been a huge fight during their recent stop at Subic Bay in the Philippines, in the Sampaguita nightclub, mostly black sailors versus white ones. Keel had been in the middle of the brawl, but he had managed to get out of it without any serious injuries, and without getting arrested by the shore patrol.

"I don't know," Keel replied. "Listen to that. That sounds like something big. I think it might be them. They could be heading this way."

Keel was in many ways typical of the sailors on the *Kitty Hawk,* but on this night he was in a unique position. He knew more about the violence that had been happening throughout the ship than most of his buddies. He had been in the middle of some of it, and he had heard nearly frantic officers discussing a violent rampage by black sailors. Keel's buddies had heard rumors that evening about blacks attacking whites, but the carrier was so big and mazelike that even a huge disturbance in one area might not be seen by sailors going about their business elsewhere. They were left to depend on the information passed from one man to another and they didn't know how much of it to believe. Some of it sounded too incredible—stories had been circulating about white sailors being attacked by black sailors for no reason, even rumors that the captain was missing and claims that black rioters were trying to take over the ship.

Eventually the sound faded away. The men didn't want to go looking for trouble if their immediate area seemed calm, so they remained where they were and tried to relax even as they worried about the rumors. A few stretched out in their bunks, a couple sat up playing cards, one wrote a letter. They were a good representative lot of the *Kitty Hawk*'s crew, mostly eighteen- or nineteen-year-old men, with a couple, like Keel, in their early twenties. They were mostly white, and unlike many black sailors on the ship, the black men hanging out with Keel that night seemed at ease. Almost all of them were riding out a tour in the Navy to avoid being drafted into the jungles of Vietnam. Earning a few bucks along the way was a plus, since jobs were pretty scarce back home for young men with little education.

Keel had had similar motivation for joining up. He had also been spurred by his father's naval career. Though he had started out as a rebellious young man he was now looking at maybe making a career in the Navy. Keel had a wife and four-year-old daughter at home to keep him motivated, and he was quickly becoming one of the most reliable hands on the *Kitty Hawk*.

Because he was a bit older than many of his bunk mates, in a situation in which a few years' experience set you worlds apart from guys still learning their jobs on the fly, Keel had some influence over his buddies. If nothing else, they respected the fact that he was on his second "WestPac" cruise to the western Pacific, already having spent one tour off the coast of Vietnam. Now he was at it again, grinding through the long days of work in compartments belowdecks, rarely seeing sunlight and seldom getting more than a few hours off in a row. The other sailors in his living area found it a little harder to complain when they knew Keel had already been through it once and survived.

Keel stuck his head out of the hatch leading from their berthing compartment and listened for any trouble, but he heard nothing. With what he had seen and heard earlier, he was still worried, however. Something was terribly wrong on the ship, and from the scuttlebutt Keel had heard, many of the sailors who had been assaulted on the *Kitty Hawk* had not known what was going on until a mob attacked them. Keel was worried that maybe that was about to happen to his bunk mates and to him, but he couldn't be certain, and he didn't want to say it out loud to the others and risk looking paranoid. He had been attacked twice that day, though, so he had good reason to be on alert.

The first attack had come when he was sitting in the aft mess several hours earlier, with a bit of free time before going on watch. Keel had been alone, taking advantage of the quiet and uncommon solitude to write a letter home. He had heard a rumble of noise—the same banging and raised voices that he had just heard outside the berthing compartment—and looked up just as a group of black sailors burst in through a hatch. They were loud and angry, shouting obscenities and screaming about getting even. The thing that most got Keel's attention, however, was the fact that they were armed. The sailors, about thirty of them, were carrying wrenches, pipes, chains, and other heavy tools. A couple were carrying fog foam nozzles—heavy metal wands, several feet long, with nozzle heads that are used to apply fire-extinguishing foam in an emergency. They were found all over the carrier as part of the crew's firefighting gear, and now sailors were wielding them like clubs.

Keel didn't know what to make of the group at first, whether they were running from a fight or looking for one, but either way they were pissed off and heavily armed, and he knew he didn't want to get involved. He just sat at the table writing, looking up as the black sailors filed by and hoping they had somewhere else to go. He was relieved when they passed by without acknowledging his presence. But then the last guy in the line did notice Keel.

"What are you doing here?" he shouted.

"I'm writing a letter home," Keel said, as matter-of-factly as he could in spite of his fear. He didn't want to provoke these guys, but he didn't want to cower in front of them either.

The black sailor looked around the mess hall and saw a stack of bomb fins, metal parts that are attached to 500-pound bombs when they are loaded onto airplanes. He picked up one and heaved it across the room at Keel, who ducked as it clanged across tables and fell away. The black sailor looked as if he were about to charge Keel, but then he realized that the rest of his group had left. Not wanting to be left behind, or unwilling to attack Keel without backup, the sailor took off.

Shaken but unharmed, Keel went to work his shift as a communications technician in damage control, the heart of the ship's emergency response system. There he was privy to news about what was happening throughout the *Kitty Hawk*. What he saw and heard left him unnerved. Then, on his way back to the berthing compartment after his watch, he was forced to hole up in a mess deck with some other white sailors and fend off a crowd of rampaging black sailors who were trying to get in. Why? Keel had no idea. He had defended himself with a chemical fire extinguisher, ready to spray the caustic purple powder into the face of any sailor who made it through the hatch.

From what he could tell, the attacks he had endured were just two examples of what was going on throughout the ship that day. The *Kitty Hawk's* leadership apparently was aware of the violence, but it sounded like the captain had been taken by the rioters. And even worse, the command structure wasn't kicking in. *That* was what worried Keel. If a group of sailors was running wild on the *Kitty Hawk* and even trying to mutiny and take over the carrier, why weren't the captain and the XO stopping it quickly? Just how bad was the situation if neither the captain nor the XO could get the job done?

Keel had related his experiences to his buddies when he returned to the berthing compartment. He had more firsthand experience with the day's violence than they had, but he still couldn't piece it all together. Were they safe?

The group of sailors sat or lay around, too tired for action but too worried to really relax. Everyone was uneasy, not sure how much of what they heard was just rumor and how much was really happening. They couldn't help but imagine the worst.

"I heard they're in control of the 04 deck," one man said.

"Yeah, I heard they got the second deck too," another said. "But I don't think they have the hangar deck. The flight deck is okay too, and I don't think they made it to the island," referring to the key part of the ship that contained the bridge and other command operations.

Another sailor said, "They're tearing white guys out of their racks and beating the shit out of them for no reason. I saw a guy whose face was messed up real bad." The chatter continued, the men passing on bits and pieces of whatever they had seen or heard during the day.

"Where's the skipper?" someone asked. "I heard them calling for him on the 1MC like he was lost or something."

No one answered right away, so Keel spoke up. He told the men what he had heard in damage control, that no one seemed to know where the captain was. That news made everyone quiet for a moment. The captain of the *Kitty Hawk* was missing?

"For all we know, he's dead," another sailor said. No one argued with him.

The men were silent as they thought about their predicament, stuck in an interior compartment of an aircraft carrier, with little means of communication and no authority to do anything but just wait and see if a mob came charging down the passage toward them.

Keel kept glancing at the hatch leading to their compartment. It was the only way in and the only way out.

"We need to seal that hatch," Keel said.

He didn't have to say it twice.

CHAPTER TWO

A NEW CAPTAIN

1972

Marland Townsend was an unlikely figure to appear before a congressional hearing in November 1972, defending himself against accusations that he had lost control of one of the world's most powerful war ships.

In 1972, Townsend, known as Doc to his friends and his crew, was at the top of his game. As captain of the aircraft carrier USS *Kitty Hawk*, a shining star in the U.S. fleet, Townsend had climbed just about as far as a Navy officer could get and still be on the water, not behind a desk in Washington, DC. This was the glory assignment for any Navy officer, the opportunity to lead thousands of men into battle and help direct the outcome of the Vietnam War. In addition to the immense pride he felt in being given such great responsibility, Townsend knew that this role typically led to becoming a flag officer. After his service on the *Kitty Hawk*, it was very likely that Townsend would retire as an admiral—well deserved after a distinguished career.

By May 1972, when he took the helm of the carrier, Townsend had already amassed a long list of achievements in the Navy, everything from winning a Distinguished Flying Cross for daring bomb raids in North Vietnam, to risking his life as a test pilot, to developing the "Top Gun" school for training the best fighter pilots in the world. His assignment as captain of the *Kitty Hawk* was the next logical step in an outstanding career. Born in 1927 in a decidedly middle-class, peaceful suburb of Washington, DC, known as Mount Ranier, Townsend knew early on that he wanted to fly jets for the Navy. After he had achieved that goal, he kept looking for another.

TALL AND HANDSOME, a hale and hearty fellow who made the uniform look good, Townsend clearly was destined for greatness. He had entered the Navy in 1945, when the service was eager to replace the many pilots returning home after World War II. The Navy's Flying Midshipmen Program paid for two years of college at Georgia Tech in Atlanta, and then Townsend went on to Memphis for flight training. By 1948, he was flying F8F bearcats with fighter squadron VF–91 out of Charleston, Rhode Island, and in 1950, he returned to Georgia Tech to complete a bachelor's degree in aeronautics. But sitting in a classroom wasn't enough for Townsend. He still had to fly, not because the Navy required it but because he needed to be in the air, so he maintained his flight skills by flying Corsairs with the Naval Reserve unit in Atlanta.

Townsend welcomed his return to active duty in November 1952, when he and the rest of VF–53 joined the carrier USS *Valley Forge* and headed to Korea to fly F9Fs in air strikes against Communist artillery and antiaircraft sites. Another deployment to the Pacific followed aboard the USS *Philippine Sea,* after which Townsend earned a master's degree in aeronautical engineering from Princeton University. But as always, he was eager to get back in the air. And the Navy wanted him flying. They knew what a good pilot Townsend was and what an asset he represented for the Navy. So in 1962, when the Navy needed a test pilot, they called on Marland Townsend. True to form, Townsend quickly conquered that role and went on to become an instructor at the test pilot school in Patuxent River, Maryland. Townsend prided himself on never being beaten by a student in a dogfight.

Townsend clearly was among the Navy's very best, moving steadily from one challenging assignment to the next. When the conflict in Vietnam started heating up, the Navy called on pilots like Doc Townsend. From July 1965 to June 1967, he was executive officer and then commander of squadron VF-143, the "World Famous Pukin' Dogs" out of Oceana, California, flying off the carriers USS *Ranger* and USS *Constellation*. It was during this time that Townsend earned a Distinguished Flying Cross for his role in an air strike against a series of warehouses and then coordinating the rescue of another pilot who had ejected. But it was also during this time that Townsend started looking at the big picture, not necessarily just what the Navy told him about the war. Though he committed himself fully to each mission, Townsend was beginning to doubt the American involvement in Vietnam. Every time the three-man crew took to the air, they were risking their lives and a $3.6 million Phantom to strike some ramshackle buildings and supplies. Townsend just couldn't see the sense in it. Risking so much to support troops on the ground was one thing, but many of their objectives didn't seem worth the danger of getting shot down. He advised his pilots to play it safe, never to take an unnecessary chance with these missions. The caution paid off; Townsend's unit suffered only two operational aircraft losses in over two thousand combat sorties under his command. That concern with men's lives didn't mean that Townsend held back or took the easy routes: On June 6, for example, he flew the mission that earned him his second Distinguished Flying Cross—a dicey strike on a target eight miles south of Hanoi, through heavy artillery and surface-to-air missile fire.

After his time in Vietnam, Townsend continued his ascent. In 1967 he went on to command VF–121 in Miramar, California, and spearheaded development of the now-famous "Top Gun" school for training elite fighter pilots, using a captured Russian MigG–21C fighter. His personnel jacket was stuffed with outstanding evaluations, so when he was ready to leave VF–121, the Navy brass was open to nearly any request he had for his next assignment. He had plenty of opportunity for more flight commands, but Townsend was thinking about taking his career in a different direction. When he heard in 1968 that there was an opening on the *Constellation* for an operations officer, he was intrigued. The ops officer is usually found on the bridge of the carrier, near the captain, responsible for controlling many of the ship's functions related to flight operations. It would be a different sort of job from what Townsend had been doing, but not too far afield, and he wanted the experience of working in the carrier system. The job was his for the asking, and Townsend found that he enjoyed the position. After six months as ops officer, he moved up the ladder to become the executive officer (XO) on the *Constellation,* working under three captains he admired and considered mentors, all three of whom went on to become admirals. Not wanting to give up his flying altogether, Townsend had worked out an agreement with the first skipper that would allow him to fly off the *Constellation* occasionally, though never on actual missions. He could hop in a Phantom once in awhile for a training mission, just to stay current and see what the deck looked like from above. It was an unusual arrangement for an ops officer, and he continued to fly every month or so when he became XO. Townsend enjoyed being able to take a plane up once in a while, of course, because no Navy pilot is satisfied to take a job where his feet never leave the ground, but the jaunts also kept him well connected with the flight operations, the pilots, and the crew. Standing up on the bridge and watching flight ops just isn't the same as actually flying off the deck and seeing firsthand how everything is working.

His 18 months as XO gave Townsend a chance to learn how to run a ship, no small feat when you're talking about one of the biggest, most complex ships in the world, and he gained a solid understanding of how valuable a good XO can be to the captain. Townsend was given considerable authority, even driving the ship during some of the most delicate operations for a carrier, such as the underway replenishments, when a supply ship comes alongside to transfer supplies. After Townsend's stint as XO, the Navy selected him for deep draft command, meaning he was in line to captain a carrier or other large ship. Until there was an opening, he was transferred to Washington, DC, to work in the air systems command as essentially a fighter design officer. There he was responsible for overseeing the technical design of Navy fighters. In 1971 Townsend was assigned to captain the USS *Seattle,* a fast combat support ship whose primary role was to resupply carriers and other ships. He welcomed the opportunity to helm this vital link in the carrier family, partly because a large part of his role as XO on the *Constellation* had involved managing the interplay between the carrier and the other vessels that make the big girl go.

Townsend was waiting for the call that would give him the most responsibility and probably the most challenge he had ever faced, which was saying something for a man like him. He had been on the *Seattle* for about a year when that call came: Townsend was to command the *Kitty Hawk,* one of the world's most powerful warships, a carrier whose years of service were already legendary. The transfer was made even easier by the fact that the carrier was nearly identical to the *Constellation,* which Townsend knew inside out, backward and forward. They were sister ships, the *Kitty Hawk* being the first in the class and the *Constellation* following a few months later in 1961. Both were great ships to command, Townsend thought, representing the very best that the Navy had at sea.

Townsend took command of the *Kitty Hawk* from Captain Owen H. Oberg in June 1972, when the ship was on duty in the western Pacific. He expected a finely tuned instrument of war, but he found troubling problems right away—some material issues and some re-lated to personnel. The *Kitty Hawk* had the best-equipped air wing in the Pacific Fleet, sporting the latest and greatest in airplanes, elec-tronics, and weaponry. The ship had nearly everything a captain could ask for in terms of equipment and technology, but as Townsend inspected the ship over several days before relieving Captain Oberg, he found evidence of a ship not run to his standards. The engineering spaces, for one thing, were not maintained properly. Two boilers were overdue for inspection, one so neglected that Townsend feared the damn thing might burn up the ship. The ship was flying only 85 sor-ties a day; Townsend knew from his experience on the *Constellation* that 120 sorties should have been easily achievable.

It didn't take long for Townsend to identify the root cause of the *Kitty Hawk*'s troubles. Simply walking around and talking to the crew told him as much or more than he got from the reports of his senior officers. The crew had a bad attitude. They didn't want to be there. They were angry that the ship had left San Diego earlier than ex-pected, and they weren't motivated to do anything more than the minimum required work. Townsend also took note of some of the other issues that would later concern the ship's XO: the lax discipline and an informal, self-imposed segregation between black sailors and white ones. Townsend's assessment of the *Kitty Hawk* helped con-firm a trend he had noticed recently: There was a marked decline in the quality of some enlisted men coming into the Navy, the result of a new effort to increase the ranks by lowering minimum test scores on aptitude and intelligence tests.

It wasn't what Townsend had hoped to find when he took com-mand of the carrier.

Our job is to do the assigned task and do it well, Townsend thought at the time. *How we got here is not the issue. The condition of this ship and this crew is a real shame, because the* Kitty Hawk *is a great ship. These men have been coddled for too long.*

A tough, seasoned Navy officer like Townsend didn't have much sympathy for sailors moping and feeling sorry for themselves, but he did understand that being in the Navy in 1972 was no walk in the park. In addition to the plain old stress of hard work, being away from home, and risking your life every day, the antiwar sentiment made some sailors feel like pariahs when they walked the streets of San Diego in uniform. Antiwar protestors demonstrated when the ship departed or returned to port, and it was not uncommon for sailors to endure insults on the street or get into bar fights when some ignorant kid in love beads accused them of doing something heinous just because they were serving their country.

Townsend knew the crew was skeptical about the war and many wondered why they were sacrificing so much for what sometimes seemed a pointless effort. It was no secret that many in the military—senior officers included—had the same misgivings about the Vietnam War, if not the same outright opposition, that could be found in the civilian population. These feelings certainly didn't help the morale and work ethic on the *Kitty Hawk*. Although Townsend shared some of the crew's concerns about the futility of the effort in Southeast Asia, prompted by his own experience as a pilot, he could never express those feelings to his crew. He had to walk a fine line with the sailors, presenting a strong, commanding presence while also trying to show concern for the issues that troubled them.

Townsend reported back to the admiral that problems on the *Kitty Hawk* would delay the carrier being fully operational. The overdue inspections on the boilers were a particular worry for him. He feared they could create a fire aboard the *Kitty Hawk*, a hazard that haunted every Navy ship's captain after several high-profile fires in the 1960s had killed hundreds of sailors and caused many millions of dollars of damage. Townsend told the admiral that he wouldn't be getting 30 knots across the bow—the standard for launching aircraft and considered the sign that a carrier is operating normally—until he squared away the safety inspections on those boilers. A good wind would only fan the flames if a fire did occur, so Townsend opted for the safer choice of delaying full flight operations. The admiral didn't argue with the new captain's judgment.

Townsend had every confidence in his ability to straighten out the *Kitty Hawk,* but commanding an aircraft carrier is not a one-man job. A captain depends on his executive officer, his second in command, to enact many of his directives and take responsibility for more of the hands-on administration while the captain determines the big picture for the ship. The XO's primary duties are to oversee the department heads, keep the ship clean, and command the master-at-arms forces—the sailors who serve as sort of the police force of a Navy ship. The captain is responsible for the operational readiness of the ship, seamanship, actually ensuring that the carrier can perform its role. The current XO was being transferred off the *Kitty Hawk.* Considering the state of the ship, Townsend wasn't going to shed any tears over the XO's departure. He had high hopes for the new XO who was to arrive shortly, a black Navy flier named Ben Cloud. Townsend did not know Cloud personally, but he had studied the man's record thoroughly and liked what he saw. If he hadn't, he could have vetoed the assignment. From what Townsend could tell, Cloud was eminently qualified and came with the best recommendations. Townsend was going to have one of the Navy's most senior black officers under his command, and the first black XO of a carrier, but he considered race a trivial issue. When Townsend approved Cloud's assignment as XO, a superior officer tried to clarify that Townsend understood the situation.

"You know, Doc, this guy is black. Is that going to be okay with you? Are you sure this is the right thing for the *Hawk?*"

"I don't give a damn what color he is," Townsend replied. "I just want a good XO. That's all that matters to me, and if the Navy wants to send him to me, I'll take him."

He didn't plan to make any fuss about Cloud breaking new ground or blazing trails, and as far as he could tell, neither did Cloud. The bottom line for Townsend was that he didn't care much about Cloud's skin color; he just wanted to see if the man would do a good job as XO. Townsend was sympathetic to the civil rights movement, but on the whole he expected all men, and certainly his sailors, to act appropriately, no matter what their race was. He did not realize, however, that some of the ship's black sailors often were driven by past experience and cultural differences that he could not understand.

Townsend, like all commanders, needed to depend on the XO to be his eyes and ears with the sailors, to have the more personal connection to the crew that he could not make without sacrificing his standing as the captain. But he only knew Cloud from his outstanding record; he didn't know the man well enough to be certain where he would stand on some of the issues they would have to address on the *Kitty Hawk*. It would not take long for them both to realize that their personal styles were very different. That could be a hindrance, because Townsend already knew this crew was stressed and in disarray.

And he knew that the way the captain and XO commanded a crew of 5,000 men at sea bore some similarity to the way a mom and dad parented a child. They might have different styles, but they had to be consistent and present a united front. That's what he needed from this new XO. The crew of the *Kitty Hawk* would need strong leadership from both of them.

CHAPTER THREE

A NEW XO

August 1972

The man who would save the *Kitty Hawk* arrived on the ship in August 1972. By December of the same year, he was testifying before the same congressional committee that had heard from Doc Townsend. Confident but not quite defiant, Benjamin Cloud told the congressmen that he had done what was necessary.

"The methods that I used admittedly were unorthodox, and I will admit unmilitary," he told the committee members who would pass judgment on him. "But I felt, and as I feel right now, sir, they were absolutely necessary to prevent loss of life and extreme destruction to the *Kitty Hawk*. And in retrospect I must say that looking back on that situation, the tempo and tenor of the situation at that time, and knowing what would be at stake, I would do it again."

IT HAD BEEN HARD to foresee the trouble coming when Cloud joined the *Kitty Hawk* in August, just three months after Townsend had taken command of the ship. By that time, Townsend had whipped the crew back into shape. The ship's standards now matched those Cloud had seen earlier in his career, when the future XO had flown off the *Kitty Hawk* as a naval aviator. Under Doc Townsend's command, the crew was performing at a much higher level, and those boilers were, by god, inspected regularly. Within seven days of taking command, Townsend had 30 knots of wind over the deck again. The new captain became a familiar face in the belly of the ship, way down deep in the engineering compartments where the crew hardly ever saw a top officer. Townsend was so pleased with how the crew had improved the material condition of the ship that he ordered a new sign placed at the aft entrance: "Home of the Best Engineers in the Navy." The engineers appreciated the gesture because theirs was one of the least glamorous and most difficult jobs on the carrier. All the high drama, glory, and excitement takes place on the flight deck, but every carrier has thousands of men belowdecks who see none of that, or sunshine either.

The crew soon came to realize that Townsend was a hands-on leader who liked to observe things for himself, and it was not unusual to see him off the bridge, meeting with department heads and getting into whatever was going on around the ship. He was seen, but he didn't make a big deal out of sitting down with the crew to shoot the bull or eating with the enlisted men just to make a show of how he was a regular guy. He wasn't a regular guy on the *Kitty Hawk;* he was the captain. Townsend was so focused on getting the ship back in order, in ways that he could see and understand and measure, that he didn't realize that many personnel issues still simmered below the surface. He had some idea that morale on the ship still was subpar, especially among the lower ranks and minority crew members, but he felt that much of the cause of that bad morale was beyond his control, intertwined as it was with what was happening in the civilian world back home. He was focused on making the ship function at its best, and he put a higher priority on the logistics than the intangibles of crew morale. Whatever the personnel problems were, he hoped the arrival of his new XO might improve the situation.

The arrival of Benjamin Cloud as the new XO on the *Kitty Hawk* caused many on board the aircraft carrier and throughout the Navy to take notice. As second in command of one of the world's most powerful warships and one with a long, colorful history, the XO would be in a high-profile position and on the fast track to even greater glory in the Navy. Cloud fit the bill perfectly; his career was already fast moving and high achieving, having passed milestones at age forty that would make any naval aviator proud. He looked the part too—a handsome, trim man with a firm, steady look in his eyes that told you he was ready to tackle anything.

Cloud had been born in San Diego, the home port of the aircraft carrier, on November 6, 1931, the son of a San Diego police officer who would retire in the late 1930s. In 1940, the family moved about 15 miles to El Cajon, California, in hopes that the drier climate would help Cloud's chronic asthma. The family settled onto a 25-acre ranch, one of many in the area, where Cloud and his brother enjoyed the open lands and horses, plus the attention of his mother, a dedicated homemaker who was nearly always at home with her boys. Cloud was not the stereotypical jock who goes on to become a fighter pilot. He gravitated more toward the arts than athletics, taking up the violin as a child and playing with the State of California Youth Symphony.

Cloud's racial heritage was a mixture of black and American Indian on both sides. His family name could be traced back to a paternal grandfather who was a full-blooded Indian in Tennessee, and his mother's family tree included Indians living in Oklahoma. Despite this rich and more complex ancestry, most people assumed the Clouds were entirely of black heritage. Racial issues did not pose significant hurdles in Cloud's childhood, and he would come to realize later that his early years were very different from those of other black men and women of the same era. The Cloud family lived in a predominantly minority, upper-middle-class neighborhood in San Diego County, where racial issues were not at the forefront of daily life as much as they might be in, say, Birmingham, Atlanta, Chicago, or New York. There certainly was racial discrimination, and Cloud's father experienced far more in his earlier life than his sons did, but Cloud's experience in San Diego and El Cajon did not create childhood memories of oppression at every turn. In San Diego, young Cloud spent most of his time in a community made up of blacks and Latinos who were decidedly middle class and who did not focus much time and energy on complaining about racism. No one denied it existed, no one pretended that it didn't matter, but it was not a reason to take your eye off the prize. When the family moved to the far more rural community of El Cajon, the distant neighbors were primarily white, with some Latinos but very few black families nearby. When he started grammar school, Cloud was among only three or four black children enrolled, and he was the only black student in the high school.

Cloud's family almost never discussed racial issues at home, not because it was taboo or too disturbing to bring up, but simply because the family had better things to talk about. Cloud's father believed that you succeeded in this world on your own merits and that no amount of racism was going to stop you if you were determined.

"If you're good enough to do something, you're going to succeed no matter what color your skin is," Cloud's father told the boys on many occasions. "You're not only going to succeed, but other people are going to want to be a part of your life."

That attitude carried Cloud's father through the harassment and discouragement that he encountered when he became the first minority police officer in San Diego. He didn't use racism and the undeniable inequities it spawned as a reason to stop pursuing his goal, and he taught his sons that nothing should hinder the pursuit of their dreams.

Cloud began studying civil engineering at San Diego State College, but before long, the growing war in Korea made men his age start wondering if they would be drafted. Rather than wait to see whether the draft would dictate how he served his country, Cloud decided to suspend his college studies and join the Navy to become a flier. He had flown a bit during high school, so he aimed at becoming a fighter pilot. It was during his training in Pensacola, Florida, in 1952 that Cloud got his first real experience with segregation. He was not welcome to get his hair cut in the same Navy Exchange barbershop his classmates used, and he was shocked to find that even as a naval officer candidate, he had to sit in the back of the bus when traveling around the base itself. He was reassured somewhat by the fact that some of his white friends insisted on sitting in the back with him.

After excelling in his flight program, Cloud was assigned in 1954 to fighter reconnaissance program VC–61 (later designated as VFP–63) in San Diego, flying F9F Panthers, the same plane in which Townsend had so much experience. He welcomed the assignment because his widowed mother and his brother were still living nearby. He wasn't home all that much, though, because his unit deployed to the Pacific several times on the carriers USS *Boxer, Coral Sea,* and *Ticonderoga.* Still determined to get his college degree, Cloud fought for acceptance in the Navy's "Five Term" program, which allowed junior college officers to go to school full time at any university that would guarantee a degree after the completion of five semesters, with the Navy paying for the education. The Navy granted his request, and Cloud was accepted at Stanford University, but then the program ended abruptly because of budget cuts. The decision greatly disappointed Cloud, and he even toyed with the idea of ending his Navy service much sooner than he had planned so he could continue his education on his own. Instead, Cloud consulted with several senior officers he considered mentors and they convinced him to stay, steering him toward another Navy program that paid for about half of his tuition. After being accepted in that program, in 1959 Cloud was transferred to a desk job at the Naval Photographic Center in Anacostia, Maryland, with the understanding that his primary duty was to get his degree at the University of Maryland. By 1963 he had received his degree in Chinese language and culture—the university had no civil engineering program to complete his earlier studies—and the Navy was ready to put him back to work. His superiors asked Cloud if he wanted to return to VC–61 in San Diego and become the team leader for a photo reconnaissance detachment scheduled to go to Southeast Asia. What would soon be known as the Vietnam War was just building steam that year, so Cloud saw no reason to consider the assignment particularly dangerous—not that that would have deterred him from taking what clearly was a good step up the career ladder. He welcomed the opportunity to lead a team of Navy pilots. His group deployed to Southeast Asia on the *Kitty Hawk* for what they all expected to be a relatively safe assignment, but they soon found that they were probing into dangerous territory just as the Vietnam conflict was beginning to heat up. Cloud's team was charged with many top-secret missions over Laos and Vietnam, and they were in the middle of it all when the situation reached full boil. One of Cloud's team, Charles Klausmann, was among the first to be wounded in the Vietnam War; captured after his plane went down on a reconnaissance mission, he subsequently escaped from a prisoner of war camp.

After his tour in Southeast Asia, Cloud left the reconnaissance team and returned to Washington, DC, where he was assigned to the Bureau of Naval Personnel and the White House, as an aide to President Lyndon Johnson. He described his job in the White House as putting on a uniform and standing around trying to look sharp until someone needed something from him. It was a radical change from flying death-defying missions over Laos in 1964, but Cloud knew it was temporary and considered an honor. He didn't spend all of his time standing around the White House, however. Cloud also represented the Navy in many community service programs around the country, making sure that minority youth, in particular, saw that a black man could be a successful Navy officer. These activities and his White House contacts put Cloud in touch with many black leaders of the day, including the Reverend Martin Luther King Jr., whom Cloud admired but never openly supported. He didn't feel it was his place as a prominent Navy officer to take a stand on the race debates going on in the country and especially on the controversial tactics used by some to raise awareness. Even King's nonviolent protests were illegal in many cases; Cloud felt that he could not align himself too closely with any such activities without risking his career or damaging the Navy's image. Better to lead by example. Cloud figured that a young black child seeing him in uniform and shaking hands with dignitaries probably accomplished more than anything he could say.

In 1966, he was assigned to a fighter squadron in Oceana, California, flying F–4 Phantoms. That tour lasted four years, including time flying Phantoms in the Mediterranean and Caribbean. From there, Cloud was assigned as the XO of VFP–63, his first squadron back in San Diego, and then he became commander of that unit— one of the first black officers to command a squadron. Cloud knew full well that this position put him squarely on the path toward becoming an admiral some day. He was honored and took his duties at the desk every bit as seriously as he did flying Phantoms over enemy territory.

As Cloud's Navy career flourished and he progressed on a track that promised even more prestigious assignments, he never once looked at himself as a "black officer" or a "black aviator," and he certainly didn't see himself as blazing any new trails for the black community. If others wanted to find some meaning in a black man—more accurately, a black and American Indian man—reaching the levels of success that he was enjoying, so be it. He didn't mind being a role model for anyone who wanted to follow the same path, black or white, but he knew that he had done it all through hard work; he hadn't had anything handed to him because of the color of his skin. When anyone ever asked him what effect his race had on his advancement in the Navy—and the question did come up—he was quick to answer "Zero. Absolutely none." And he made it clear that he meant it went both ways. The color of his skin had offered him no advantages over anyone else; neither had it posed any real obstacles. He gave credit to the Navy for not treating him any differently than his white counterparts when it came to training and advancement, and he damn sure didn't want anyone to think that his success was the result of anything but hard work and perseverance. He was one of the top officers in the Navy, not one of the top *minority* officers, and it was insulting to him to suggest—to even inquire about—the possibility that the Navy had moved him to choice assignments as some sort of ad hoc affirmative action. His father had told him that his race shouldn't be a concern as he pursued his goals, and he felt he was living proof that his father was right. He was quick to anger if anyone suggested otherwise.

Despite Cloud's justifiable pride in his own accomplishments, there was no denying that others noticed his success not just as an individual but also as a black man. This was, after all, 1972, and race relations were a prominent concern throughout the country. When Cloud was assigned as XO on the *Kitty Hawk,* no one seriously thought it was because he was black, yet it was still noteworthy in a Navy that was only beginning to accept the idea of blacks in senior leadership positions.

His assignment as XO came when Cloud was a student at the Navy War College in Newport, Rhode Island, awaiting his next assignment. Admiral Bernard A. Clarey, deputy commander in chief of the Pacific (CINCPAC), was a guest speaker at the college one day. Cloud had met Clarey earlier while being debriefed after photo reconnaissance flights over Vietnam, and apparently the younger flier's accomplishments and attitude had impressed the admiral. Seeing that Cloud was up for assignment after completing his studies, Admiral Clarey asked Cloud if he would be interested in coming to work as his aide. Cloud was flattered and interested in the position, but he had to be honest about one potential problem.

"Sir, I know that an officer in your position and his deputy are involved in a great deal of social activities and that one's wife gets heavily involved in the CINCPAC life," Cloud told Clarey. "Admiral, I don't have a wife and I really do not anticipate getting one in the fore-seeable future."

Clarey agreed that a single man might not be the best choice for his aide, and asked Cloud what other assignment he was interested in. Cloud told him that he had been thinking about becoming XO of a major ship. With his seniority, he should be a fine candidate for such a position, he told the admiral. Clarey agreed and got the ball rolling, eventually asking Townsend about assigning Cloud as his new second in command. Townsend pointed out that there were two other officers on the ship who were senior to Cloud and should be considered. After more discussions, Clarey and Townsend agreed that Cloud was the right man for the job. A ship's captain has ultimate approval over the XO, and Townsend indicated that he would welcome Cloud aboard.

Cloud was extremely pleased with the assignment to the *Kitty Hawk,* which almost felt like home to him. His first experience on the carrier had been as an ensign, when he was detailed to the *Kitty Hawk* as it was being built in Camden, New Jersey, responsible for installing some advanced photographic equipment in the ship's photo labs. Cloud had made five cruises aboard the *Kitty Hawk* as an air squadron member, and it had been the platform for many of his flights over Vietnam. The *Kitty Hawk* was only one of several carriers that Cloud had flown from throughout his career, but he had spent enough time on the great ship to get to know her well. He felt a special affinity for the carrier.

When Cloud joined the *Kitty Hawk* in August 1972, he found a carrier that was operating at top speed, meeting goals that would daunt lesser carriers and crews. This was the kind of ship on which a hard-charging, ambitious officer like Cloud wanted to serve. The day he took on his role as XO and settled into his quarters, Cloud knew that he was taking a bold step forward in his Navy career, and he was eager to get to work.

The carrier that Cloud boarded showcased the best and the worst of the Navy in 1972. The crew was hardworking and dedicated—most of them anyway—but the *Kitty Hawk* wasn't without difficulties. Like any Navy ship then or now, the crew had their own personal issues to deal with while they performed their duties, and the more men you put together in one big tin can on the ocean, the more those personal issues grow into something much more onerous. Racial issues were a prime concern in the United States in 1972, and there were reports of incidents on Navy ships and bases around the world—everything from minor fistfights among sailors to substantial vandalism against ships. But for the most part, the Navy was avoiding the topic and simply declared that race would not be an issue on its ships. Sailors sometimes disagreed.

Cloud saw some signs right away that suggested black sailors were struggling with what they perceived as racial discrimination on board, and he noted that their concerns bore watching. Real or imagined, he knew that their perception of racism on the *Kitty Hawk* could become a problem. It was evident right away that the sailors naturally grouped themselves by the same racial, ethnic, and socio-demographic differences that separated them back home in the States. Latinos from Texas or California tended to congregate with each other, as did black sailors from Chicago or Los Angeles. Cloud also could see that the officers on the *Kitty Hawk* tended to take a very hands-off approach to the sailors' time away from work, interfering little with how the men associated and not enforcing much discipline in berthing areas. Some such areas were totally black, some all Latino, some strictly white—all segregated by the sailors themselves. There also were areas of the ship where *Kitty Hawk* officers—mostly white—did not go because they knew they were not welcome. Some areas, regardless of the occupants' race, were filthy because the sailors were allowed to live however they wanted. Some of this disturbed Cloud right off the bat, but he knew it was not unique to the *Kitty Hawk*. It all reflected the Navy of 1972. Many senior officers recognized the existence of such problems but did not know how to address them.

Cloud and Townsend meshed well from the start, though they had somewhat different styles: the captain was more reserved and formal, while the XO was more gregarious. Townsend was pleased right away with the new guy. After Cloud spent some time with the outgoing XO to learn the ropes, the captain felt that he was entirely capable of providing the kind of leadership the crew needed and he expected. Their initial impressions of each other were favorable. Everything bode well for a good working relationship, possibly even a good friendship.

Townsend was pleased to see that, as he expected, Cloud clearly thought of himself as the XO, not the "black XO" or the "first black XO." The black sailors noticed that there now was a black man on the bridge, and Cloud encouraged them to come to him with concerns, but he never did so in a way that undermined junior officers or made it appear that black sailors had a special conduit to the top because he was of the same race.

Early on, Cloud got word from other senior officers that the black sailors were known for griping about mistreatment, spending a lot of time sitting around their berthing areas bitching and moaning about what the Navy was doing to them. Nothing but bellyaching and whining all the time, always something the white man was doing to them. "They piss on their shoe and somehow it's whitey's fault" was how one officer put it.

The description took Cloud back to his childhood. Even after the family moved to the white community of El Cajon, the family owned property in a black neighborhood in San Diego, including a small barbershop that was popular with local black men. Cloud, his father, and his brother went there regularly on Saturday mornings in the late 1930s and early 1940s for their own haircuts. As a child, particularly one who was growing up in a white community and whose father taught him not to dwell on race, Cloud was always intrigued by the conversations of the men in the inner-city barbershop. Half of them weren't even there for a haircut; they just enjoyed hanging out and socializing with the other men. The conversation was always about what the white man was doing, how they were being oppressed by the white man, the latest injustice perpetrated by the white man. Rarely was there any talk about the kind of things Cloud heard adults talking about in other settings—their jobs, their families, what their children were doing in school, the latest sports scores. No, it was always about the white man—what the white man did to keep them down and what they did to thwart the white man. Cloud noticed that they seemed to enjoy the interchange, in a sense, even when they were complaining. The men fed off each other's sense of righteous indignation, whipping each other into more resentment and anger about white discrimination. Cloud realized, with some amusement, that the black men usually tried to best each other with their tales, each one trying to top the last story with a little more injustice, a little more outrage. "You think that's bad? Let me tell you what a white man said to me at the bus stop yesterday!"

Listening to the black men tell their stories gave Cloud a better understanding of how some were living lives very different from his, both in terms of how they were treated and how they focused their energy. But he also realized that it was their way of coping, a strategy for dealing with the inequities that they faced every day. It wasn't the way Cloud was raised, but as he looked back on it years later, he realized it was a coping strategy that was deeply ingrained in the male black culture, a traditional way to blow off steam and deal with the stress of being a black man in a mostly white world. The young black men on the *Kitty Hawk* had probably grown up sitting around barbershops or gas stations or on front porches listening to their fathers and other men gripe and groan about how hard it is to be a black man in a white world. They brought that culture to the carrier and used the same coping technique when they felt stressed and put upon.

Cloud figured the gripe sessions on the *Kitty Hawk* served the same purpose, and he hoped they were just as harmless.

It would take some time for Cloud to get a good handle on the culture of this floating city, and he was being assessed at the same time. The men on board took their time to size up Cloud, and the black sailors were some of the most wary. Rather than welcoming the black XO with open arms, some of them wanted to wait and see if he really was a black man like them or just another officer. An even more important relationship for Cloud was with Townsend, his new boss. Though it was off to a good start, they didn't really know each other.

CHAPTER FOUR

AMERICA AT SEA

The crew of the *Kitty Hawk* was a microcosm of America in 1972: mostly young men, with the same interests, vices, and problems as any other eighteen-, nineteen-, and twenty-year-olds back home. But these young people also were thrown into a claustrophobic warship a long way from home, with danger at every turn and extremely demanding work schedules.

The ship's crew members were diverse in as many ways as they were similar. Robert Keel grew up in San Diego, the son of a career Navy officer, which largely accounted for how he ended up in the Navy. He had been in JROTC in high school in 1966 when, at seventeen and pumped full of testosterone and bravado, he asked his father to sign the papers that would allow him to join the Army. Keel excitedly told his father that he had his heart set on joining the Army's Special Forces. Keel's father, who had served in the Navy during World War II and had seen plenty of action, looked at his son like he was out of his mind.

"You have no idea what you're talking about," the elder Keel said. "I'm not signing anything."

So Keel had to put off his gung-ho plans, and over the next few years he lost interest, beginning to focus more on his new wife and finding a path for his future. The military option came up again one evening in 1968, when the nineteen-year-old Keel was talking with his father, who pointed out that the war in Southeast Asia was heating up and more young men were being drafted. "If you don't do something yourself, you may not have a choice," he told his son. "You need to think about joining the Navy."

Fathers and sons were having that conversation all over the country. The older men, especially those who had been through World War II or the Korean War and knew the brutal reality of ground warfare, urged their sons to consider joining the Navy before they got drafted into the infantry. The Navy was a fine way to serve your country, they said, and though it certainly was no easy ride, at least you could be pretty sure you weren't going to die in some godforsaken jungle. Keel took his father's advice and was accepted into the Navy's nuclear submarine school, a prestigious appointment that would assure the young man of specialized duty, and which could lead to a technical career after his military service. But then Keel learned that he hadn't passed the Navy's rigorous moral tests because he had followed his recruiter's advice to be totally honest on his induction questionnaire and recount every single encounter he had ever had with a policeman—every traffic stop, every meaningless scolding from a cop. The Navy decided that was too many police contacts and tagged Keel with a history of delinquency. They rejected him for nuke school, and Keel felt like a fool for detailing what were really nothing more than typical teen antics. From there, he went through the motions of requesting the assignment he wanted, a destroyer, but he was assigned to the *Kitty Hawk* instead. An aircraft carrier needs lots of warm bodies to make it go, so plenty of the men assigned to it didn't necessarily want to be there. Keel had entered the Navy with a fine attitude, but being rejected for nuke school had left him disillusioned. His early months on the *Kitty Hawk* were rough, as they are for most sailors, but Keel's attitude kept spiraling down until one day he found himself sitting on the beach watching the ship sail out of Puget Sound without him. He was absent without leave, a criminal. The ship was pulling out after repairs and headed back to its home port of San Diego, after which it would go to sea for weeks and then months at a time. Keel didn't want to go with it. The twenty-year-old was so fed up with the Navy that he was toying with the idea of running away to Canada; not reporting for duty had felt like the right decision.

Until he saw his ship sailing out of port without him. The image shook him, and he knew he had screwed up. Big time.

Shit . . .what have I done?

Keel realized, with sudden clarity, that this was a turning point for him. The Navy offered opportunities, and he had responsibilities to his shipmates and to his family that he couldn't shirk just because he was feeling sorry for himself. This was the moment when Keel felt he had to be a man and do the right thing. He left town that night and made sure he was in San Diego when the *Kitty Hawk* docked. He went aboard and turned himself in, receiving twenty days in the brig. Oddly enough, his time in the brig helped turn around his attitude toward the Navy. It was easy time—none of the hard work that makes up most of a sailor's day, three meals and no waiting in the chow line, and he got to be good buddies with his Marine guards. Keel's only responsibility was to keep the brig spotless, just the way Marines like things. Keel spent his eighteen days in the brig, earning two days for good behavior, and came out with a much healthier attitude toward the Navy and life in general. The only bad part was that he had missed a couple weekends with his wife and baby daughter. To celebrate his release, Keel had the Marine guards over to his house for a party.

Keel went back to duty as a 4.0 sailor, squared away, the model of a good seaman, and kept that attitude up as he focused on his work in interior communications (IC). He and his fellow IC men were responsible for the operation and upkeep of the carrier's telephones, intercoms, equipment control, and telemetry systems. Keel had been on board the *Kitty Hawk* more than three years in 1972, and he enjoyed the overseas travel. Along the way he made a lot of friends on board, and learned to play poker. After he got over his initial disillusionment about Navy life, Keel thought life on the *Kitty Hawk* wasn't so bad. He could see the racial tension on board, however. Keel was like many white sailors who paid little attention to race and didn't let something as simple as skin color guide their impressions of other sailors, but he recognized that other white sailors had very different thoughts. One white man in Keel's department was from Texas and tried to explain to him how blacks were different.

"They're a different species, man. Can't you understand that?" the man said to Keel, incredulous that he even had to explain this to another white man. "Their bones are different, their muscles are different, they're put together different. They are not human."

Fuck, this guy is out of his mind, Keel thought. But he didn't try to argue, and Keel got along fine with most everyone on board. The ship had its share of extremist nut jobs, both black and white; the best strategy was to just steer clear of them. Most of the white sailors felt that way.

JOHN TRAVERS, ANOTHER white sailor from California, agreed that the *Kitty Hawk* was a decent way to serve your stint in the military. He went aboard the ship in July 1972 and spent the first two weeks belowdeck, so busy trying to settle into life on a carrier that he hardly realized he hadn't seen the sun for so long. When he got his first chance to step up on deck for a breather, the bright sun felt like ice picks in his eyes. Travers also learned to be careful with the ship's drinking water; if the crew didn't properly purge the lines when filling the water tanks, sometimes it became polluted with jet fuel. At times the water was so foul that you could light it on fire.

Daily hardships aside, Travers was pleased to be on a ship with a reputation like the *Kitty Hawk*'s. It was pretty badass. The carrier USS *Enterprise* might get all the glory, the crew often said, but we get the dirty jobs and we get the job done. He was satisfied with what he saw of the captain too. Townsend's reputation went up a few notches with a number of sailors one day when the ship was cruising in winds that were blowing like hell and kicking up waves that looked big even against a massive aircraft carrier. Travers was in the chow line on the hangar deck, one of dozens of hungry sailors. Captain Townsend came onto the deck trailed by his ever-present Marine escort, whom the crew referred to—mostly good-naturedly—as the "the captain's dog." Like all the Marines on board, but especially one who walked alongside the sharply dressed skipper all day, the captain's dog's uniform was always impeccable. All the sailors were watching as Townsend and the Marine stopped in the big elevator doors on the side of the carrier—huge open portals, wide enough for two jets side by side—to look at the swells. They should have noticed that the deck there was very wet. Suddenly a wave hit the ship broadside, splashing high up onto the sponson jutting out over the elevator door and right into the open portal, hitting the captain and his dog full force with what must have been a hundred gallons of seawater. The Marine instinctively jumped back. The captain, however, just stood there in his dark brown leather flight jacket and got drenched, taking the full brunt of the wave, hands on his hips, staring out to sea like Leif Ericson. The sailors could have laughed as the captain stood there with water pouring off of him, but instead they roared with admiration and applauded the sight of Doc taking it like a real sailor. They did laugh a bit at the Marine for flinching.

THE CAPTAIN'S CONFIDENCE also reassured Chris Mason, a young white sailor from Gadsden, Alabama, who came to the *Kitty Hawk* by way of the Navy Reserves, trying like so many of his fellow sailors to avoid the draft. When he graduated high school in 1968, as the Tet offensive was dealing a hard blow to U.S. troops, he listened to the warnings from friends who had already served their times in the jungles of Southeast Asia. To a man, every one of them told Mason,

"Don't go." Running from duty was never an option, so, to avoid being drafted, Mason joined the Reserves and then went on to active duty on the *Kitty Hawk*. Even before he sailed for Vietnam, Mason realized that he was in the middle of something momentous. Many of his fellow sailors were caught up in the antiwar tumult of the time. Though Mason put more value on military service than many of them, he couldn't help but be fascinated by seeing servicemen openly defying their orders, refusing to report for duty, and participating in antiwar protests. Mason felt like he was watching history unfold in front of him, an unexpected development for a small-town Alabama boy. Assigned to the captain's mail room, Mason was way too busy learning the ropes to be concerned with issues of race, which had never bothered him much anyway. His best buddy on the carrier ended up being a black guy from San Pedro, whom he worked with, and they spent their rare downtime shooting the breeze with hardly any acknowledgment of their differences beyond the kinds that make for idle chitchat and some harmless ribbing. Mason actually felt a sort of reverse discrimination on the *Kitty Hawk;* upon hearing his Southern accent and learning he was from Alabama, black sailors, and even some whites, automatically assumed he was some stereotypical racist. The epithets "redneck" and "cracker" came flying at Mason with some regularity, but he tried to let them just roll off. Once people got to know him, they realized he was just a good old boy with no grudge against anyone for their skin color. But one problem on all ships of this size was that it was hard for 5,000 men to get to know each other. And the more the sailors self-segregated, the more the black sailors could imagine the worst of the whites.

Mason's eyes were opened a little to the differences in how black and white sailors perceived the racial issues on the *Kitty Hawk* when the carrier had a "tiger cruise"—an opportunity for sailors' relatives and close friends to join them for a short cruise to see the ship's inner workings and gain some appreciation for how the crew lives and what their jobs entail. One afternoon Mason was in the chow hall and had just gotten his food when he spotted his black buddy at a table with his family. Without giving it a second thought, Mason took his tray over and sat down at the table with his buddy, greeting his friend's family in that Southern drawl and welcoming them aboard. His friend looked at him with surprise, as if Mason had just committed some obvious faux pas, but went through the motions of introducing his family. Mason didn't understand the tension and ate quickly before excusing himself. Over the next months, as the racial tension on the *Kitty Hawk* came to the surface, he came to realize that his friend felt Mason had put him in an awkward situation, not only with his own family but with the other black sailors who saw them together. It was one thing for them to hang out when it was just the two of them, Mason found out, but the presence of his friend's family and the other black guests on board made his socializing with the Alabama white boy something much more.

"Didn't you feel uncomfortable?" his friend asked soon after the incident.

"No way. We're work mates, man. We always hang out," Mason replied. His friend shook his head like Mason just didn't get it. And he didn't.

"Man . . ." His buddy started and stopped, looking for a way to explain. "People were *looking.*"

GARLAND YOUNG GREW UP in Hamilton, Ohio, just outside Cincinnati, living in the projects after his father, a World War II veteran who became the town drunk as he continued fighting the war in his mind, lost yet another job. Living there meant Young had to learn to cope with being a white kid in a nearly all-black neighborhood. He was in the third grade when he moved to the projects, so he was largely ignorant of the racial issues involved, though he did come to think that his fifth-grade teacher, Mrs. Flowers, didn't like him because he was white and that was why she beat him so much. He also noticed that his sixth-grade teacher, Mr. Gallagher, a black man, was such a whiz with rocketry that he was woefully underemployed as a school teacher and should have been working for NASA. Young's father left home when Garland was eleven years old, leaving his wife to raise five sons. The war in Southeast Asia was heating up at just about the same time Young was old enough to be drafted. At that time, Ping-Pong balls with birth dates were picked out of a little wire cage to determine the order in which men would be drafted. Men with Young's birth date were number two in line. Unless the United States made a sudden turnaround and started pulling soldiers out of Southeast Asia, Young knew that it was only a matter of time—and probably not much time—before he was drafted. He considered signing up for a longer stint than the two years that came with being drafted, but his preacher reminded Young that they had seen his Sunday school teacher come home from Vietnam in a box.

The preacher urged Young not to go to war, to obtain a hardship deferment and stay home to help his mother. He'd vouch for the hardship, the preacher told him. But Young refused, saying his family never shirked military duty.

"At least go to the Navy," the man told Young. "Stay out of the infantry."

Young promised he'd think about it. The preacher's pleas were on his mind the next time he ran into the two Navy recruiters on his paper route. He ended up chatting with them, and one, Chief Robey, persuaded Young that he could serve his country with honor by joining the Navy. Robey made a good pitch for the Navy—travel, see the world, spend your days on the glorious high seas, meet plenty of women, learn a skill, build a career—and he included many promises about what kind of assignment Young could get, where we would be stationed, anything that Young needed to hear before signing the papers. Robey left Hamilton before Young actually signed the papers to enlist, so he was not listed on the forms as the recruiter.

By the time Young enlisted, was through boot camp, and trans-ferred to the *Kitty Hawk,* he was already finding that some of those promises weren't coming through. Young was just another warm body to be used however the Navy needed, and it didn't seem to care what he preferred or what the recruiter had promised. Young asked for a carrier assignment, figuring that if he was going to sea, he might as well go all the way.

Soon after his arrival on the *Kitty Hawk,* Young had a break from his job as a mess cook—the crappy job nearly every enlisted man got when first aboard the ship, no matter what their normal as-signment would be later—and spotted a familiar face: Chief Robey. Young walked up and said hello to the man who had promised so much. Robey's face went white when he saw Young. Recruiters weren't supposed to end up serving with anyone they had re-cruited—for exactly this reason. Young shook the man's hand and told him not to worry, that he wasn't angry.

And Young meant it. He was pleased to be on the big carrier, though he was finding out that life on the *Kitty Hawk* was going to be a long, hard ride. He would become an airman after his stint as a cook, and Young soon found out that the work—long and hard cer-tainly—was only part of the challenge of this Navy assignment.

JOHN CALLAHAN WAS A white sailor who probably would not have ex-changed pleasantries with his recruiter if he had seen him aboard the *Kitty Hawk.* Callahan also was spurred to join the Navy when he got a low draft number. Very much the all-American kid with a paper route and a quiet personality, Callahan came from a Navy family so he de-cided it would make sense to enlist in that branch when faced with a choice. He knew it offered relative safety during a time of war com-pared to the other military options. When Callahan talked to his local recruiter in the suburbs of Long Island, New York, he was assured that if he enlisted, he could be kept stateside and trained as a Navy journalist, which suited the young man's career ambitions and his antiwar sentiment. As soon as he enlisted, however, those promises went out the window. He went to boot camp, then to radar school and directly to Vietnam on the *Kitty Hawk*. He was not happy, and it was more than just that the recruiter's promises were broken, more than just not wanting to be at sea on a carrier working on radar. Callahan deeply opposed the Vietnam War, and he saw a real difference between serving in the Navy stateside and sitting on the carrier in the Gulf of Tonkin while it launched airplanes to bomb Vietnamese people. Callahan wasn't on the ship long before he filed the paperwork requesting to be declared a conscientious objector (CO), which he hoped would get him pulled off the carrier. Such a request was not uncommon during the war, and Callahan's superiors didn't make a big deal out of it. The paperwork would take a while to be approved or denied, however. In the meantime, Callahan was put in a noncombat role on the mess deck, helping to feed the thousands of men on the ship. It was supposed to be a nonviolent role for the potential CO, but Callahan later would see the irony in that assignment.

NOT THAT YOUNG, CALLAHAN, or the other white sailors really saw trouble coming. Racial tensions surfaced on the ship every now and then, but that happened in any American city just as much and sometimes more. The black sailors on the carrier were no more homogenous than the whites. Perry Pettus was a black sailor who, unlike many of his fellow blacks on the *Kitty Hawk,* thought the Navy was treating him pretty well. He had grown up in Hopkinsville, Kentucky, part of a large family that worked his grandfather's 600-acre farm. Pettus routinely worked on the farm after school, which had been segregated until he was in the eighth grade. He had tried a couple years of college, which yielded a lot of bills and not very good grades. Pettus's draft number was 52, so he wasn't in imminent danger of being drafted, but he decided that enlisting might be a better use of his time and would eliminate any future fears about the draft. Prompted in part by his memories of a first cousin home on leave, strutting down the street in his sharp Navy blues, Pettus decided to save his parents some money by quitting school and joining up. He studied aviation in the Navy and was thrilled to be assigned to the *Kitty Hawk*. His first night on the ship, he got an opportunity to go to the flight deck and see flight operations, where he would soon be working. The sight of planes taking off and landing in the dark, with just minimal red lights and men in danger everywhere he looked, scared him more than a little. This was serious business, he realized. People die on flight decks.

Pettus had already heard about the division officer who died a couple weeks earlier when he stepped just a hair too close to the jet intake of an A–7 Corsair. He was sucked into the blades of the jet engine in a heartbeat. Young had seen the same thing happen to a friend of his. For a nineteen-year-old farm boy from Kentucky like Pettus, the deck of the *Kitty Hawk* was like a different world—a scary but exciting place to be. Once he got over the inevitable shock of a first-timer, Pettus came to love the fast-paced, carefully choreographed action on the flight deck, where men communicated more with elaborate hand gestures than with words, where each man depended on the others to do their jobs well and keep everyone safe while fulfilling their combat missions. Pettus loved his job, and when he was working, the only colors that mattered were the color-coordinated jerseys worn on the flight deck to differentiate the men's various duties—purple for fuel handlers, red for weapons specialists, blue for plane handlers. As long as he was on deck helping get planes on and off the ship, he didn't feel like anybody gave a damn what his skin color was. Belowdecks was a different matter, but sometimes it seemed the black sailors cared more than the whites. Although Pettus was about as content as anyone on a carrier crew could be, it wouldn't be long before he found himself victimized because of his skin color.

IN STARK CONTRAST TO most of the other sailors, and even Cloud and Townsend, were the Marines on the *Kitty Hawk*. Captain Nicholas F. Carlucci, commander of the seventy Marines who were in charge of securing the most sensitive areas of the ship, had joined the Corps in 1965 when he was twenty-one, as the draft loomed for him also. His college degree earned him a transfer to Officer Candidate School at Quantico, Virginia. He served admirably in Vietnam in 1967, seeing extensive action and playing a key role in the rescue of a unit that had been ambushed. After completing his tour, Carlucci was a Marine instructor for two years, itching to go back to combat. When the Marines didn't have an appropriate assignment for him, he requested a ship detachment, figuring it would be a change of pace and a way to get back into the action in some way. The Marines assigned him to command the detachment on the *Kitty Hawk* and Carlucci tackled the job with his usual gusto, diving deeply into studies of every task he might be called on to perform on a carrier—everything from running a brig, to safeguarding nuclear weapons, to quelling a riot. Carlucci was a Marine, a damn good one by anyone's estimation, and he did things the way Marines did everything: by the book.

Carlucci's men followed his lead and had zero tolerance for what they considered the slack discipline of the modern Navy. The Navy in 1972 might let its sailors take a casual approach to uniforms and nearly every other aspect of military decorum and discipline, but not the Marines. Carlucci's men were squared-away, ramrod-straight Marines with short, regulation haircuts, and they had no respect for slovenly sailors who looked more like hippies than military men. The Marines on the *Kitty Hawk* didn't seem to care much whether you were white or black or Latino, but they openly disdained any sailors with scraggly beards and sloppy uniforms. And they didn't have much tolerance for any kind of misbehavior. In an era in which even the Navy was affected by the Age of Aquarius, the Marines were from a different age altogether. They were an island of conservatism among 5,000 sailors who, despite their Navy uniforms, weren't all that much

different in attitude, interests, and activities from the typical nineteen-
year-olds back home.

THAT THE CREW of the *Kitty Hawk* were still young people in an increasingly youth-oriented, anything-goes society was clear to anyone
who saw the sailors in their off time, either in the berthing areas and
mess halls or when they left the ship for liberty calls. Just as they were
for their counterparts back home, drugs were a frequent escape for
those on board the *Kitty Hawk* and other Navy ships, with top-qual-
ity heroin, marijuana, hashish, and LSD picked up easily on shore in
the Philippines and sold on the ship's black market. In these days
long before drug testing became commonplace, sailors found it easy
to escape from the rigors and boredom of carrier life with their drug
of choice. The many nooks and crannies of a vast aircraft carrier
made it an easy feat to smoke pot or even inject heroin without being
caught. Captain Townsend and XO Cloud were aware of the drug
use, as was Carlucci and every other ranking officer on the ship, but
stopping it was altogether another matter. Townsend was under the
impression that the drug use was relatively uncommon, estimating
that only 5 percent of his crew used drugs while at sea. But his sailors
knew it was much more than that.

The drug use was obvious to Tom Dysart, another white sailor
whose journey to the *Kitty Hawk* was spurred by the looming draft.
He joined the Navy Reserves while at Southwest Missouri State University in Springfield, and went on to serve his two years of active
duty. He was assigned to the *Kitty Hawk* in the summer of 1971, serving his first three months as a trash-and-garbage guy before moving to
the E division as an electrician. Like many of those on board, he was a
typical child of the 1960s, smoking pot at every opportunity and just
riding out his military service on the *Hawk*. In that respect, Dysart fit
in just fine with the rest of the crew. There was no noticeable racial
tension, as far as he could tell, though life on board the carrier tended

to be just as segregated as it was in civilian life. There weren't any hard-and-fast rules about where blacks and whites could be or any Navy-sanctioned separation of the races, but people just knew. Dysart could see that, especially when it came to berthing areas, some parts of the *Kitty Hawk* were the black neighborhoods, some were Latino, and most were white. People mixed sometimes, just as they might in the civilian world, but the unofficial demarcations were clear.

The extent of the drug use on the carrier did surprise Dysart some. He met a sailor from Detroit who struck him as a nice guy, a typical fresh-faced young kid. Soon after joining the *Kitty Hawk,* the young man confided that he had scored a big stash of heroin and was hoping it would help him get through the long days at sea. Before long, the kid looked like a scarecrow.

The extent of the drug use was obvious to others, too. John Travers, for instance, knew of pilots on the *Kitty Hawk* who were bringing in drugs from Thailand. He also knew that drugs were present throughout the military, easily found on any ship, on any base. On his way to his assignment on the *Kitty Hawk,* he and some other sailors stopped at Clark Air Force Base in the Philippines. They were informed that a helicopter had just come in and would ferry them closer to the carrier as soon as they unloaded the passengers and baggage. Travers overheard people at the base talking about how the helo had just brought in the Navy's top brass—Chief of Naval Operations (CNO) Admiral Elmo Zumwalt, who was already becoming legendary for his leadership and innovative, sometimes controversial, policy decisions. Zumwalt and his family were returning from a trip to Southeast Asia.

Travers and the other sailors got to work unloading the luggage, which looked like what a family might travel with, along with various duffel bags and other items that had been aboard the helo. As they tossed the items out, one bag fell and out spilled several large jars of white tablets. Travers and the other sailors stopped and stared at them, wondering what they were and what to do. Everyone figured out pretty quickly what they were, and they silently agreed that they didn't want any trouble, no matter who those drugs belonged to. No one suspected that Zumwalt or his family members were transporting a duffel bag of heroin, but the fact that someone had put the shipment on the CNO's helo said a lot about the brazenness of the drug trade in the Navy.

The men stuffed the jars back into the duffel bag and sent it on its way.

CHAPTER FIVE

A LONG, DIFFICULT JOURNEY

Their backgrounds and motivations may have been varied, but there were many black men on the Kitty Hawk with a bad attitude. Many of the most unhappy black sailors on the Kitty Hawk were there because of Project 100,000, a Navy program that set out to recruit primarily inner-city youths who were previously considered ineligible for military service because of low test scores. Standards were lowered to help the Navy fill the need for more warm bodies during the war. Military applicants had been screened since 1950 with the Armed Forces Qualification Test (AFQT), which included verbal and math questions and was aimed at assessing recruits' ability to be trained, which in turn predicted their likelihood of advancing, feeling satisfied with serving in the military, and completing the term of enlistment. Test scores placed applicants in categories 1 through 5, with 1 representing the highest scores. The armed services used the test scores, in conjunction with each applicant's education, to screen all applicants and draftees.

During the mid-1960s, it became apparent that up to a third of young men would be ineligible for military service because of their low test scores. A significant number of them came from disadvantaged backgrounds and had little education. Because a great many also were unemployed, some activists and political leaders called on the military to change the standards as part of President Lyndon Johnson's ongoing War on Poverty. Secretary of Defense Robert McNamara declared on August 23, 1966, that the military would help disadvantaged young men by establishing a sort of affirmative action policy for recruiting: "The poor of America have not had the opportunity to earn their fair share of this nation's abundance, but they can be given an opportunity to serve in their country's defense, and they can be given an opportunity to return to civilian life with skills and aptitudes which for them and their families will reverse the downward spiral of human decay."

Project 100,000 was launched on October 1, 1966, and the Department of Defense began accepting men who previously would not have qualified for military service. The stated goal was to enlist 40,000 men under the less stringent standards during the first year and 100,000 every year thereafter. Applicants with AFQT scores in category 5, the lowest, were still not eligible, but some in category 4, who scored between the tenth and thirtieth percentiles on the tests, were. Having a high school diploma helped a category 4 applicant be approved despite the low scores.

Many of the Project 100,000 recruits, referred to as "New Standards Men" (NSMs), were assigned to what the military called soft-skill jobs that required little training or intelligence—food service and supply jobs, for instance. The project ended in December 1971 after 354,000 men had entered military service under its relaxed standards, so in 1972 the Navy still had many sailors who had been admitted through the program. And because an aircraft carrier requires a large crew, the *Kitty Hawk* was certain to have its share of Project 100,000 sailors. Just over half of all project sailors, 54 percent, were volunteers. The other 46 percent were draftees who otherwise would have gotten a free pass from serving because of their inability to be trained. According to Department of Defense statistics, Project 100,000 recruits had an average age of twenty. About half came from the South, and 41 percent were minorities. Their average reading ability was at a sixth-grade level, and 13 percent read below the fourth-grade level.

Project 100,000 succeeded in opening the world of military service to more young men, and the influx of recruits helped keep the services staffed as the war continued in Vietnam. But its effects were decidedly mixed. One unexpected result—or some would say the entirely predictable result—was that many black sailors were finding themselves in the lowest-level assignments with virtually no chance of being able to work their way up because they didn't have the necessary intelligence, education, or skills. Many felt their recruiters lied to them, making the same promises of career advancement and glorious assignments that they made to everyone else, despite knowing that the men's low test scores would make it impossible for them to advance. These sailors were stuck at the bottom when it came to job assignments, and no amount of hard work was going to earn them a promotion.

The Navy was finding that many Project 100,000 recruits also were not useful assets. A 1969 assessment of their performance concluded that the enlistees performed worse than other recruits and that the program "is not in the best interest of the Navy, unless dictated by a manpower shortage or other non-military considerations." A 1990 analysis also determined that Project 100,000 did not bestow any long-term benefits on the men admitted to military service under the lowered standards. Contrary to McNamara's hopes that the men would "return to civilian life with skills and aptitudes which for them and their families will reverse the downward spiral of human decay," the 1990 analysis of the men's experiences after serving in the military found no such results. "These data provide no evidence to support the hypothesis that military service offers a 'leg up' to [low-aptitude] and disadvantaged youth as they seek to overcome their cognitive and skill deficits and compete successfully in the civilian world," the report concluded.

While the Navy positioned Project 100,000 as a progressive effort to open up the benefits of service to the inner-city youth who needed jobs, some critics said the project was a well-intentioned but misguided effort to use the military as a means of social change. Still others called it an intentional effort to trick young black men into the Navy and keep the rosters filled for the war in Vietnam. The antiwar movement, especially the most militant factions in the Revolutionary Communist Party, USA, and other communist groups, openly derided the project as just a way of "using the nigger against the gook."

The true motivation for Project 100,000 was probably neither as noble as McNamara claimed nor as nefarious as the communists contended. Nevertheless, the project was one reason why the *Kitty Hawk* was staffed with plenty of disgruntled black sailors who had little to lose by disobeying orders or performing poorly. Marland Townsend had already seen the effects of the project when he served on the *Constellation,* and he saw the same problems as soon as he took command of the *Kitty Hawk.* After his initial refurbishment, the ship was in great shape logistically. He recognized, however, that some crew members seemed to be in over their heads. Whether they had good attitudes or not, enlisted men whose test scores indicated that their IQs were well below average were of limited use to Townsend on the *Kitty Hawk.* Without the most basic intelligence, they would never advance beyond the lowest-level grunt work, he realized. This troubled Townsend in two ways. First, he had a carrier to run, and his ship was operating at maximum capacity in a war zone. He couldn't afford to have crew members of limited potential. And second, he worried that these New Standards Men were growing frustrated with their lot in the Navy.

These guys could not have understood the contract they signed to get in the Navy, Townsend realized. *There's no way. They didn't understand what they were doing.*

He was right on target, though he didn't know how bad the problem was or what to do about it.

CONTRARY TO SO MANY other young sailors on the *Kitty Hawk,* and ironically so as it would turn out, eighteen-year-old Terry Avinger actually wanted to be there. The young black man from Philadelphia volunteered to join the Navy as a means to escape not the draft but his troubled, violent life. In a moment of clarity, determined to make something better of himself, Avinger signed up for the Navy and joined the *Kitty Hawk* with a positive attitude. He knew that he was on a path to disaster if he continued with his life of drugs, crime, and violence back home; for him, the *Kitty Hawk* was a way out, a way to create a new life. Avinger soon found out, however, that his personal demons followed when he joined the carrier crew, and some of the same issues that frustrated and enraged black men back home could be found on the *Kitty Hawk.* Avinger's optimism would not last.

Terry Avinger shared many traits in common with the young sailors on the *Kitty Hawk,* particularly with the other young black men. He was born in 1954, the sixth of his mother's eleven children. The Avinger family originally was from Savannah, Georgia, but his parents had moved to Philadelphia some years earlier because, as Avinger heard his mother and father say many times, "Too many of the men in our family were being killed down there." Whether the deaths were at the hands of racist whites or from other causes, Avinger didn't know. But he heard his parents talk of the pervasive racism in the Deep South.

Avinger was raised from the age of two to ten years by his grandmother and great-aunt, who had previously lived under one roof with the extended family but decided to ease the crowding by getting their own place and taking the baby with them. They lived in a mostly white, middle-class neighborhood of Philadelphia, along with a cousin who was seventeen years older than Avinger. Then when Avinger was ten years old, his comfortable and calm life was interrupted: He was sent back to live with his mother and his ten brothers and sisters in a poor black section of Philadelphia. The family lived in a small townhouse with one bathroom. Avinger's father was an Army veteran who worked as a barber but did not live with the family. Moving to the North Philadelphia neighborhood was a shock for the black boy who had grown up surrounded by whites and who felt comfortable in that environment. Suddenly he was among black people nearly all the time, and Avinger found himself enjoying a fellowship with blacks that he never knew he had been denied. His mother was well known in the community, which helped the youngster make friends. He attended a Baptist church with his family regularly, but it wasn't long before Avinger found another aspect of the North Philly neighborhood that was more attractive. He began spending a lot of time with boys who seemed more streetwise than he felt, tougher and wiser in the ways of the world, brash in their black pride and in their defiance of anything they perceived as discrimination from whites. As Avinger grew older and started feeling the rebelliousness of a teenage boy, joining the local gang seemed the natural step. He became an enthusiastic member of 28th and Oxford, the violent gang named after the neighborhood corner they called home. Fights with other gangs were a regular part of Avinger's life, sometimes organized on a schoolyard almost like formal boxing matches and sometimes random assaults. Though he often came home with cuts and bruises from vicious fights featuring any improvised weapons the gang members could find—bricks, car antennas wielded like steel whips, even the occasional handgun—Avinger mostly avoided serious injury. Despite being shot at on more than one occasion, Avinger felt the invincibility of youth and saw the gang as a second family. That satisfaction diminished when he was thirteen and playing a game of stickball with his fellow gang members. A moment of carefree play turned tragic when a rival gang member appeared and started shooting. A close friend of Avinger's died that day, and he realized that the gang life was not just about bravado and bonding. For what would be the first in a series of attempts, Avinger decided to turn his life around. He joined a local youth club and soon quit the gang. Rather than attend the regular high school in the neighborhood, Avinger decided to go to a vocational school to study auto mechanics, figuring this would put him on a path toward a decent job. He was doing his best to do the right thing, to stay on the straight and narrow, and he was successful until a series of tragedies overwhelmed him and sent him on a downward spiral. First a younger brother died of spinal meningitis, a devastating blow to his family, and then a year later Avinger's father was shot to death in a bar. Avinger fell into a deep depression, with no idea how to deal with his grief. His grades suffered so much that he was held back in school two years in a row. During this time, Avinger began using alcohol and marijuana on a regular basis and sometimes heroin—the same weakness that engulfed many men of his generation, but also a young man's attempt to deal with what felt like all-encompassing grief.

As Avinger neared adulthood, his tall and skinny frame beginning to fill out, he was mired in a lifestyle that promised nothing good. He was using drugs and alcohol frequently, and he attended school only sporadically. No longer was Avinger the essentially good kid who got into various scrapes. He was now moody, and prone to violence. Drugs and alcohol were his main focus and his main escape. He was quick to lash out at others, always likely to hit first. He was angry most of the time, angry at anyone and everyone, especially authority figures. He was angry at God. He was angry at the racial disparities he saw around him, in particular the segregation of Girard College, a private kindergarten-through-twelfth grade school in his own neighborhood, an all-white boys' school in an almost entirely black neighborhood. The school had been established in 1833 by a merchant seaman, before the neighborhood was mostly black, but it became a focal point for the community's growing outrage over racism and segregation, the focus of frequent protests and demonstrations. Like the protestors, Avinger wasn't upset because he wanted to attend the school. The cost of a private school was way beyond his family's means. But the school was his introduction to institutional racism, and it became one of his most hated symbols of white America. This wasn't just one ignorant white man saying something cruel, and it wasn't just one shop owner who refused to serve blacks. It was an institution that was set up specifically to exclude blacks, and it was right in their community. It was in Avinger's face every day, a glaring example of racism in America. For Avinger and many other young people in the community, the children going to the school, their parents, and the all-white teachers and administrators were practically the only white people they ever encountered. Despite years of protests and legal challenges, Girard College did not admit its first black student until 1968, and only grudgingly then. By Avinger's late teens, the school was officially desegregated, but it remained an example of institutional racism to many black Philadelphians. He hated the school, and he felt pretty much the same way about white people in general.

But even with all the anger raging inside him, Avinger still had enough insight to see that he was going nowhere fast. For the second time in his young life, he decided to make a dramatic turnaround. While many young men were finding ways to avoid military service altogether, Avinger went down to the local recruiting station one month after he turned seventeen and joined the Navy. He chose the Navy partly because the infantry just didn't sound like a good experience, even if you didn't go to Vietnam, and partly because he had always been fascinated with boats and ships. He also had an uncle and a cousin who had been in the Navy, and he loved the movies featuring Navy ships in World War II. Avinger, a true city boy, was fascinated by the idea of so many men living on a ship out on the ocean for months at a time. Carriers in particular captivated him because of their size and power. The recruiter told Avinger he could be a jet mechanic, which fit with his mechanical interests and could lead to a civilian career. Things were looking up.

And then another stumble. Avinger, like many of his fellow recruits, had minimized his drug and alcohol use before joining up. The hitch came when a boot camp instructor saw needle tracks on his arms, evidence of past heroin use. The Navy threatened to discharge him immediately, and Avinger had to wonder why he was being singled out. The young man convinced his superiors that he was turning his life around and that he was no longer using drugs. He was relieved when the Navy agreed to let him continue on to aviation school in Memphis before assignment to a squadron. It was there that Avinger started to see more examples of the racism that fueled the anger still simmering deep inside. A black man in Tennessee in 1971 couldn't be surprised to find discrimination, but Avinger was frustrated, and more than a little disappointed, to find it institutionalized in the Navy just as it was in Girard College.

By the time Avinger arrived on the *Kitty Hawk* as an airman apprentice in 1972, he had lost much of his initial enthusiasm for the Navy and his optimism about creating a better life for himself. His inner turmoil had taken over again, and his experiences with racism were causing him to focus his anger on the white race. There were times when he could redirect his thinking and promise himself that he would do his best to succeed in the white man's world, that if he just applied himself he could prevail despite all the obstacles put in his way. But most of the time he was a young black man with a chip on his shoulder, just waiting for someone to knock it off.

TOWNSEND REALIZED THAT THE *Kitty Hawk* crew was working hard, but he still thought the carrier could perform better. Drawing on his instinct for technical analysis and hard numbers, the captain looked at the situation and realized the carrier could be more productive without asking the crew to work any harder. In fact, he might be able to ease the workload at the same time he improved performance. The *Kitty Hawk* was there to win a war, and Townsend thought the carrier could improve flight operations by changing how the crew were scheduled. The standard for carriers at the time was for flight ops crew to work from 6 A.M. to 6 P.M. for ten days, then switch to the noon-to-midnight shift for ten days, then on to the midnight-to-noon shift for ten days before starting the cycle all over again. These hours kicked the crew's ass. Not only was the ship performing the incredibly complex and dangerous flight ops around the clock, but crew members could never settle into a daily pattern. It was hell on their minds and bodies. So Townsend convinced his admiral that the *Kitty Hawk* should have flight ops only from midnight to noon, with the rest of the day set aside for the aircraft maintenance. Townsend's plan actually resulted in a significant increase in the number of sorties flown per hour.

This was the kind of captain Townsend was. Townsend couldn't be out glad-handing with every sailor every day, but he always figured the men's welfare into his calculations aimed at making the *Kitty Hawk* the best she could be. It was the kind of effort that the crew often had no idea was even going on, much less how much they were benefiting from it.

Crew members were more likely to take notice of the edicts from above regarding cleanliness of the ship and other requirements. Townsend was old school Navy in some ways, and like the Marines onboard, he had no tolerance for the Navy's newly relaxed attitude on some issues. Just like the rest of American society, the Navy in 1972 was changing, and not all change was good. Mirroring the rest of America, the Navy let its hair down—both figuratively and literally. Sailors were allowed to have longish hair and beards, and uniform standards were relaxed to the point that many more seasoned Navy officers were disgusted by the sloppy appearance of some sailors—and their officers' lack of interest in correcting them. The relaxed standards were officially sanctioned, part of Admiral Zumwalt's many initiatives to respond to the changing face of young America, promote better treatment of minorities in the Navy, and avoid having the ranks dwindle because no one was willing to meet the past standards of Navy dress and decorum.

Townsend considered Zumwalt's efforts well reasoned and well intended, but he could see that some of the initiatives weren't working out as planned.

The same issues of cleanliness in berthing areas and throughout the ship that troubled Benjamin Cloud when he came aboard also grated on Townsend. The captain informed the crew early on that he would insist on a higher level of cleanliness, inside and out, than they might have been used to. In particular, he informed them that some men would get one of the most dreaded assignments for a young sailor.

"When we're in port—you're not going to like this—but we're going to have side cleaners," he told his senior staff. "We're not going to have a rust bucket sitting out here with rust running down the side. And we're not going to do it only on the starboard side either. We're going to do it on the port side, the side people don't see."

That meant that while their buddies were ashore enjoying some R&R, some unlucky sailors were going to be hanging off the side of the carrier, scraping, washing, and painting. It was work that couldn't be done while the ship was at sea. The crew hated the new policy, but Townsend was adamant: "We're going to keep this ship clean. That's just the way it's going to be."

That kind of attitude led to a scathing attack on the captain in the *Kitty Litter* newspaper published on board the carrier by anonymous crew members. The article was headlined "The New Captain, Another Queeg?" a reference to the paranoid, maniacal, and abusive captain portrayed in the 1951 Herman Wouk novel *The Caine*

Mutiny and the 1954 movie of the same name starring Humphrey Bogart. The writer said: "Townsend has shown himself to be one of the original 'law 'n order' kids" through the harsh punishment he handed out for "such tiny and meaningless 'crimes' as unauthorized absence." The article went on to accuse the captain of outright racism in his handling of disciplinary matters and then mocked him for giving speeches in which he praised the crew's accomplishments in carrying out bombing runs. "Probably the only person these actions are 'good' for is the Captain and other lifers who want feathers in their caps for murdering their fellow human beings," the article said.

TOWNSEND WAS NOT NEARLY so draconian as the writer claimed, and he certainly was no Queeg. Much of that kind of ranting could be dismissed as sophomoric, the kind of name-calling that the bottom ranks aim at the top dog in any operation. But it does give insight into the general disdain some of the carrier's crew felt for the war, the Navy, and their captain. The *Kitty Hawk* was not unique in facing crew resistance, and one captain like Townsend could not reverse the changes going on in the Navy. The lowered expectations for discipline and military protocol meshed in a dangerous way with the growing war resistance in the late 1960s and early 1970s. The antiwar movement was in full swing back home, and the young people in the military were not immune to its charms. In fact, sometimes they were the most fervent of antiwar protestors because it was they who would be going to Vietnam, either on the ground or on a ship in the Gulf of Tonkin. The *Kitty Hawk,* like any Navy ship with a large crew, had a mix of the same young men you could find back home: sailors who were proud to serve their country and despised the long-haired hippies who protested and called them names in port, and sailors who vehemently opposed the war and weren't going to stop protesting just because the government forced them into a white uniform. There were plenty in the middle too. Combined with the growing black power movement and the prevalent dope culture, sailors in this period could be far from the disciplined and obedient ideal that the Navy sought. Like teenagers who think they're smarter than their parents and too big to be spanked, sailors sometimes spoke their minds freely. Sometimes they paid a price for the insolence, and sometimes, perhaps too often, superiors just let it go.

Resistance was more than just vocal, however. By 1972, the Navy was well aware that some of its own men were interfering in the war effort by sabotaging equipment, organizing work strikes, and deliberately slowing down operations. At first, resistance within military ranks was instigated by those who had been active in the antiwar movement before entering the service, but then the movement began to grow and involve more service members. Many of the early incidents involved desertions and refusals to report for duty; then the resistors turned to violence. Sailors of all races participated, but black sailors often were motivated by a mixture of antiwar sentiment and black pride, in the same way those movements were deeply intertwined in the civilian world. The black power movement prominent in cities back home could be found on U.S. bases in Germany, the Philippines, and elsewhere. In the jungles of Vietnam, the Viet Cong (VC) enemy actively played on black soldiers' disillusionment with the white establishment. VC propaganda suggested that blacks and Vietnamese were both being abused by the white man and should not fight each other. A popular phrase among disgruntled black soldiers was "No VC ever called me a nigger."

Black pride and black power were prominent components of the growing resistance to the Vietnam War, and more militant factions of the black community called on black servicemen to rebel openly. For example, the Black Panther Party called on black soldiers, sailors, and airmen to fight the white system from within, to stop the American war machine from using more young black men as cannon fodder by any means necessary. "Either quit the Army now or start destroying it from the inside," Black Panther leader Eldridge Cleaver told them in

1970. The message resonated with more than a few black service-men. One poll found that 76 percent of black servicemen supported Cleaver and were in favor of the armed overthrow of the U.S. govern-ment. A publication of the Revolutionary Communist Party, USA, quoted one black Marine as explaining how some of his fellow black soldiers were smuggling mortars home from the battlefield to use on the streets of America. After showing a reporter how the men broke the mortars down into smaller components, the Marine pointed to one mortar and said, "Now, that'll take out a police station for you."

The flashpoints often came where military personnel were held on criminal charges. One of the most prominent uprisings was at Fort Bragg, North Carolina, on July 23, 1968. Prompted by the beating of a black inmate being held at the stockade, a group of black and white soldiers took over the detention center and held it for forty-eight hours before troops from the 82nd Airborne division forced them to surrender. Similar incidents occurred more often in 1969, many times in the stockades or brigs, but violent uprisings also took place that had nothing to do with prisoners. Military authorities usually la-beled them race riots, partly because of the number of black service-men involved but also because similar disturbances were going on in the civilian world at the time. A more accurate description would be that they were both racially motivated and anti-authoritarian, again a mirror of what was happening in American civilian communities. A great many of the incidents amounted to black servicemen going toe to toe with white military police (MPs) and officers. Another incident at Fort Bragg occurred on August 11, 1969, when about two hundred servicemen got into a fight at the base's club for enlisted men. All but one of the MPs called to stop the fight were white. The arrival of armed white MPs caused the fight to escalate; before it was over, twenty-five soldiers were hospitalized. In another incident, two hun-dred soldiers at Fort Hood, Texas, almost all of them black, took over a six-block area of the base and damaged many buildings, including the recruitment office. They fought with MPs for hours, and eventually forty soldiers were arrested. Just four days later, another major uprising took place at Fort Carson, Colorado, where a couple hundred black soldiers seized control of a portion of the base and held off MPs for hours by throwing rocks, bottles, and other debris at them.

Even the stalwart Marines could not avoid dissension within their ranks. A particularly bad uprising took place at Camp Lejeune, North Carolina, on July 20, 1969. What began as a black versus white fistfight in the enlisted men's club grew until eventually there was a huge brawl outside the barracks area of the 1st Battalion, 6th Marines. Fourteen men were injured, and one white Marine corporal died. After the riot, it was revealed that the base commander had been worried about growing racial tensions and had formed a commission to investigate. That board had issued its conclusions just before the melee occurred. According to the report: "[A]n explosive situation of major proportions" existed at Camp Lejeune, partly because "many white officers and NCOs retain prejudices and deliberately practice them." The investigation concluded that MPs regularly harassed black Marines.

In the Navy, until 1971, resistance to the war and racially charged incidents were mostly minor: individual desertions or refusal to follow orders, or sabotage, such as throwing a wrench in the machinery of a ship to delay deployment—things that have always happened with some regularity. But in 1970, the antiwar, anti-authority, black power movement gained force in the Navy with the formation of the Movement for a Democratic Military (MDM), one of several organizations—many openly or more discreetly allied with the communist political movement in the United States—that stoked the fires of outrage among service members and encouraged them to resist. MDM, based in Southern California, was more closely allied with sailors than the other groups. With its locally published newspapers *Duck Soup, Out Now!* and *Up Against the Bulkhead,* MDM was militant and strident, arguing as much for black liberation as for ending the war in Vietnam. One of the group's first shows of strength was on May 16, 1970, when it organized a demonstration outside the building where four black WAVES—females in the Navy—were being detained. While MPs were busy with the protest, other MDM supporters committed acts of sabotage throughout the base. Similar acts of defiance, sabotage, and work slowdowns occurred frequently at Navy bases and training stations. Townsend recognized that the growing movement was a coordinated, organized effort to subvert the military's goals in Vietnam. He recognized the risk of such an uprising on his ship, but he felt that the best strategy was to run a tight ship, look after the crew as best he could, and not stir things up by overreacting to every incident on board.

THE NAVY WOULD RECORD a total of seventy-four incidents of sabotage to vessels in the Pacific Fleet in 1972, ranging from the creative and surreptitious to the plain old method of banging on some delicate instrumentation with a hammer when no one was looking. The techniques spanned the gamut: cutting electrical wires, putting sugar in oil supplies, throwing foreign objects in gears, causing oil spills, throwing equipment overboard, starting fires. Clearly any Navy ship in 1972 was at risk for sabotage, violent assaults, and, even worse, mutiny attempts. The carriers were more susceptible than smaller ships, simply because of the much larger number of crew forced to live and work under demanding conditions. Shortly after assuming command of the *Kitty Hawk,* Townsend had received classified messages to keep a sharp lookout for a growing risk of sabotage. A "Stop the *Hawk*" movement was expected to materialize during the deployment, in which a large number of sailors would sign a petition calling for a return to San Diego.

Townsend, and to a lesser extent Cloud, because he had only just arrived on the ship, overlooked or failed to act on some issues that fed the crew's growing dissatisfaction, but the errors can be seen far more clearly in retrospect. Some factors that exacerbated racial tensions and could have been ameliorated by directives from the captain or XO were not so evident at the time. The segregated berthing on the *Kitty Hawk* is one example. The Navy had not officially segregated berthing of sailors since 1948, when President Harry S Truman signed Executive Order 9981, which required all branches of the military to treat service members equally without regard to race. As in the rest of society, however, a pledge of nondiscrimination was not enough to ensure that minorities actually received equal treatment. For many years after the order it was common to see black sailors relegated to stewards, cooks, and other jobs traditionally reserved for minorities. Segregated berthing continued as well, though it was at least nominally voluntary. By 1972, self-segregation in berthing areas was standard on many Navy ships, though the captains always had the option of ordering that work units or other groups of sailors bunk together without regard to race. The reason for the self-segregation on the *Kitty Hawk* was simple, on the surface at least: Black sailors typically liked to spend their off time together, as did whites, Latinos, and Asian Americans. There was some mingling, but it was common knowledge on the *Kitty Hawk* that some berthing areas—usually three spartan bunks on each side of a narrow cube that formed the sailor's personal home when off duty—were all black or all white. Townsend had considered but decided against prohibiting this self-imposed segregation.

The first fifteen minutes on your watch, you don't change anything. You just observe to see what's going on, Townsend recalled from his early training as a naval officer. *You don't change anything that seems to be working until you fully understand why it is the way it is.*

Townsend felt he was still in the first fifteen minutes of his watch. There had been no reports of trouble related to the segregated berthing. Rather than insist that the division officers desegregate the berthing, he let it go.

The captain did not realize that the segregated berthing was contributing to the growing racial tension on the ship, further isolating the black sailors from the larger community and enabling disgruntled crew members to feed off of one another's anger. The gripe sessions that Cloud heard of were common occurrences in the all-black berthing areas. Contrary to his hopes, they were not always harmless exercises in blowing off steam. These segregated living spaces encouraged the polarization of the black crew members, playing into the idea that they were not truly accepted and treated as equals. The all-black groupings also fed the paranoia and often-misplaced sense of brotherhood among black sailors. The grievance of one black man—whether real, exaggerated, or completely imagined—became the grievance of many as he told and retold the story to his buddies. The men often complained about the captain's mast, the disciplinary hearings on board the *Kitty Hawk* when a sailor was accused of breaking any rules—coming back from shore leave late, being out of uniform, disrespecting an officer, failing to report to duty on time, possession of drugs, any of the many ways a sailor could get in trouble. In a scene that went back hundreds of years to the earliest sailing ships, the offender was required to stand before the captain and hear his punishment. The sailor did not appear before the captain until first having gone through a series of investigations, preliminary hearings, a review by the XO, and being apprised of his rights. It was, in all respects, a criminal court proceeding at sea.

Black sailors felt they received harsher punishment for infractions than whites, an impression that was at least partly true, because Navy rules required the captain to consider a sailor's past disciplinary record—*civilian* as well as naval—when determining a suitable punishment. The result was that some black sailors went before the captain with a strike against them already, and many would say that was only because the civilian justice system had treated them more harshly than their white counterparts. Those watching the mast didn't realize what the captain had to base his decisions on; they only saw some blacks being punished more severely than whites. The public nature of captain's mast was, in fact, part of the problem.

Townsend continued the previous captain's policy of airing captain's mast on the ship-wide television network, meaning every sailor with a few minutes of free time could watch friends and strangers being chastised for misbehavior—and many found captain's mast to be far more entertaining than sitcoms and movies. It was all a very public way of dealing with what Townsend really thought should be handled privately and with more dignity, but as with the segregated berthing, he didn't want to change policies on the *Kitty Hawk* too quickly. The previous captain had told Townsend the practice promoted a sense of openness, enabling everyone to see justice happen. There also was the deterrent effect, of course, of seeing your friends go through captain's mast and not wanting to be in their place.

For much of the crew, however, the public display of the captain's mast had a different effect. Pettus, the black sailor from western Kentucky, sensed the bitterness about the captain's mast as soon as he joined the ship. Chris Mason, the white sailor from Alabama, also sensed that many viewed parading defendants in front of their ship mates as degrading; blacks reacted especially negatively to seeing black sailors standing in front of the white captain for a dressing down over what was usually a minor infraction. As with some other sources of contention on the *Kitty Hawk*, the black sailors saw discrimination and the continuation of age-old racist practices where whites saw a straightforward and sometimes entertaining judicial proceeding.

Terry Avinger and Pettus both had firsthand experience with the captain's mast, and their incidents fueled the fire that was growing on the *Kitty Hawk*. On June 8, 1972, Avinger was among a group of black sailors who assaulted J. L. Finley, a white sailor who was passing through their berthing area. It began with what seemed petty harassment—throwing a fistful of popcorn kernels at the man's face—but soon Finley was chased and attacked by fifteen or twenty black sailors. Punches and a trash can were thrown, then Finley was tossed down an escalator. The next day, Avinger and another black sailor, Melvin J. Newson, went before the captain's mast, accused of leading the assault on Finley. Newson was sentenced to a period of correctional custody, during which time he was allowed to pursue training as a barber. Avinger pleaded not guilty and was sentenced to three days in the brig on bread and water—not the harshest sentence Townsend could have imposed, but one many blacks considered excessive and cruel. Avinger was incensed, and so were many of the other black sailors on the ship.

Townsend maintained that he had been entirely fair, even lenient, with Avinger. Avinger's offense and his record up to that point were serious enough to warrant a dishonorable discharge. During his time in the brig, Avinger wrote a letter to the captain saying he had seen the error of his ways and wanted to ensure an honorable discharge in the future. Townsend was moved by Avinger's plea to help him get involved in jet maintenance to keep him focused and motivated. As soon as he was released, Townsend had Avinger transferred to the jet shop, where he excelled. Unfortunately, Townsend would come to regret extending his hand to Avinger, eventually concluding that the sailor should have been dishonorably discharged.

Townsend and Cloud both heard the rumblings of discontent following Avinger's sentencing, and the captain met with a group of angry black sailors the next day. He was satisfied that he had explained his reasons to the men and that they felt better at the end of the meeting, but a day later another captain's mast stirred the pot again. This time the mast involved a white sailor who was supervising a black sailor manning a high-pressure water hose. The black sailor lost control of the hose, and when he hesitated in picking it up again, the white man was accused of shoving him and saying "We don't take no static from niggers down here." As sailors throughout the ship watched, the charges were described. Townsend resolved the case with only a strong verbal admonition to the white sailor. He knew he could have been a hero to the black men in his crew by coming down hard on the man, and the thought had crossed his mind. But after hearing the evidence, the captain decided that the incident was little more than a shoving match and cross words borne from frustration.

Black sailors on the *Kitty Hawk* didn't see it that way at all. They saw the captain sentencing Avinger to the brig on bread and water and then handing down essentially no punishment to a white man who shoved a black man and called him "nigger."

ANOTHER FREQUENT SOURCE OF frustration was a Navy tradition that already had caused many fights and assaults. Nearly every enlisted man coming on the *Kitty Hawk* had to first serve a stint as mess cook, dishing out chow to the sailors coming through the line or bussing tables. They weren't actually cooking and learning any skills or doing anything that felt important. That was the job of sailors permanently assigned to the mess decks. Rather, they were just warm bodies doing the grunt work required to feed 5,000 men a day. This requirement wasn't intended as a hazing but ensured that everyone got a taste of the most basic and least-liked jobs on the ship—and kept these positions filled. Though the policy was not required by the Navy, Townsend liked it because it helped promote the idea that no one was too good to work the chow line. Black sailors tended to see the assignment differently. Even though whites and other minorities worked as mess cooks when they were new to the carrier, either the black sailors did not understand that the policy was nondiscriminatory, or they suspected that their assignments were manipulated to make sure they spent more time in the mess than others. The mess cook assignment was one of the lowest assignments, requiring zero skill, and it previously had been one of the "Negro jobs" on Navy ships. So when a black sailor had to serve as mess cook, it was easy for him to feel like he was being treated as a second-class sailor. And in the case of some Project 100,000 enlistees, they probably were.

Even the white sailors serving as mess cooks hated the detail and were angry the whole time they slopped chow on sailors' trays or cleaned the mess decks; the black sailors working the chow line were even more resentful. Short tempers resulted in many fights, most of them racially based, in the mess halls. This was where men were off duty, not under the eyes of their immediate superiors, and they were more like themselves—quiet and easygoing or looking for a fight. More than anywhere else on the ship, the mess hall was where even a seemingly innocent comment, the most minor or misperceived slight, could prompt a snarled threat or a punch. The mess cooks working the line seemed almost on a hair trigger, almost eager to take offense at anyone and anything. Travers, the white sailor from California, served his time as mess cook when first coming aboard the *Kitty Hawk,* and he didn't like it any more than the others. He was eager to begin his job in electronics, but first he had to spend forty-five days with a big metal spoon putting mashed potatoes on trays for hours at a time. He hadn't even had a chance to meet the people he would work with in electronics.

He learned, however, that the mess deck was one of the few places on a carrier where one interacts with others from all over the ship, men from every department. This could be good, but it also could be bad when some of those men were angry and perceived everyone but their closest friends to be racist enemies. Travers encountered more than a few of those crew coming down the line, but he did his best to dish out food without a confrontation—not a simple task. Day after day there were confrontations in the mess decks. The mix of men who didn't normally see each other, the sullen mess cooks who didn't want to be there, and the crew members' dependence on the food they were served to sustain them through exhausting workdays and to give them a moment of comfort in what otherwise might be a miserable day: It all came together to make the mess line a scene of surprisingly high tension. Someone would say something that would be misinterpreted or taken way too seriously and suddenly fists were flying or a serving spoon was lobbed at someone's head. As with most matters on the *Kitty Hawk,* race often infused these confrontations, with the black mess cook who felt degraded in the position taking offense too easily at a snarky comment by a white sailor in line, or a black crew member assuming his race was the reason the white mess cook splattered him with gravy. Sometimes racism really was at work, but more often, the men were just being petty or not realizing that everyone else was facing the same indignities.

Most of the mess deck fights were nothing more than face-offs between men shouting insults or maybe inflicting a bloody nose, but one young crewman would soon find that some sailors took the confrontations quite seriously. Twenty-year-old James W. Radford, a white airman from Miami, Florida, was serving out his days as a mess cook after joining the *Kitty Hawk.* One day in October 1972 he saw six or seven black sailors jump in line, clearly daring others to protest. After some quiet grumbling, the men in line did nothing. Radford didn't like seeing the black sailors break the rules and he didn't like their bullying ways, but he began serving them without causing any trouble. Then he noticed that one was out of uniform. This was too much. He called back to a nearby cook who was superior to him.

"Hey, do I have to serve this guy? He's not even in uniform."

The cook confirmed that Radford didn't have to serve anyone who came through without a tray (meaning they had jumped the line) or anyone who wasn't in uniform. So Radford followed the rules and said no. The black man mumbled something profane and reached over to get a sandwich for himself. Radford grabbed his hand and told him no, and he warned the man not to reach again or there would be trouble.

The black sailor was incensed. Probably in part because his buddies were watching, he puffed up and threatened Radford.

"Do you want me to climb over there and kick your white ass?" the sailor said.

"Hey, if you're feeling froggy, you go ahead and leap," Radford replied, feeling just as indignant.

"Why don't you come out here and say that?" the black sailor replied.

Radford had had enough of this kind of crap, so he threw off his apron and went around the serving counter to square off. Radford was ready to fight, and so was his adversary. But just then, another black man stood up from the table where he was eating and shouted for them to stop.

"No! You are not going to fight out here. This is not the time or place."

The black sailor responded immediately, putting his fists down and stepping back. Radford was happy to do the same. He returned to the serving station and put his apron back on. *Fine. I guess that's the end of that,* he thought.

But it wasn't. The sailor and his friends were not done with Radford.

Other incidents started over equally meaningless confrontations. A white mess cook refused to give a black sailor an extra helping, so the hungry sailor called the other man a honky, prompting said honky to punch him in the face. On another occasion, a black sailor stepped away from his tray but didn't put an "occupied" sign on it to signal that he would return, so a white mess boy cleared the tray. When the black sailor returned and found his meal was gone, he went after the white sailor.

On and on it went, every day. Tension was building on the *Kitty Hawk.* John Callahan, the sailor who was trying to get conscientious objector status and was assigned to the mess deck until the request was handled, saw the fights and heard the slurs day in and day out. After a while, he started to wonder if something was seriously wrong on the ship. It seemed like too much, more than just random spats. He was one of the few white sailors who gave any serious thought to the prospect that there could be a serious blow-up between the races on the *Kitty Hawk.* But he was in no position to do anything about it.

THE VIETNAM WAR WAS already weighing heavily on the crew's minds when the *Kitty Hawk* made its way to the Tonkin Gulf to continue the bombing campaign aimed at stopping North Vietnamese forces. The ship's rapid departure from San Diego in February 1972 meant many of the men had had to scramble to get on board; some had departed with little or no good-byes from their family. Keel had been on leave back home, thinking he had several weeks before deployment, when, while watching television one night, there was an interruption for a news announcement. "Attention. These military members are to report to their duty stations immediately." Then the announcer recited a list of ships and other units, including the *Kitty Hawk*. Keel had to go to the airport immediately, with no idea why the deployment had been moved up. He worried that it meant something very bad, perhaps growing international tensions leading to nuclear war. The actual reason had to do with changes in the plans for continued bombing in Southeast Asia and the need to get the *Kitty Hawk* to work right away.

Once at sea, there was little relief from the highly demanding work of an aircraft carrier in a combat zone. The crew performed admirably for the most part, launching thousands of sorties and carrying through on President Nixon's desire to continue the bombing until the nation could find a way out of the war. The work was long and hard, even for an aircraft carrier, and some men got very little rest. The sailors stayed on station longer and longer, despite frequent promises that the cruise would end soon and return to San Diego. The men had no way of knowing they were headed toward a nearly unheard-of 247 days at sea. Each time the promise of going home was broken, the crew became more restless, more tense. Many found solace in drugs.

At the same time, the black sailors on board were bonding in a way the white sailors and officers did not fully comprehend. The black sailors on the *Kitty Hawk* created their own community within the ship in which each member was far more closely allied than those in any other racial group. What seemed like collegiality between black sailors actually was, for some at least, much more: It was, as XO

Cloud suspected, an extension of the way black Americans had long leaned on each other to cope with a mostly white society and the wrongs inflicted on them by racism.

For some black sailors on the ship, like Perry Pettus, it was only that. He enjoyed bonding with the black brothers on board, but he never saw it as anything more sinister than simply buddies showing a little black pride and having fun with the slang and fashions of the day. It was buddies hanging out, talking smack about the officers, griping some about the white man, nothing serious. But this only means that Pettus wasn't involved in the highest level of the black power structure of the *Kitty Hawk,* a sub rosa society in which the men fed off each other's gripes about being put down by the white Navy and secretly formed their own command structure and planned for the day they could truly stand up for themselves.

Townsend and Cloud did not realize the extent of the secret command structure until it was too late. What the captain had perceived as simply bonding among black "brothers" had actually become a formally organized command structure in which some sailors held rank and delivered orders to others on the ship concerning protests and ways to counter what they saw as pervasive racial discrimination. In the following months, Townsend looked back and concluded that a black sailor whom he respected as a hardworking, intelligent, and ambitious sailor who wanted to be promoted to chief, actually had been the sub rosa leader of the black community. Townsend had wondered why the young man had not yet made chief; only later did he learn that the master chief always distrusted the younger man. The sailor sometimes worked on the bridge and his presence there made him privy to conversations among the top officers. Once violence erupted on the *Kitty Hawk,* Townsend saw this sailor's face at the front of every mob of black sailors.

Unlike many crew members on a huge carrier, many black sailors knew each other as individuals, not just nameless faces. They took the time to bond at every opportunity—most prominently through "dapping"—the long, elaborate handshakes popular among many back home. Pettus learned the daps along with every other black sailor on board, but he saw them as harmless bonding. Other black sailors knew that the dap could serve as a "salute" to other members of the sub rosa command structure, the exact nature of the dap connoting where the participants stood in the hierarchy. There were dozens and dozens of dap variations—The Rowboats, The Steamboats, The Over the Mountains—some of them intricate and time consuming. Many involved meaningful symbolism, such as crossing the chest to signify that you were willing to die for the other person or tapping the other man's forehead to signify passing the power. Some of the daps were well known back home, but the sailors also created their own, choreographing intricate routines in their downtime and passing them on. Dapping became a standard practice among blacks, so much so that it was hard for two sailors to pass each other without at least a short dap. Townsend and Cloud tolerated the practice; there was no Navy directive against it, and they also did not realize that the daps held any particular significance. By 1972, dapping had become so pervasive that it was common to see whites backed up in the narrow passageways, waiting for two black sailors to finish a dap. At times it became an open challenge to the white sailors and officers, with black sailors intentionally blocking a busy passageway for a long dap, silently daring the impatient whites to interfere. Chris Mason once saw a black sailor take a swing at a white officer who got impatient waiting and pushed his way past two black sailors.

One dap, known as Kill the Beast, was recognized even by Pettus as more than just a harmless handshake. The white man was the "beast" because he controlled everything and had the black man's fate in his hands. When black sailors felt they were being abused by a petty officer or some other white man on the *Kitty Hawk,* they would dap Kill the Beast to let each other knew they were thinking the same thing and would someday overcome. The last part of the dap was a pantomime of squashing the beast on the ground underfoot. It wasn't a dap that Pettus used, but he saw it among the more militant blacks on board and, unlike most whites, he knew what it meant.

Dapping on the *Kitty Hawk* became a decidedly non-military greeting between men in uniform that signaled an allegiance to something other than the Navy—but it could always be defended as just a harmless handshake. If Townsend, Cloud and the other leaders had realized how much dapping was an open symbol of defiance, they might have been clued in to the serious rebellion brewing beneath the surface. The white men on board, from the lowliest sailor on up to Townsend, completely underestimated the anger of some of these black men. Even those who were not especially angry when they joined the *Kitty Hawk* crew were pressured into joining the underground black movement; resistance meant being labeled a sellout, an Uncle Tom. XO Cloud already was under suspicion because he was a high-ranking officer who made no overt effort to celebrate his black heritage or show solidarity with the black brothers. As the XO, of course, he could never display black pride the way some of the black sailors wanted. Sailors without Cloud's rank and responsibility could go along, however. Pettus knew the drill for fitting in with the black brotherhood: Learn the daps, use them openly in front of whites, and dress during shore leave to show that you're proud of your black heritage. That meant wearing red, black, and green to signify Africa and some type of honor for Martin Luther King and/or Malcolm X. There were those who took all the symbolism very seriously, and there were plenty like Pettus who just wanted to fit in and not be singled out for harassment by more militant black sailors, such as Terry Avinger, whom Pettus would remember as a "hard core black American."

MANY OF THE WHITE CREW, like John Travers, admired Cloud and figured that the presence of a black XO could only help calm any racial tension. Travers realized, however, that he was just a naive white kid from California and might not understand the black sailors on board. Chris Mason, the white sailor from Alabama who had formed a tenuous friendship with a black sailor, probably had a better appreciation of the situation. He had seen how his black buddy, an easygoing guy, not at all like some of the angry, inner-city, militant black sailors, nevertheless was allying with those rougher sailors.

One evening Mason was reading in his bunk when his black buddy came to their berthing area, which, like some on the *Hawk*, was racially mixed. Mason knew that his friend had been to a clandestine meeting in a secure space near the captain's wardroom, and he couldn't help asking why his friend was hanging out with those people.

"Man, it's not like I really have a choice," he told Mason. "If I blow them off, they're gonna call me an Uncle Tom and cause all kinds of trouble for me."

His friend looked troubled by the whole affair. After a minute, Mason asked what they talked about in the meetings.

"I can't tell you much about it, Chris," he said. "But these guys are really out there. They're rough, man. Some of these guys were in gangs back home, and now they're taking all kinds of crazy stuff."

Mason didn't want to trouble his buddy any more, so he let it go and went back to his book. But Mason could tell his friend was scared by what he knew.

CHAPTER SIX

THE DAP FIGHT

October 10, 1972
Subic Bay, the Philippines

By October 1972, the *Kitty Hawk* had been at sea nearly nine months under some of the most demanding conditions that a carrier crew had faced since World War II. The work pace was fast and unrelenting, the heat off the coast of Vietnam (on the map grid known as Yankee Station) was almost unbearable, and racial tensions were approaching a fast boil. The crew was eager to go home, but the demands of the war kept putting the *Kitty Hawk* back on line. Every time they thought they had finished their job and could return to San Diego, the captain would come back on the horn and tell them that they were staying in the waters off Southeast Asia. Every time Townsend made that announcement, morale sank a little lower and frustrations moved a little closer to the surface. Tempers were hot. Every sailor was on a short fuse. It didn't take much to spark an argument, a fistfight, a shouting match.

All of these factors came together on the *Kitty Hawk* in October 1972. Trouble had been brewing for a long while but came to a head when the carrier visited Subic Bay in the Philippines for some desperately needed R&R.

The carrier had left Yankee Station on October 3 after its fifth online period (the fifth time it was stationed off the coast and launching attacks almost around the clock). As the *Kitty Hawk* sailed to Subic Bay Naval Base, many of the young men on board thought that, finally, this had to be it. Surely after their scheduled six-day stay in Subic, the *Kitty Hawk* crew would be sent home. They had earned it.

Captain Townsend was not as eager to go back to San Diego. He was ready to continue fighting as long Washington told him to, but he knew that his crew had earned some respite. The crew had been running about 120 sorties a day and had suffered no casualties while on line, so Townsend and XO Cloud were damned proud of them. The *Kitty Hawk* had become the ship to depend on, the one that would stay on line and cover for other carriers while they went into port to deal with casualties or damage, and that dependability had cost the crew some much-needed downtime. But perhaps the long journey was finally about to end. Townsend and Cloud talked about the progress of the peace negotiations and the fact that the war might be nearing an end. And they knew that the USS *Ranger* was supposed to arrive at Yankee Station soon, which meant the *Kitty Hawk* wouldn't have to be the primary flight platform. Like the rest of the crew, they both suspected that the carrier might be sent back to San Diego after the Subic stop.

Townsend and Cloud, the two men at the top of the command on the *Kitty Hawk,* didn't realize how troubled the ship was when it arrived in the Philippines. They didn't know how much volatility lay just beneath the surface. They were well aware of tension among the crew, but they attributed most of it to the long cruise and figured several nights of R&R would cure much of what ailed the men.

In fact, when the *Kitty Hawk* pulled into Subic Bay Naval Base on October 8, 1972, the carrier was about to burst at the seams with the pent-up frustrations, anticipations, and hostilities of 5,000 testosterone-driven men. These men needed to get off the ship and let go of some energy. They needed to get drunk, get high, get laid, and then maybe go home. The ship docked at Alava Pier, closest to the bars and nightclubs, rather than on the Naval Air Station Cubi side of the bay, as Townsend usually chose for its accessibility to maintenance resources. For this port call, Townsend decided to do the crew a favor and dock where they could walk to town instead of relying on taxis and buses. The ship could still be serviced, but the crew could spend their money on the important things, like beer and women, instead of transportation. As the crew members were getting their uniforms in order and trying to collect on any overdue loans and poker winnings, they heard a dreaded sound. It was the captain on the 1MC, the public address system that reached the entire ship.

"Men of the *Kitty Hawk*. This is the captain. I have to tell you that there has been a change in our schedule. After three nights R&R in Subic, we will be returning to Yankee Station. I don't know when we're going home, and that's all there is to that."

The announcement was like swiping candy away from a baby. A wave of depression washed over the crew. Robert Keel, Chris Mason, and Garland Young all joined the chorus of curses that rang through the air. *Not again! Goddammit, when are we going home?* Not only were they going back to Yankee Station, but they weren't even going to get their full six days in Subic. *Three nights? What a rip-off!*

Townsend had no choice in the matter. His orders came from the Pentagon, and he took the carrier where they told him to go. But he knew the crew would hold the news against him. They would resent that he had kept them at sea for so long. Even if the sailors understood that he didn't make the call, he still was the face of the Navy command that did.

As had happened before, it fell on the *Kitty Hawk* to cover for another carrier that couldn't fulfill its obligations. In this case, the other ship was the *Ranger*, which had been sabotaged. In July, a white sailor had jammed an eighteen-inch steel rod in the carrier's reduction gear, creating major damage that required a long repair in August. Then, when the ship was operational again, the crew had to catch up with disrupted training. That training was taking longer than expected, so the *Ranger* could not relieve the *Kitty Hawk* until November 16. That meant that instead of being relieved soon, Townsend's ship had to get right back to Yankee Station and keep the war going.

Both Townsend and Cloud regretted the truncated port call, knowing how disappointed the crew would be. And they wondered if the few nights in Subic were going to help release some of the tension or if the change in plans would just make everything worse. All they could do was to let the men go out for liberty and hope that they came back capable of another month or so in a war zone. Townsend's main concern, as far as any possible problems in port, was drugs. Once the men stepped off the ship, they could obtain just about any illegal drugs they wanted, and Townsend didn't want men sauntering back on to the *Kitty Hawk* with a duffel bag full of heroin. So, as he had done for the previous three port calls in Subic, Townsend ordered Nicholas Carlucci, the head of the Marines on board, to post guards at both brows, fore and aft, where the sailors returned to the ship. They were empowered to search the returning sailors for contraband, and they also had orders not to allow any foreign nationals aboard except those involved with the ship's maintenance. Without the Marine guards, it was not unusual for sailors to sneak a local working girl aboard or for a local drug dealer to board to sell his wares.

WHEN THEY STEPPED OFF the ship in Subic Bay on October 8, most of the sailors had not seen their families in eight months. For most of them, the recreational opportunities provided on the naval base were not their focus. They marched right past the wholesome offerings of the golf course and the beautiful beaches—they'd seen plenty of water already, thank you—and right out the gates to the raucous offerings in the town of Olongapo. The young single men needed some female companionship, and so did some of the old married ones. Nearly all of them needed a drink or two or twelve, and more than a few needed to score some pot or heroin. It was all waiting for them in Olongapo.

Everything a sailor could want was easy to find in this classic example of a town that thrives on drunken sailors spending their money on booze, tattoos, and cheap women. (And these were very experienced women. At the height of the war, the base sometimes hosted more than two hundred ships per month.) Much of the entertainment, particularly the many whorehouses, was segregated by race, as the Filipinos were no more racially enlightened than much of white America at the time. A black sailor looking for love in the white section of Olongapo, known as the Strip, would be flatly refused and directed to the whorehouses in the Jungle, easily found by taking a left out of the main gate at the base.

As USUAL ON PORT calls, Townsend and Cloud went ashore each night for dinner at the officers' club on base but then returned to the ship to continue the administrative work that always came with maintenance and repairs. For most of the crew, the first two nights of R&R were wild and woolly affairs, with the men blowing all their money on booze and women. The much-needed downtime was working wonders on morale, though everyone knew that wouldn't last after the ship headed back to war. Chris Mason and Garland Young just tried not to think too far ahead, to stay in the moment and have fun. Young always enjoyed their stops in Subic, throwing himself into the bars and nightclubs, enjoying the local ladies, and even organizing parties on the beach for his buddies, both black and white. He considered Subic to be one place where the races could socialize pretty easily, though there were the clearly segregated areas, and he enjoyed spending his liberty with both blacks and whites he considered good friends. All of the *Kitty Hawk* men knew that R&R could get wild as men under stress blew off a lot of steam. Fights were possible, even likely, among the men, but they usually amounted to a few drunken sailors and Marines screaming insults at each other and throwing a sloppy punch in the general direction of the other fellow before staggering off or being dragged away by more clearheaded friends. Robert Keel and Young both were present, however, for something more serious on the first night of liberty at Subic. They had gone separately to the enlisted men's club at Subic, known as the EM club, and were enjoying time with their friends. Young was sitting at a table near the stage with his friend Martin, who was black, another friend named Kirk, who was half Mexican, and another sailor from New York. The music was provided by local groups and the surprisingly good bands that often formed on Navy ships. Young regularly sang with some buddies on the carrier, their band putting on shows for the crew on the fantail. The *Kitty Hawk* sailors and men from other ships were partying hard.

At one point a small fight broke out, and Keel tried to stop two sailors from swinging at each other. As Keel grabbed one of the guys, who happened to be black, and pulled him away, he thought he was just doing what any not-so-drunk bystander would do. But Keel suddenly found himself fighting the black sailor, and then he was thrown to the ground, where a half dozen of the other guy's friends began kicking him. By the time he was able to scramble to his feet, all of Keel's assailants had fled. Sore from his beating and seething with anger, Keel wandered the club for half an hour in a near rage, his shoulder aching from what would turn out to be torn cartilage. He was looking for the men who had beaten him. Lacking those targets, he trolled for anyone else who looked at him the wrong way. He was ready to fight, but no one took him up on the offer. Keel wondered if the men had attacked because he had made the mistake of grabbing the black sailor in the fight.

The joint was hopping with a local band that did amazing covers of Santana, Jimi Hendrix, Janis Joplin, and other popular performers from back home. At one point Young leaned over to Martin and said, "Man, you just haven't lived until you've heard a Filipino guy sing Janis Joplin!" The night was going great until a black sailor took the stage between songs and started screaming to the crowd about black power. Young didn't recognize him as a *Kitty Hawk* sailor, though he could have been.

"Black power! This war is the white man's war! The Black Panthers are taking over!"

The man's rant went on and on, and the initial eye rolling from the whites in the crowd soon turned to anger. As whites started screaming for the black sailor to shut up, Young's friend Kirk saw what was coming. "Okay, here it comes," he said calmly as he turned his chair to the side so he could move quickly. Just then a glass went flying and hit the black sailor in the head. That prompted more bottles, which set off a fight between black sailors and white ones and anyone else who felt like throwing a punch or a chair. Young and his buddies didn't want to join in the fight. Instead, they dropped under the table.

"Let's get the hell out of here!" Young said, and his buddies agreed. Using the table for cover, they maneuvered toward the door like an awkward turtle. As they got to the exit, they discarded the table and rushed out into the night, still on their hands and knees. Young looked over at Martin and said, "Whooo, I'm glad that's over." But just as he started to get up, Young noticed that a phalanx of Marines had formed outside the EM club, shoulder to shoulder and holding wooden truncheons.

"Get back down on your knees!" one burly Marine yelled at him. Young complied. Soon the Marines were ordering everyone coming out of the club onto their knees and then onto a waiting bus. The men were ordered to stay silent on the ride back to the base. At the dock, the *Hawk's* officer of the deck, a white lieutenant, greeted the returning buses and put all the sailors in formation. They waited at attention for all the buses, and then the lieutenant started lecturing them.

"This is not going to happen on my ship!" he told them. "Is that clear? This is not going to be tolerated. Now, who can tell me what happened at the EM club?"

No one seemed eager to explain, and probably no one had a clear idea of how the fight started, so finally Young spoke up. "Some black guy started mouthing off and got everybody pissed off," he told the lieutenant. "We didn't even know him."

The lieutenant didn't seem satisfied, but he ordered all the sailors back to their berthing areas. The men ran off. The next afternoon, Young and his buddies were in their compartment, still grumbling about the fight, the way the Marines handled them, and the lieutenant's dressing down. Just then they heard someone yell "Attention on deck!" and saw the lieutenant striding toward them.

They sprang up and waited for another lecture, but instead the officer spoke quietly and intently to Young.

"Young, I need you to tell me what happened at that club last night. I really need to know," he said. "There are things happening all over the fleet, and I need to know what happened here."

Young told the lieutenant that he couldn't be of much help.

"The guy was screaming about Martin Luther King and the Black Panthers. All we did was roll the table and get out. Then here comes the Marines with ax handles, so we did what we were told and got out."

The lieutenant asked the other men if Young's story was true, and they agreed, saying they didn't know any more than that. The officer seemed to believe them, but clearly he wasn't satisfied.

"All right, well . . .do me a favor," he said to the sailors. "Don't go back to the EM club. If you want to go out, go out on the town. Stay out of the EM club tonight."

They told the officer they would.

WHAT YOUNG AND THE lieutenant didn't know was that there had been another noteworthy incident at 12:30 on the morning of October 9, as a black *Kitty Hawk* sailor, Airman Dwight W. Horton, was returning to the ship. The shore patrol arrested him for fighting outside the base gate with two white petty officers, though he said it was less a fight than a beating from the other two, particularly since he already had one arm in a cast. After being returned to the *Kitty Hawk,* he reported to his black brothers that he had been mistreated by the white shore patrol officers and the base provost marshal's office. They sat around their berthing compartment talking about the incident and getting more and more worked up.

"Not surprising," one of the men said. "Even halfway around the world, a black man can't walk the street without whites giving him a hard time. And then, of course, the white lawmen have to take their turns with the black man. Typical."

But they would get even. The evening of Oct. 9 passed without incident, but the next night, October 10, was their last in Subic and the black sailors decided they would protest Horton's mistreatment by disrupting one of the favorite white hangouts on the Strip: the Sampaguita Club.

THE WHITE SAILORS ON the *Kitty Hawk* had no idea that any retribution was planned that night. Neither did many of the black sailors. Likewise, Townsend and Cloud had no inkling of what would occur as they had dinner ashore, then returned to work on the carrier.

Keel's sore shoulder left him laying low for the rest of the port stay, so he didn't end up in the Sampaguita Club on October 10, even though it was the hot destination. The club was hosting its weekly "Soul Night," which meant that black sailors were welcome in this usually all-white club, and it also guaranteed good entertainment. The club was packed, full of sailors along with some civilians, such as the wives of men stationed at the base and locals—black, white, and Filipino. Everyone, of all races, loved soul music, and opening the doors to everyone usually guaranteed a big crowd—one that was raucous and loud, ready to dance and have a good time. But on this night, the racial tension that had been fomenting among the *Kitty Hawk* sailors would come to the club with them. The brawls started almost immediately. One fight broke out about 9 P.M. and appeared to be nothing more than the typical scuffle over something meaningless until a white shore patrolman from the oiler *Savannah,* also in port for R&R, stepped in. He tapped a black sailor on the shoulder, and that man immediately swung around and slammed the shore patrolman in the face with his fist. Others in the crowd rescued the shore patrolman from a group of black sailors who surrounded him. The rescuers pulled him into the manager's office at the club and called for an ambulance. Other shore patrol officers called the base headquarters to report that the Sampaguita Club was heating up. The base operations command center sent over another fifteen shore patrolmen, doubling the number at the club.

The additional show of force helped settle the crowd down, but all over the club, men were eyeing each other warily. The booze was flowing and the men were on edge. The bands carried on, playing covers of the great music of the day—crowd pleasers like "Push and Pull" by Rufus Thomas and "Jody's Got Your Girl," about the much-hated Jody stealing your girl while you're away, by Johnny Taylor. The crowd responded to the hot soul hits like Curtis Mayfield's "Freddie's Dead (Theme from Superfly)" and "I Gotcha" by Joe Tex. At nearly 1 A.M., on the morning of October 11, Alabama boy Chris Mason was enjoying himself with some buddies, ordering another round, while they waited for the band to resume playing. John Callahan, the would-be conscientious objector, was there too. The band looked like it was just about ready to hit it again, but then about ten black sailors walked up on stage, dressed in what Mason thought was a parody of how black soul brothers were portrayed in the movies: civilian suits in loud colors and big hats with feathers. Mason had never seen such a sight in person and wondered if they were part of the show. Sailors sometimes performed with their bands in the club.

Soon it became clear that the men weren't on stage to sing. The crowd watched as the men started dapping, performing an elaborate soul handshake that was clearly meant to be "in your face" for the whites in the crowd. An audible groan went up, especially from the whites who just didn't want any more dapping rubbed in their faces and wanted to get back to the music. As the dap went on and on, shouts were hurled from the crowd.

"Get the fuck off the stage!"

"We want the music!"

"Enough with that nigger shit! Get out of there!"

Black sailors responded, in part as a true show of support for their brothers on stage, and in part to defend the men from the abuse.

"Right on, brother!"

"Black power!"

At about the same time, Horton, the black sailor who had incensed his buddies with his story of being mistreated the night before, arrived at the door to the club and swung at a shore patrolman stationed there. The scuffle that ensued as Horton was subdued occupied several shore patrolmen just as the crowd inside was growing rowdier.

With the band waiting behind them, the black sailors continued with the dap. Their smug expressions told the crowd they were getting exactly the reaction they wanted. It wasn't long before the first beer bottle flew through the air. Soon it was raining broken glass. The band ran for cover, and most everyone else in the club ran for the nearest sailor of a different color and started swinging. Chairs flew. Bottles smashed. Tables broke. Men bled. It was a full-scale brawl.

A shore patrolman called the base command center, desperate for backup.

The base sent over twelve Marines and ten provost marshals to supplement the thirty shore patrolmen already on site. When they arrived, the backups found a scene of destruction. A civilian investigator from the provost marshal's office who had come along to help was told by white sailors that a group of blacks had dragged a man into a bathroom and were beating him. The investigator forced his way into the head with six shore patrolmen and rescued the white sailor, then had the Marines throw the most violent black sailors out into the parking lot, where shore patrolmen guarded them until paddy wagons could take them to the brig.

As Mason ducked to escape the flying debris and fists, he noticed that the shore patrol and the Marines were making their offensive. The helmeted men were wading into the crowd swinging their batons, knocking any heads within reach until men stopped fighting. Mason made his way to the nearest exit and escaped, racing away as fast as he could. Callahan did the same thing.

With the most violent men out of the crowd and under guard, the club finally began to settle down. Then a black sailor threw a bottle that smashed near the front door, and the noise set off the sailors being held outside. They broke free of their guards and rushed back into the club, turning over tables, throwing chairs, and assaulting whites. The Marines who tried to block the exits were thwarted by some black civilians who helped the rampaging black sailors escape. They darted off into the darkness of Olongapo and toward the base, along with many others trying to escape the melee and the shore patrol.

PERRY PETTUS, MEANWHILE, WAS heading back toward the main gate of the naval base after having spent the evening with other black sailors at Harlem, the most popular club in the Jungle. He and several black friends were making their way to the *Kitty Hawk* when they saw a couple of white sailors arguing with a few black sailors. Pettus could tell that the blacks were giving the whites a hard time about going into the Jungle. Pettus and his friends didn't pay much attention, thinking it just a stupid argument among drunks, and when they saw the shore patrol coming over they certainly didn't want to get involved. As they got close to the scene, they saw the shore patrolmen turn around suddenly and run toward the Sampaguita Club. The men didn't know what was going on, but they assumed the shore patrol had bigger fish to fry. Then they heard the commotion, looked toward the noise, and realized that something big was happening.

What the hell?

A horde of men, black and white, was running toward them. It didn't take long for Pettus and all the other men standing there to decide that they didn't really need to know what the crowd was running from. Whatever it was, they'd better run too. Pettus and the others turned and ran. At first they were in front of the surging mass, but soon they were outpaced by some of the more motivated sailors spilling from the club. Pettus could see that some were bleeding, their clothes torn, and a few were still screaming insults at each other as they ran.

The Marines guarding the enlisted men's brow saw the mostly black crowd racing down the pier. The men piled onto the *Kitty Hawk* as fast as they could, some pushing past the Marine guards who insisted on checking their identification cards, jumping the turnstiles instead of waiting to board in an orderly fashion. The men knew that if they didn't get back to sanctuary on their ship, they'd wind up in the brig or the hospital. The Marines let them board without any explanation for their torn uniforms, black eyes, and bloody lips, but they also took notice of the sailors because of their disheveled appearance and panicky efforts to get aboard.

Man, what was that all about? Pettus wondered as he made his way to his berthing compartment. Other sailors told him of the big fight at the club and how sailors were being thrown in paddy wagons.

That had to be one hell of a fight, he thought. *Glad I was at Harlem.*

The officers chalked up the fight as just another wild night in Subic Bay. They did not realize that many of the black sailors and some of the white ones still seethed with anger after the brawl. They had brought their anger back to the ship with them. All they needed was an excuse to let it fly.

CHAPTER SEVEN

SAILING INTO TROUBLED WATER

October 11, 1972

L ater in the day on October 11, the *Kitty Hawk* pulled away from the Alava Pier at Subic Bay, and Captain Townsend set a course for Yankee Station. By now the men on the bridge hardly needed much direction in getting the ship back on line. After such a long cruise, the *Kitty Hawk* helmsmen could find their way back to Yankee Station almost on instinct. Some of the sailors on board, and the officers too, were beginning to wonder just how long the Navy could keep one carrier at sea and on duty. The accepted scuttlebutt was that a carrier could stay on line for up to a year, with periodic replenishment at sea and relatively minor upkeep at nearby ports, before having to return to its home port for more extensive maintenance. A year at sea was a long time. Even the best port calls were no substitute for being back home with friends and family. It was clear to the sailors that their time at sea would be dictated by the physical needs of the ship and the strategic needs of the war, not any concerns for the crew.

The *Kitty Hawk* was sailing back for its sixth on-line period, and the ship's commanders knew they were asking a lot of the crew. Townsend felt a twinge of regret as the big carrier sailed west toward Southeast Asia, but his sympathy for the men on the long cruise wasn't going to get in the way of fulfilling his mission. By 1 P.M. on October 12, the men of the *Kitty Hawk* would be within range of her targets and launching aircraft as she continued to Yankee Station. The aircraft would launch no matter how hung over, bruised, angry, or homesick the sailors might be. Cloud knew he could depend on the crew to do their jobs, but at the same time, he worried about their mental state. They were being pushed hard, they'd been away from home a long time, and now they were being dragged away from Subic too soon.

Both Townsend and Cloud had heard about the fight at the Sampaguita Club and how so many of the sailors had returned to the ship showing signs of having been involved. Before sailing, the captain received a report from the chief of staff at Subic Naval Base, whom Townsend happened to know personally.

"It looks like it was a good number of your black sailors" involved in the fight, the officer told Townsend. "We're not sure how it started, but you know how these things go. I just wanted you to know because it was a really big fight, pretty much a riot. We had to send a lot of Marines but even then most of the troublemakers got away."

Townsend thanked the man for the heads-up and then called his officer of the day for a report. The *Kitty Hawk* officer confirmed to Townsend that a crowd of sailors, many of them black, had rushed aboard in the early morning with their clothes disheveled, seeming frantic to get back aboard.

"Some of them were armed too," the officer reported. "They had those nunchakus, sir, those sticks with the chain between them that you twirl around. Apparently some of the men are quite proficient with those things."

Townsend questioned whether the men had caused any trouble on returning, and the officer reported that they hadn't. That was why the officers on watch did nothing and made no special report of the incident, he told the captain. Townsend, satisfied, wondered whether the information from Subic constituted any real reason for concern or if it was just another bar fight. Though he had known his crew for only about four months, and even with the tensions he knew existed on the ship, Townsend didn't think any of his men would go ashore and create such problems. He radioed back to the Subic chief of staff for more information. "Was the fight really that bad? Are you sure it was my men? I've never had that kind of trouble from them before. I find this difficult to believe."

The Subic officer confirmed that it was that bad and that the sailors who escaped from Marine custody that night had been seen returning to the *Kitty Hawk*. Townsend ordered his staff to investigate and report back to him. In particular, he told them, he wanted to know if the disturbance had been planned or organized. That would be quite different from a spontaneous bar fight, no matter how big. Carlucci, the leader of the Marines on the *Kitty Hawk,* had the two Marines who had been posted at the enlisted men's brow walk through the ship with him, looking for any faces they recognized from the night before. They found some, but each sailor questioned told Carlucci that it wasn't him, that he had returned to the ship much earlier and hadn't been involved in the Sampaguita fight. Without any way to dispute their word now that the ship had left port, Carlucci had no choice but to end the investigation.

Townsend knew as well as any other Navy leader in 1972 that the black power movement and antiwar sentiment could result in organized uprisings on Navy bases and on ships at sea. But on the morning of October 11, he could only exercise caution and wonder what he might not know about his crew. Cloud was at more of a disadvantage even than his boss. Townsend didn't have much time on board but he still had twice as much experience with the crew as Cloud's two months. In fact, both men were woefully unaware of the underlying tension as they sailed back to Yankee Station. Each suspected that something might be afoot, but Townsend was focused on the mission at hand and trusted his crew. Cloud was more suspicious, but he didn't know exactly what was wrong. As for how it might erupt, neither Townsend nor Cloud had any idea.

The official reports from Subic and from the *Kitty Hawk* officers did not adequately relay to the top brass the level of disharmony on board. Frustrations and anger had been growing ever higher during the Westpac cruise, and some black sailors on the ship were just waiting for the right moment to strike back at the white Navy and the white sailors who oppressed them every day. The disturbances at the clubs at Subic Bay were like dry timbers on a long-smoldering fire. When the *Kitty Hawk* sailors returned to their ship, their animosity simmered, and as the ship churned through the sea to Yankee Station, a great many men were on a hair trigger. A great many more were at risk because they were *not* so agitated by the pervasive but easy-to-ignore racial issues. These sailors, most of them young and innocent, were not on high alert and did not see trouble coming. They did not know to be cautious.

On October 11, as the ship was in transit, the workload was relatively light, so the men were able to relax and rest up for the hard work that would face them the next day when full flight operations began again. But many of the sailors did not really relax. The EM club fight on the first night was still a fresh memory for some, and even more were still worked up about the last night in Subic. The stories and the rumors flew. Everyone who had been at the Sampaguita Club told tales about how wild the fight had been and how they didn't know whether it would be worse to face the rioters inside or the Marines outside. Everyone's account of the brawl was somewhat different, but the white sailors generally told the same story about black sailors starting the fight and seeking out white sailors for beating. Black sailors told their version: The white sailors didn't want them in the club and viciously attacked the men who were dapping. With each retelling, the riot became even bigger, the story more sensational, and the racial tension more pronounced. The trash talking never stopped. Sailors passing each other in ship would mumble an insult under their breath about honkies, niggers, or spooks. Black sailors warned white ones that they wouldn't make it through the night. White sailors told them to bring it on. And yet many white sailors remained oblivious. On a huge ship made up of thousands of tiny compartments, even the most volatile situation can be unknown to those on the other side of a steel wall.

It wasn't just the fights at the EM club and the Sampaguita Club that had so many of the black sailors seething. Word was going around of how a white sailor from the *Kitty Hawk* had hired a group of locals from Subic to beat up a black sailor. According to the tale, the two men had a fight while the ship was still at sea. Then the white sailor supposedly hired the Filipinos—all karate experts—to exact retribution while the black man was in the Jungle. A group of black sailors from the *Kitty Hawk* stumbled on the scene as it was about to begin and were able to run off the Filipinos. The veracity of the story didn't matter; true or not, it was fueling the fire.

Perry Pettus was going about his duties that day, not especially concerned about any of the fights or the rumors that were flying throughout the ship. As always, he was minding his own business and not getting involved in any of the crap that can get a sailor in trouble. He felt solidarity with his black brothers certainly, but he didn't hate whitey and he wasn't looking for trouble. He also wasn't well connected to the most extreme black sailors on board, so he didn't know of any plans they might have for the *Kitty Hawk*. But soon he would be reminded that some whites on the *Kitty Hawk* saw only his race, and along with it their worst prejudices.

The carrier was conducting some flight ops while making its way to Yankee Station, mostly touch-and-go landings to help pilots hone the skills required for returning to a huge ship that suddenly looks

quite small when you have to land on it. Though the work was relatively light for the flight deck crew, the constant heat made any activity
demanding. Around lunchtime, Pettus took a break from his job of
driving tractors around the flight deck, moving planes from here to
there, and went to the mess deck to eat with his friends John and
Lawrence, both black. As they were in line, Pettus noticed that, as
usual, the mess deck was where all the hotheads seemed to let fly with
their tempers. He saw one black sailor, whom he knew to be particularly militant in his black pride, grow agitated at the white sailors
ahead of him in line. Apparently they were moving too slowly, and the
sailor also didn't like some comments the whites were making about
the slop on their trays, taking it as an insult to the black mess cook
who had served them. They exchanged words, and Pettus noticed
that the black sailor was stewing about it while he ate lunch, soon
stomping up and flinging his tray through the window at the dish-
washers. That set off a scuffle that got everyone's attention, but it wasn't
so bad that Pettus and his buddies interrupted their lunch. They
watched and, when the skirmish was over, they finished their meal
and headed back to the flight deck.

To get back to their assignments, they went through the hangar
bay, a cavernous area directly below the flight deck where airplanes
are stored and maintained, making their way from the forward area to
the aft, where they could take a hatch up to the flight deck. The men
were chatting, joking around with each other, and had almost reached
the end of the hangar bay when three white Marines stepped out and
told them to halt. Pettus and his buddies stopped and asked what was
wrong.

"Y'all can't walk in groups of more than two at a time," one Marine told them.

"What? Who is 'y'all'?" Pettus asked.

"You black people. Can't have three blacks together," the Marine
explained.

Pettus and his friends looked at each other like they thought the Marine was crazy. They had never heard of any such rule, and it sounded to them like some bullshit the Marines just made up to hassle them.

"What are you talking about?" Pettus asked. "We're just going back to the flight deck. We've got work to do."

"Well, y'all ain't going together. No more than two at a time," the Marine repeated.

Pettus and his friends laughed a little, rolling their eyes at these Marines trying to give them a hard time. The Marine's "y'all" really rubbed them the wrong way, making them feel like they were being hassled by some hick sheriff. Pettus and the other two men needed to get back to the flight deck right away or they'd be counted late coming back from lunch. They didn't have time for this crap.

"Man, you crazy," Pettus said to the Marine, shaking his head with disgust. "We have to get back to the flight deck. We got a recovery coming in."

Pettus turned to walk away and proceed out of the hangar bay, and his friends moved to follow him. In a heartbeat, the Marine who had been doing all the talking grabbed Pettus and pushed him up against a nearby airplane, roughly shoving his wooden baton under Pettus's chin and nearly choking him. With his hands on either end of the baton and using it shove the sailor up off his feet, the Marine got in Pettus's face.

"No more than two at a time," he growled. "I'm not telling you again." Pettus was waiting for him to add "boy," but the Marine didn't go that far. He didn't need to. Pettus could see that the other Marines had grabbed his friends and were holding them just as roughly, watching the lead dog for cues on what to do. His buddy John was a big guy who worked on the crash crew, ready to wade into the flaming wreckage of an airplane to rescue the pilots, but he wasn't fighting back. Lawrence, short but stocky and known for having a mouth on him, also just stood there with his eyes wide, waiting to see what would happen. Pettus feared they were about to get a good white-on-black ass whooping right there, but instead the Marines handcuffed all three men and called for a master-at-arms to take them to the brig. Pettus and his friends were reeling, completely confused about why they had been assaulted and detained. They were just trying to get back to work, for God's sake. What they didn't know was that the Marine detachment on the *Kitty Hawk* was well aware of the growing racial tension on the ship and had been instructed to be on the lookout for trouble. Exactly when they were instructed to prohibit gatherings of more than two black sailors would later be disputed, but they did receive that order at some point in the day.

Pettus, John, and Lawrence were quickly moving from bewilderment to anger as they were taken to the brig. They couldn't understand what was happening to them, but they were damned sure it was happening because they were black. The men were still in handcuffs in the brig area, waiting to be locked up, when the phone rang. They could hear the voice of the young white lieutenant who was processing them snap to attention when he heard the other voice on the line. The captain's order was loud enough that Pettus could hear it himself. "Get those men up here right now!"

The lieutenant responded with a crisp "Yes, sir" and started moving the prisoners out. Pettus didn't know what this meant. *How the hell did I end up here? In handcuffs and being taken to the captain?* As the lieutenant hustled them to the captain's quarters near the bridge, they passed many sailors who stared at them with wide-eyed wonder and some who looked on in anger. Three black sailors being run through the ship in handcuffs by a white officer.

Pettus had no idea what to expect when they reached the captain's quarters, but as soon as the door opened, Townsend barked at the lieutenant.

"Get those handcuffs off! Take them off now!"

Townsend had the men sit and explained that their detention was the result of a misunderstanding. He hadn't given any order to prohibit gatherings of more than two black sailors, he told them, and the Marines apparently had gotten their wires crossed. Townsend knew that, most likely, the Marines were being vigilant about prohibiting sabotage in the hangar bay in light of the fights at Subic and the rumors floating around the ship. He didn't tell the sailors that, but he did apologize for the mistake. The captain said that they were completely free to go and that there would be no disciplinary action against them. Pettus and the other two men said "Yes, sir" and left, relieved that the incident was over but still upset.

As the day wore on, the more he thought about being roughed up by the Marines and humiliated in handcuffs, the more Pettus felt like the captain's apology wasn't enough.

Other flare-ups happened, predictably, in the mess decks as the day wore on. With the day's somewhat relaxed work schedule, the men had more chances to linger and chat—or to look for trouble. When airman Terry Avinger, the troubled young black sailor who kept trying to find the right path for his life but who was known as one of the most hard-core black power proponents on the ship, made his way to the mess deck for dinner around 6:30 P.M., he brought along the usual chip on his shoulder. And, as usual, the white mess cook on the other side of the chow line was in a foul mood because he was back at his lousy job. Both had heard the black versus white trash talk that was going on that day. As Avinger went down the chow line with his tray, he decided he was feeling pretty hungry, so he asked for two sandwiches instead of one. The mess cook said no. Avinger knew the mess cook was just being a dick about it, so he reached over and tried to grab the second sandwich anyway. The mess cook told Avinger to keep his hands to himself, then the men began shouting insults and threats, Avinger insisting that he could have a second damn sandwich if he wanted one and that no white boy was going to push him around. The white mess cook was screaming just as loudly that he would say what happened on the damn chow line and Avinger wasn't going to just grab whatever he wanted. The incident ended without violence when others intervened, but it left both men angry. It was a typical dispute in the mess deck, so petty that it could have even been comical except that it was an indicator of how short everyone's fuse was. Avinger didn't forget the incident, feeling disrespected by being denied a simple sandwich by a white man as others watched. And he wasn't the only one noting every little indignity that day, piling them on to the heap of injustices that the black sailors had felt for a long time. Another spat broke out when a white mess cook accidentally stepped on a black sailor's foot as he was stacking trays. What might have been excused with a simple "sorry" instead turned into a heated argument between the races. Again the incident came to an end without anyone throwing a punch, but just barely.

And so it went, on into the evening. As the sun began to set, darkness did not bring much relief from the unrelenting heat. It never did. The tons of metal that made up the *Kitty Hawk* had been sitting in the sun for the entire day, soaking up the heat, and with nightfall it retained much of what it had absorbed, making the ship a hot box full of hot tempers on this night. Pettus had completed his shift on the flight deck after being hassled by the Marines, and after dinner he went back to his berthing compartment still hot, sweaty, and supremely pissed off. He found several of his buddies, along with other black sailors he knew but didn't necessarily consider friends, sitting around talking about Subic, the rumors flying around the ship, and the various minor incidents that had taken place that day. Pettus recognized Terry Avinger in the group, taking notice because he knew that some of the black sailors considered Avinger, a hothead, to be a leader. On any other day, Avinger and Pettus would have had little in common other than their black skin, but tonight Pettus was feeling just as oppressed as Avinger usually felt. For pretty much the first time, Pettus was "an angry black man."

Avinger, a charismatic type who was a natural leader, was holding forth on his experience that day, telling how the white mess cook had disrespected him and regretting that he didn't just beat the racist cracker's ass right there. This wasn't the first time that Pettus had walked into a bull session where black sailors were trading stories about how the white man was mistreating them, but this was different. This wasn't just the cathartic complaining that Cloud remembered from the barbershop of his boyhood. Pettus realized he shared a visceral anger with these men, the kind that can almost scare a man when he realizes how much is in the room with him. Avinger was urging the men to get mad, telling them the black sailors on the *Kitty Hawk* had had enough and it was time to stand up for themselves. Pettus found himself screaming "Yes!" right along with the others. And when there was a pause, Pettus jumped in to tell his story about being jacked up by the Marines and handcuffed. All of the black sailors within earshot were outraged but not surprised, and Pettus could see that he had raised the temperature a few more degrees. And he didn't mind. Maybe these boys from the streets of Detroit, Chicago, Philadelphia, and New York had the right idea all along. *I'm not going to be treated like this,* Pettus told himself. *Maybe it's time we stand up to this bullshit.*

Pettus was in the middle of it now, helping Avinger and some other vocal black sailors whip the crowd into a near frenzy.

"We don't have to take this anymore!" they shouted. "We have to stand up for ourselves!"

"Black power!" others yelled. "Black power! It's time the white man gets what he deserves!"

Avinger repeatedly pointed to Pettus and cited his story, whipping the crowd up further, declaring that Pettus's abuse had to be the final straw, the final indignity heaped on the black men of the *Kitty Hawk*. Pettus felt proud that his black brothers were standing up for him, that they also felt outraged by his treatment. *Yes, my black brothers are here for me,* he thought.

Pettus imagined that his buddies John and Lawrence were some-where on the ship also talking to their friends about their mistreat-ment that day. The incident of harassment was becoming a catalyst for the dangerous mood throughout the *Kitty Hawk*. The men in that berthing compartment were working themselves into a fury of righ-teous indignation, and then, without warning, the emotions reached a tipping point. The black sailors spilled out of the compartment and charged down the passageway, shouting encouragement to each other and insults about whites, and declaring that they wouldn't stand for the abuse any longer. Pettus ran with the mob, fully a part of it and eager to exact some retribution. Most of the men had no particular purpose in mind, but some of the more militant group members rec-ognized that this was more than just a random flare-up of some angry sailors. They knew it was the beginning of an uprising that they had planned for a long time.

Pettus rumbled along with the group, making as much noise as they could, shouting epithets at any white sailor they encountered, pulling gear off the walls, and smashing whatever they could as they passed. The group roamed through the passageways and they soon began accosting white sailors, beating them until the men could scramble away to safety. Pettus was in the thick of it, cheering on his black brothers and even dealing a righteous blow here and there, though his punches never connected with anyone. Running with the mob was cathartic for Pettus. If some white guy ended up with a bloody nose, well, too freakin' bad. It felt right.

SOME OF THE MEN, particularly the most dominant and vocal among them, had grabbed makeshift weapons along the way—broom han-dles, wrenches, anything they could find. The mob was racing down a passageway, looking for trouble, when Pettus saw a young white mess cook turn and walk straight into their path. The short blond sailor stopped abruptly, startled by the sea of angry black faces closing in on him. Pettus's heart sank. The sailor was so small in stature that he looked like a child playing dress-up. Any notion of retribution and vengeance evaporated as Pettus looked into the young man's eyes and saw a deep fear, mixed with confusion and panic. He looked like a very young, very scared boy.

Though the white sailor had frozen in his tracks, his instincts were kicking in and he turned to run just as someone from the crowd screamed "Get him!" The mob surged forward and engulfed him. The black sailors beat the white sailor viciously, but Pettus held back. Then he saw everyone in the crowd retreat a few steps, leaving just one black sailor standing over the mess cook, the blood soaking his denim work clothes and pooling on the floor as he feebly tried to ward off the next blows.

The black sailor took a foam fog nozzle off the wall, where it was stored at a firefighting station. This heavy metal wand was used to apply firefighting foam, but it also made a deadly club with the big fist of metal at the applicator end. The black sailor raised the foam fog nozzle high and slammed it down onto the poor kid, over and over, bashing his head in as most of the crowd urged him on. When he was done, the black sailor dragged the white man to a nearby hatch and tossed him down a flight of steps.

The mob cheered and screamed its approval, then moved on in search of more trouble. But it went without Pettus. He was sickened by the kid's beating, disgusted by the vicious assault on someone who, as far as he knew, was totally innocent. He stood there in the passageway, still smelling the sweat of the crowd and the sickly sweet stench of blood. He was breathing heavily and thought he might throw up.

This is too much. This is more than I bargained for, he thought. *My God, I don't want to be a part of this.*

AFTER CHECKING THAT OTHERS had come to the aid of the white sailor, Pettus made his way back to his berthing compartment, where the riot began. The mob continued its rampage, assaulting any white sailors unlucky enough to get in its way. By now the mob had quieted down, no longer shouting and instead becoming an eerie, imposing force moving through the ship, weapons in hand. The men had no destination, no real plan, but they wanted to break stuff and hurt some whites.

All over the ship that evening, there were similar blowups. Without much warning, white sailors were attacked and crowds of black sailors rampaged. John Travers, like most of the white sailors, was in his own berthing area, oblivious to the trouble. Around ten o'clock that night, the berthing area was jammed with not just the sailors who bunked there but another handful who were hanging out while the ship was in transit and they had little work to do. Travers was preoccupied at the moment with combing his hair. He had longish hair, like many in the Navy those days, and he prided himself on keeping a sharp look. Because he had lost his own comb some time back, he was using an afro pick that he had found. After cutting off half the length of the teeth, Travers still struggled to make the comb work for his Caucasian hair. He recognized a black friend named Jerry from the same berthing area. As Jerry squeezed between him and the mirror, Travers thought his friend might find it amusing that he was using an afro pick, and not all that successfully. With a smile, Travers called out, "Hey, man, you guys got screwed-up combs." Oddly, Jerry didn't respond and just kept walking, turning the corner a few feet away. Travers thought his little joke deserved some kind of reaction, so he stepped in Jerry's direction and called out louder.

"Hey, man, didn't you hear me? I said you black guys got really screwed-up combs!"

As soon as the words were out of his mouth, Travers realized he was standing in the narrow, congested passageway surrounded by black sailors, many of them armed. He wasn't sure where they had come from, because they weren't all from his berthing area. Travers also noticed right away that they didn't look too happy. Suddenly one short guy punched him in the face with a right hook, leaving him reeling. Travers regained his senses and looked at the guy for a moment, wondering what the hell was happening, then the fist popped him in the face again. When he was able to see straight again, Travers was about to start wailing on the guy, not willing to just stand there and take a third punch for no reason. But then he noticed that his friend Jerry had stepped back from around the corner and was watching. Travers could see that Jerry was trying to make eye contact with him, shaking his head no, as if warning Travers not to make a move. Packed in tightly with the black sailors and recognizing the danger, Travers swallowed his pride and didn't fight back.

When he backed down, the black sailors turned away from him and entered the berthing compartment, where they pulled the white sailors out of their bunks, beat them savagely, and trashed the area. Fights also were happening in several areas nearby, and Travers just backed away.

Good god, what's going on? Are they really that upset about what I said?

For years, Pettus and Travers would both think that they had started the riot on the *Kitty Hawk,* the black man by urging a crowd to seek retribution for his mistreatment and the white man by making an ill-advised comment about an afro comb.

CHAPTER EIGHT

A RAISED FIST

John Travers could see that the fight was getting bigger. More and more men were coming to his berthing area, both blacks and whites, and he had no idea who was fighting whom or what the whole mess was about. He fought off a couple of black sailors who came after him and then as he paused in a passageway with another white sailor, Travers asked what the hell was going on.

"I don't really know, man," the other sailor said. "I heard it was something about that fight in the forward mess deck last month. The one where the guy stepped on some black dude's toe and they got to fighting."

"Yeah, I remember. That white guy was a black belt and he ended up beating up four of the black guys, right?"

"Uh-huh. And then the master-at-arms put him in protective custody for thirty days. They just let him out, and the black guys are going after him. That's what I heard."

Travers realized that he was in a bad spot. He couldn't tell which way through the maze of passageways might lead to safety and which might throw him right into the melee again. It was clear, however, that this passageway outside his berthing area wasn't a safe place to stay. He felt very vulnerable just crouching there empty-handed, so he started looking around for a weapon. If one of those guys came after him with a pipe, he wanted something to defend himself.

My knife. I have to get that knife.

Travers had bought a switchblade with a six-inch blade in the Philippines, mostly just because he thought it looked cool, and it was stuffed in his locker. Making his way through the melee without having to engage anyone, Travers made it back inside the berthing area and to his locker. He found the knife, then grabbed some heavy-duty tape used to wrap packages. With the tape he fashioned a three-foot lanyard that attached the switchblade securely to his wrist, ensuring that if he lost his grip on the knife, it wouldn't fall far. Watching the beatings continue around him, breathing heavily from adrenaline and ready to defend himself, Travers popped the blade open and looked at it. The blade looked huge.

Maybe this is stupid. I've just tied a big knife to myself. I think I just provided these guys a weapon to kill me with.

Travers used the knife to cut the tape lanyard off his wrist and threw the blade away, behind some cabinetry so it wouldn't be found easily. *Maybe getting the hell out of there is the better choice.* He saw an empty passageway and took off.

THE LEADERS OF the *Kitty Hawk* did not have any idea of the violence that was seizing their ship. The captain was asleep in his sea cabin near the bridge, where he often stayed. Most of the other top officers, including the XO and the Marine commander, were in the officers' wardroom watching a movie.

At about the same time that Travers was running for his life, another group of angry men was escorting a black sailor named Rowe to the ship investigator's office for questioning. Like the mob that was whipped into a frenzy by Avinger and Pettus, this group of black sailors had also been worked up by someone who felt aggrieved by his treatment at the hands of whites. Airman Rowe had been charged that day with disobeying, being disrespectful, and assaulting a petty officer, along with drug possession. When he was summoned for questioning, Rowe showed up with nine other black sailors and then refused to make a statement. Told that the investigation would continue and that he would have to face the charges, Rowe and his friends left angrily. The black sailors railed about the white man's justice system while making their way back to their berthing areas, pumping up each other's anger over what they saw as harassment of Rowe.

By the time they made it to the aft mess deck around 8 P.M., they were primed for a fight. As they entered the mess deck, they saw a young white sailor stacking trays. One of the black sailors walked up and threw a punch, knocking the young man down and scattering trays. That first punch acted as the signal for the rest of the group; they took off after any white face they could see. Their rampage seemed interminable but really lasted less than half an hour, joined by another five black sailors who jumped right in. After the crowd had run off all the white sailors and had made a mess of the area, they agreed to talk with a commissaryman—a sailor assigned full time to meal preparation—who happened to be a member of the ship's human relations council, the group designated to hear the grievances of men on the *Kitty Hawk*. The black sailors went to a training room near the mess deck with the commissaryman and two food service officers, all white. Now calm and reasonable for the most part, the black sailors explained that they were upset about Rowe's treatment and the events in Olongapo. The officers dutifully noted the black sailors' complaints and got them to agree that trashing the mess deck wasn't the right way to get attention for their cause. Then they allowed the black men to leave without being punished for their actions. The officers were hearing rumors about skirmishes and worse from all over the ship. They felt that it would be better to let the sailors go and hope that calmed down the tense atmosphere than to detain the men.

They didn't want to escalate the violence by trying to hold the men or discipline them.

Unfortunately, their efforts to calm the men didn't work. After the black sailors went back to the part of the ship that housed their berthing areas, they started getting each other fired up all over again. More and more black sailors were gathering in the same place, groups of rioters joining to make one much bigger, much more volatile mob. The group that included Terry Avinger was in this area now. At about 9:15 P.M. the group's anger reached a crescendo, and black sailors started assaulting whites again, first in the aft berthing areas, then making their way back to the aft mess deck. There they chased down and viciously beat white messmen, some of whom were still cleaning up after the earlier riot. Then they went after other white sailors in the area. The riot in the aft mess deck was on again, bigger than before.

CHRIS MASON, MEANWHILE, had finished his shift in the mail room and was making his way to his berthing area under the aft mess deck on the starboard side. He had just gone down a ladder when suddenly two white guys came running toward him in a panic. The looks on their faces instantly made Mason's mind start cycling through all the bad things that can happen on a carrier—fire, enemy attacks, explosions, gas leaks, steam leaks, and on and on. While he was still trying to think what could scare them so much, he heard one of the sailors scream "Call the Marines!"

What the hell?

"Get the Marines! There's all kinds of hell going on in the aft mess deck!"

Mason didn't know what they were talking about, but he figured it was a fight. Not so unusual, but those guys looked scared. Since he didn't see any other indication of trouble, Mason proceeded toward his berthing area by the most direct path, which would take him right to the aft mess deck. As he got closer, he could hear a lot of screaming and the sound of things being smashed. Mason's curiosity got the better of him. Instead of turning around, he went on to the entrance of the mess deck and looked inside. He could hardly believe what he saw. Black sailors were running around and screaming, throwing chairs, ketchup bottles, anything they could pick up. A couple of white mess cooks were being tossed around too, but it looked to Mason like most of the whites had already fled. Mason hung out on the perimeter with some other sailors, white and black, who were too curious to turn away.

As the rampage continued, a chief on the mess deck called down to the Marine detachment and asked for help. About twenty Marines were in their centrally located berthing area, just below the hangar deck. A black gunnery sergeant named Robert L. Sellers took the call. Tall, with a receding hairline and black rimmed glasses, he gave the impression of maturity and authority. He soon hung up the phone and volunteered to go check on the situation.

"There's some kind of disturbance. They need me to calm somebody down," he told the other Marines. "I'll take care of it."

The chief had told him the problem was black sailors going nuts, so Sellers figured it would be better for him to go instead of sending a white Marine. Sellers didn't want to alarm anyone unnecessarily, but he told his fellow Marines to stay on the alert.

"Just be ready to go if anything's happening down there," he said.

Sellers, a large, imposing authority figure, hustled to the mess deck. He was astounded by what he saw there, and concerned. Every bit the Marine, he seized command of the situation and ordered the sailors to knock it off and leave the deck. Perhaps because the order came from a black man, even if he was a Marine, the rioters grew calmer. Sellers thought his mere presence might be enough to keep the men settled down. Like other authority figures on board, he didn't want to exacerbate the situation by bringing in a show of force if it could be avoided. Apparently Sellers was imposing enough on his own.

But the nearly twenty Marines back in their berthing area hadn't heard anything from Sellers and were still waiting on alert for any sign of trouble. It soon came in the form of a panic-stricken, breathless mess cook covered in all manner of food, ketchup, and something else that might not have been ketchup. He rushed into the Marines' berthing area and shouted between heaving breaths.

"We need Marines in the aft mess deck!" he yelled. "They're going crazy in there! We need Marines down there quick!"

The Marines, some in green fatigues and some in nothing more than boxer shorts, T-shirts, and boots, grabbed their wooden batons and spilled out of the compartment. They met up with a few more Marines, including Corporal Anthony Avina, who was wearing a sidearm. As the Marines double-timed it to the aft mess deck, their boots stomping on the metal plate flooring and creating a thunderous warning to anyone about to be run over, they passed by the officers' wardroom where their commander, Captain Carlucci, was watching the 1969 movie *Paint Your Wagon,* with a number of other officers, including XO Cloud. It was the first chance Cloud had had to watch a movie since joining the *Kitty Hawk,* and it turned out to be a western musical with Clint Eastwood and Lee Marvin singing to each other. The din of the passing Marines caught the attention of the men in the wardroom, including Carlucci, who leapt up to see what was going on. Seeing his Marines racing by, Carlucci yelled for a report and the men yelled back without stopping.

"Trouble in the aft mess deck!"

"Something big!"

"Gunny went up there and he's in trouble!"

Carlucci took off after his men and others in the room shouted for Cloud, who was toward the front of the wardroom and hadn't seen the commotion. Cloud made his way to the hatch as others told him about the Marines charging by. When he heard others in the room saying that they were calling the captain, Cloud took off after Carlucci and the Marines.

A legal officer who had been watching the movie, Lieutenant James P. Martin, picked up the phone in the wardroom to call the captain.

The phone rang at 9:47 P.M. in Captain Townsend's sea cabin, the berthing area just steps away from the bridge that he often used instead of his main quarters, particularly when he needed to stay close to the action. Townsend was asleep but used to waking instantly when the phone rang because it could mean any number of problems with flight operations or control of the ship. The phone woke him.

"Sir, this is Lieutenant Martin. There's some sort of big disturbance in the aft mess deck. The Marines are on the way so I thought you should know."

Townsend shot a curt "Thank you" and hung up. His first concern was to protect the *Kitty Hawk*. All of the black power, antiwar incidents throughout the fleet and the other services came to mind. Was he facing that kind of threat? he wondered. Townsend thought of the classified message that had warned of sabotage attempts and the "Stop the *Hawk*" movement that he expected to materialize. He also recalled the fight at the Sampaguita Club and his worries that it had been premeditated. If this business in the mess deck was really anything serious, he had to keep the troublemakers from sabotaging the ship and taking her off line. The most vulnerable and high-value targets for saboteurs were the airplanes on the flight deck and in the hangar bay. Any violence on the mess deck might spread or be used as a diversion for men damaging the aircraft. Townsend immediately went to the bridge and issued orders, first to the navigator, whose position on the bridge gave him a clear view of the flight deck.

"I want a sharp lookout on the flight deck at all times. Keep your eyes out there. If you see any unusual activity, you get somebody on it right away."

Then he turned to the air officer and ordered full illumination on the flight deck instead of the minimal deck lights normally used at night. "I don't want anybody out there who shouldn't be. Don't give them anywhere to hide."

With the flight deck brightly lighted and the bridge officers on high alert, Townsend called the master-at-arms. "Get some people out there on the flight deck and in the hangar bay. I don't want anybody messing with those planes."

MASON HEARD THE MARINES coming before he saw them. By the time they stomped down the passageway, he and the other gawkers had cleared out of the doorway to make a path. The Marines burst into the mess deck, ready for a fight, They had their batons at the ready and instantly sized up the situation. Black sailors were tearing the mess deck apart. And where was Gunny?

Sellers was standing there in the mess deck, perfectly fine, and surprised to see the rest of the Marines charge in. The Marines took up positions to begin retaking control, Sellers in line with his buddies. The twenty-five black sailors, who had been mostly calm under Sellers's control, reacted immediately. Avinger and Rowe were among the most vocal of those shouting insults. The black sailors taunted the Marines, raised their fists in black power salutes, and reveled in their defiance of authority. A bunch of Marines showing up with batons wasn't going to make them stand down.

If anything, the presence of the Marines in such force only inflamed the black men. From their perspective, the Marines—including the few black Marines—were not friendly faces and they weren't there to ensure order. Quite the opposite. To many of the black sailors on board, the Marines were the Navy equivalent of the white police force that harassed them back home, the most visible and most dangerous face of the white establishment. They were the enemy. They lived apart from the rest of the crew and had little interaction except when brute force or intimidation was needed. Black sailors, and even some white ones, saw the Marines as the enforcers for the system that mistreated them in so many ways, the troopers who were eager to kick some black ass and bash heads at the first opportunity. To many on the *Kitty Hawk,* a Marine was just another pig. Even on a normal day, many sailors took every opportunity to taunt the Marines, lobbing a bit of trash at them from an upper deck, spitting on them, or shouting an insult when they could get away with it. The Marines thought too many of the sailors looked and acted more like hippies than good military men. As far as they were concerned, a lot of them needed a good Marine to set them straight. They were ready to do it right here.

Cloud knew that a confrontation between the Marines and the angry black sailors could be disastrous. That was why he was racing to the mess deck.

They'll go crazy if the Marines go in with a show of force, Cloud thought. *I've got to get there fast and keep this thing from blowing up.*

As Carlucci and Cloud neared the mess deck, the temperature was rising, just as the XO had feared. The black sailors were incensed that the Marines had come in and, just by standing there with batons, were threatening them. Then the sailors started throwing anything they could find at the Marines: ketchup bottles, salt shakers, metal trays, chairs. Others raised the broken bottles in front of them as weapons, ready to take on the Marines when they charged. The Marines dodged the items thrown their way but stood their ground and waited. Only when the black sailors overturned tables and tried to block the entrance to the mess deck did the Marines move, forming a half circle to defend the entryway. That's how Carlucci found them when he made it to the mess deck. He saw his Marines holding a line, assisted by a handful of masters-at-arms, facing off with a row of black sailors who appeared equally determined to defend their position. Carlucci knew his Marines were just waiting for the right moment to make their move.

The scene was loud and raucous, but at the moment there was no direct contact between the two groups, and Carlucci wanted it to stay that way. He stepped between them, and with the assistance of a Marine first sergeant and the commissaryman who had heard the sailors' earlier complaints, ordered the two groups to separate. Cloud arrived at this point. Just as he had feared, the presence of the Marines was creating a flashpoint. The two groups had to be separated as soon as possible. Cloud joined Carlucci and the others in ordering them apart.

"All Marines out of the mess deck! All white crew outside! Off the mess deck right now!" Cloud ordered, and then Carlucci repeated the call.

"Black sailors, you stay here! We're getting the Marines out, so you stay put!"

Cloud's idea was to separate the groups and then deal with the black rioters without them feeling under siege. The mess deck was a good place to isolate them; its watertight hatches could be sealed from the outside. Cloud ordered Carlucci to have his Marines remain near the mess deck and police the hatches from the other side. That way the rioters wouldn't go anywhere but Cloud could talk to them inside. The Marines immediately followed orders and started moving toward a hatch, prompting the black sailors to hurl more insults and claim victory. The Marines had to accept a chorus of black power shouts and one-finger salutes.

Corporal Avina, a San Antonio, Texas, native who had been aboard the *Kitty Hawk* for two years and three months, was the last Marine to make his way out of the mess deck, and he was one of the few with a pistol on his belt. He had been on guard duty that evening; he had to be armed as he made his rounds through high-security areas like the flight deck and the brig. He had been checking the brig when he heard of the trouble in the mess deck and joined the other Marines. Avina was just about to step through the hatch leading to the passageway when he felt a tug on the shoulder strap that held his holster in place. He looked up to see a black sailor yanking him back, pulling him off balance. Avina reacted as he had been taught. *Protect your weapon.* He instinctively reached for the loaded pistol at his side and placed his hand over it to make sure no one could take it from him.

Everything else happened in a blur. The black sailors saw Avina's move as aggressive, thinking he was trying to draw his gun. Some hadn't caught the first action, the black sailor grabbing Avina. The rioters moved to help the man whom they thought Avina was about to shoot. The Marines saw Avina being attacked by a black sailor and moved to defend him. The corporal was being pushed and pulled as the men all screamed at each other, but his focus was on keeping that weapon in his possession. His hand was firmly planted on the holster, and though he had no intention of drawing it, he wasn't going to let go until he got out of the mess deck. The black sailors misread Avina's determination, as did one black officer who was trying to help him get away from the rioters. Thinking Avina was trying to draw his pistol, the officer pushed Avina up against the wall and spoke directly in his face.

"Don't draw that pistol! The guys here are going to get hurt. *You* may get hurt!"

At that point the Marines surged and took hold of Avina, pulling him out of the mess deck. Carlucci yelled at the Marines to go on back to their quarters and wait for further orders, but since Avina was on guard duty, he reminded him to go first to the guard shack and report the incident. The Marines left the mess deck but knew the trouble was not over. As they left, they could hear the black sailors cheering and continuing with their demonstration. Chris Mason had seen enough and left at the same time, heading for his berthing area.

Cloud ordered all the doors leading to dining room sealed off, leaving him and a few other senior men alone with the rioters, who now numbered about forty. The incident with Avina had ratcheted up the vitriol to a new level, and their anger was now directed at Cloud.

"He tried to shoot us!"

"What are you going to about that, XO? That white man tried to pull his pistol on us!"

Cloud also heard threats about getting the Marines later, that a Marine was going to die. It took several minutes for him to calm the crowd down, to get them to stop shouting and throwing things. He had to give direct eye-to-eye orders to several men, including Avinger and Rowe, to get them to shut up and listen. After he got the most vocal men quieted, the rest followed suit.

"All right, now listen to me," he said to the men. "I'm here and I want to hear what you're upset about. But we can't have all this screaming and disorder. I want to hear what you've got to say."

The men grumbled and groaned, and some just couldn't help piping up with a smart comment, but they did listen to Cloud as he asked about their grievances and assured them that they would get a fair shake from him and the captain. When Cloud asked what they were so upset about, the men immediately went back to the incident with Avina's gun. The XO assured them that the incident would be investigated. If the corporal had acted improperly, he would be punished to the maximum, even removed from the ship if the captain felt it necessary. Then Cloud asked what else was bothering the men. They presented a laundry list of complaints, many involving their treatment by the Marines, their experiences in the mess decks, their assignments, this long tour with no end in sight, and the events in Subic Bay. Cloud listened patiently, and sympathetically, to the men. He was interested in restoring order in the here and now, but he wasn't giving short shrift to the men's complaints. He felt genuine concern for their situation, despite the manner in which they got attention for it. Cloud assured the men that he would take their complaints seriously, and he reminded them of some of the options available on the ship, such as talking to the human resources staff, who could respond to their problems. The crowd stayed calm and responded mostly in a positive way to the XO, but a couple of the ringleaders weren't buying it. They heckled Cloud as he spoke and tried to get the crowd riled up again.

"He's lying to you, man. He's just the white man's boy," one man called out. "Don't believe him just because he's got brown skin. He's just as white as any officer."

Another of the black sailors warned the crowd, "If you listen to what the XO says, you will be no better off than you have been in the past."

Cloud took the abuse in stride but knew he was being tested, that his blackness was at issue. *I'm being put to the test as to whether I'm white in practice or black in practice. I've only been here eight weeks, and plus, they've never seen a black XO.* He tried to assure the men that they could trust him.

"Look, I'm not talking to you just as the XO now. I'm talking to you as an executive officer who has a greater understanding of your problems than probably any other executive officer in the U.S. Navy because the problem of being black has been one that I have lived with all my life," he said. "I would hope that you all would understand that I don't have to be told what it's like to be a black man. I'm an authentic black man, just like you. There doesn't have to be any compromise in terms of being an effective naval officer and being black. The two can be very compatible."

As Cloud was talking with the men, Townsend got a report from Carlucci about the scene in the mess deck, including the incident in which a gun may or may not have been drawn, and rioters may or may not have tried to take it. Still uncertain as to the extent of the problem, Townsend made a decision for which he later would be criticized long and hard. Although the standard procedure is for the captain to stay on the bridge in times of crisis, Townsend decided to go down to the mess deck and see for himself. If something serious was happening, he needed to know about it. If it was a bunch of hotheads who just wanted to hear from the captain, maybe he could put an end to it all pretty quickly.

Townsend walked into the mess deck and was shocked at the destruction and disorder. The men on the other side of the room were so involved in their conversation that they didn't even notice the captain enter, so he stood there for several minutes just listening. What he heard alarmed him.

Townsend had walked in as Cloud was trying to assure the rioters that he could be trusted, that he really was a true black man. Cloud would later admit that his methodology was unorthodox and not very military in nature, but at the time he felt military discipline had already been lost.

"For the first time," Cloud told the men, "you have a brother who is the executive officer. My door is always open."

Townsend was surprised to hear Cloud talk that way, identifying himself as a "brother" and being so conciliatory to a bunch of hooligans running wild on his ship. And then it got worse. The men continued talking and Townsend could hear some of the sailors shouting "Right on!" and "We can trust this brother." Several of the men raised their fists in a black power salute and stared directly into Cloud's eyes, waiting for him to return the gesture, to show that he really was a black man.

Cloud didn't know what to do. He had never given a black power salute in his life. It just wasn't his style, no matter how proud he was of his heritage. Feeling that he couldn't let this moment slip away, that he needed to take advantage of the headway he was making with these guys, for the first time in his life Cloud raised his clenched fist in a black power salute. The sailors cried out "Black power!" and cheered the XO as a brother.

Townsend was not pleased. No one had acknowledged his presence, and now his XO was giving a black power salute with the rioters. What the hell was this?

I'm going to either have to throw the XO out right now or turn around and walk out. My authority is being eroded if I let this go on.

Townsend left, troubled by what he had seen. The violence and destruction were bad enough, but he was particularly disturbed by Cloud's behavior. The second in command of a United States aircraft carrier had given a black power salute and assured a bunch of rioting thugs that he was one of them. What in the world was going on? Townsend didn't know Cloud all that well, but he had a hard time believing the XO was going to side with the rioters just because he was black.

He's handling this all wrong, Townsend thought. *Is it because he's black? I really didn't think he was like that.*

After half an hour, in which he checked other areas for trouble, Townsend went back to the mess deck to see what was going on. Cloud was still meeting with the black crew, still talking about being a black man, still getting cheers from the rioters, and *damn it all,* he gave another black power salute while Townsend was watching. Soon after, Cloud noticed that the boss was in the room. He pulled the captain aside to suggest that he be allowed to handle the situation without interference.

"I've got something going with these guys now, Captain. Maybe it's best if I continue with this on my own."

Townsend wasn't eager to comply with Cloud's suggestion but reluctantly turned to leave. Before he got out the door, though, some of the sailors called out that they wanted to question the captain as well. Townsend agreed to take a few questions. He gave pretty much the same assurances as Cloud had that there were structures in place to resolve any legitimate complaints by the black sailors. When he was finished with the questions, he ordered the men to disperse peacefully.

Cloud left first, to check out another report of trouble. As the black sailors began to break away at about 10:45 P.M., a few of them had one last question for the captain.

"Are the Marines going to bother us?"

"No, they're not," Townsend told them. "Exit through the hangar deck so you don't run into the Marines. They're on the way back to their area."

Townsend knew that by dismissing the men, he had taken control of the situation from his XO, but he thought Cloud had done enough talking with these men already.

Cloud, however, wasn't sure Townsend fully appreciated the gravity of the situation—or how hard he was working to resolve it. The XO knew he was using some unorthodox methods, but he was confident that such measures were called for to keep the peace. *Can't the captain see that I'm making progress here?*

What the captain saw was a man he thought he could trust doing something deeply disturbing.

If Cloud does any more of that stuff, we're going to have a real problem, Townsend thought. *If he gives any more black power salutes or anything like that, I'll just fire him. I can't have an XO like that.*

"USS Kitty Hawk*"*
The USS Kitty Hawk *in 1977 (courtesy of the U.S. Navy)*

"Sailors Performing"
Kitty Hawk *sailors performing for the crew on the fantail of the ship. Garland Young is on the left, singing with KJ Ulma. (courtesy of Garland Young)*

"Out on the Town"
Kitty Hawk *sailors on liberty at the Silver Star night club in Olongapo, outside the gates of the naval base at Subic Bay in the Philippines. From left to right: Bill Jordan, Jim Clausen, Barry Taylor, and Mike Cuff. (courtesy of Jim Clausen)*

"The Mess Line"
Sailors on the Kitty Hawk *go through the chow line at meal time. The mess hall was a frequent site of violence and arguments, some of it motivated by race. (courtesy of the U.S. Navy, 1972* Kitty Hawk *cruise book)*

"Dining"
Black and white sailors dine together on the Kitty Hawk in 1972. (courtesy of the U.S.
Navy, 1972 Kitty Hawk cruise book)

"Captain Marland W. 'Doc' Townsend"
Captain of the Kitty Hawk *in 1972. (courtesy of the U.S. Navy)*

"Executive Officer Benjamin W. Cloud"
XO of the Kitty Hawk *in 1972. (courtesy of the U.S. Navy, 1972* Kitty Hawk *cruise book)*

"The Captain and XO"
Captain Townsend and XO Cloud confer on the bridge of the Kitty Hawk *in 1972.*
(courtesy of the U.S. Navy, 1972 Kitty Hawk *cruise book)*

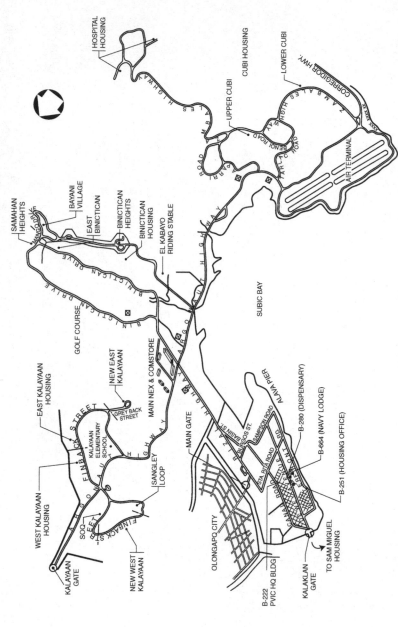

Subic Bay Naval Base, showing Alava Pier where the Kitty Hawk docked and the main gate leading to Olongapo City. (from U.S. Naval base phone book, 1990)

CHAPTER NINE

"THEY ARE GOING TO KILL US ALL!"

As Cloud and Townsend talked with the black sailors in the mess deck, they grew increasingly wary of each other's approach to the problem. Meanwhile, the Marine commander was preparing his troops for the next clash, which he thought was inevitable. Carlucci gathered his Marines in their berthing area—the ones who had confronted the rioters and those who had been elsewhere at the time. Carlucci wanted his men to know exactly what he expected for the duration of this crisis on the *Kitty Hawk*. As part of his due diligence in commanding the Marine detachment on the most prominent aircraft carrier in the U.S. fleet during this time of racial unrest, and because it was his nature to study manuals and guidelines in his free time, Carlucci had recently read a study of race riots by the Marine Corps and reviewed the procedures on responding to civil disobedience in Army Field Manual 19-15. He was ready, and he needed to tell his Marines what he expected. As he prepared to speak to his men, Carlucci received a phone call from the captain, who was still in the aft mess deck. Townsend confirmed that Carlucci's thinking was on target.

"I'm concerned about the security of the aircraft and the associated equipment on the ship," the captain explained. "You and your men are to protect that equipment from sabotage."

The Marine commander affirmed his orders and then discussed how they should respond to the black sailors in the mess deck. Carlucci proposed that the captain, with the Marines' backup if necessary, take a hard line with them. Unaware that Cloud had taken a conciliatory approach, Carlucci suggested that Townsend and the XO collect the ID cards of all the sailors at the meeting, to record the identities and provide a solid basis for any future legal action.

"It might shake those kids up a bit if you take their cards, sir," Carlucci said. "That might discourage them from doing this kind of thing again."

Townsend declined, explaining that taking the men's ID cards might get them riled up again. That answer might have made more sense to Carlucci if he had known that the men were already dispersing after bonding with their "brother," the XO. Carlucci moved on to his next suggestion: He wanted permission to find and detain the most vocal and visible of the ringleaders from the mess deck incident, including Avinger and Rowe. This move would be in accordance with the Marine protocol on riot control. Again Townsend said no, telling Carlucci that having the Marines hunt down those black sailors would only inflame the situation.

Carlucci hung up, frustrated that the captain wasn't allowing his men to respond as firmly to the rioters as he thought necessary. But they still had a clear job to do: protect the *Kitty Hawk* from sabotage.

"We're going to have three-man patrols in full uniform, full utility uniforms with nightsticks and whistles," he told the men. "I also want a twelve-man reaction force to stand by here in the Marine compartment so you have quick access to the hangar deck and the flight deck."

The Marines listened attentively as Carlucci continued.

"The three-man details are to patrol the hangar deck and flight deck. Protect the aircraft, the firefighting stations, the light water stations, and things like that. Summon help with your whistles if you encounter any resistance."

Carlucci was, as usual, playing it by the book and following accepted military wisdom on how to respond to mob violence and threats of sabotage. Remembering what he had read in Manual 19–15, he then went on to his next order.

"And as you are patrolling, you are to break up any groups of three or more men together. I don't care what color they are, white or black, if they are not actually working on the airplanes or the equipment, you are to tell them to disperse."

One of the Marines asked what they should do with sailors who refused the order to disperse.

"If anyone gives you trouble, get his name. If he refuses to give you his name, take his ID card or ask for it. If he completely refuses, then you should apprehend him and use common sense in your response. If the situation is such that you need to use force, then use some. But also request assistance. Blow the whistle."

Carlucci's Marines understood their orders. They put on their green utility uniforms, grabbed their nightsticks and whistles, and set out in three-man patrols to the flight deck and the hangar deck, leaving the reaction force behind in the berthing compartment.

AFTER LEAVING THE MESS deck, which was truly a mess by this point, Cloud continued talking with a number of the black sailors and suggested that they go to his cabin and discuss the issues they had brought up. Ever since he had arrived on the *Kitty Hawk,* Cloud had told the crew that they were welcome to talk to him at any time, in part because he had heard that they previously felt they didn't have ready access to the top command on the ship. His office had a pair of red and green lights outside the door and a sign: "Executive Officer: If light is green, knock any time day or night, then open the door and come in." A red light meant the XO was having a private conversation with someone. Cloud was always careful to make sure the crew had followed the proper channels before coming to him with a problem, but he wanted the sailors to know that he was available. So it was natural for him to invite the sailors to his cabin after the mess deck fight.

About a dozen of them agreed, and they were joined by the ship's legal officer and a few other white officers, with the men crammed into Cloud's office and taking up every available chair and spots on the floor and desk. The meeting was productive. Cloud continued the themes he had discussed in the mess deck, assuring the men that their concerns were being taken seriously, and countered some skepticism voiced by Avinger, Rowe, and the others who had doubted the XO's credentials as a real black man. The black sailors continued voicing their complaints and challenging the XO's sincerity, and Cloud felt that he was making progress simply by having the men talk to him calmly and rationally about their grievances. They still weren't completely buying what he was selling, but they were amiable, even pleasant with one another. They were having a real conversation. Cloud was pleased.

Suddenly the calm was broken as a young black sailor burst into Cloud's office, blood pouring from a gash across his head. The wound had been bleeding profusely for some time, as the man's white T-shirt was drenched and his face was crisscrossed with rivers of blood. The young man was panic stricken, in tears, nearly hysterical with fear.

"Oh my god, oh my god, oh my god," the sailor cried as the others stared, shocked by the sight. Then he looked up at the men in Cloud's stateroom and his voice rose to a terrified scream. "They're at it again. They are going to kill us all!"

The black sailors erupted, scrambling to get out of the stateroom as fast as they could, screaming that they never should have trusted the XO. They raced into the passageway and back toward the mess deck, leaving the XO and the white officers standing there, helpless.

The fire that had been tamped down to smoldering embers by Cloud's work was stoked into a full-fledged blaze again, the violence prompted by a series of miscommunications among the captain, the executive officer, and the Marines. Cloud and Townsend had told the black sailors to leave the mess deck through the hangar bay, but at the same time the captain ordered the Marine commander to make preventing sabotage a top priority, and that meant protecting the hangar deck. Though Townsend wasn't privy to Carlucci's specific orders, and they may not have met with his approval, Carlucci was following Marine protocol for riots when he told his men not to let sailors congregate in groups of three. After their experience battling the black sailors in the mess deck, the Marines could hardly be faulted for assuming the order was aimed at black sailors, and especially the black sailors from the group that had taken over the mess deck. So everyone was doing as they were instructed when the black sailors still on the mess deck—those who didn't go with Cloud to his office—left through the hangar bay and when the Marines showed up there with orders to prevent congregating. The outcome was inevitable.

The black sailors were still pumped from their apparent victory in the mess deck but feeling satisfied enough to follow the orders to disperse. The Marines were still feeling indignant about being chased out of the mess deck, and they had clear orders from their captain.

When the two groups came together in the hangar bay outside the mess deck at about 11 P.M., it was like two rival gangs meeting in the street. The black sailors started insulting the Marines, and the Marines responded by telling the sailors to disperse.

"You can't be in groups of more than two," one Marine told them. "You need to break it up and get out of here."

That prompted more jeers and threats from the black sailors, who were doing exactly as they had been instructed by the captain and the XO. They told the Marines to fuck off. The exchange escalated until someone pushed someone else, then both sides went at it. The Marines were outnumbered from the start, but the fight wasn't exactly equal because the Marines were armed and trained in hand-to-hand combat and riot control. No matter how experienced some of the black sailors were from the hard streets of America, the deciding factor usually was the Marine's nightstick, wielded by men who had plenty of time on the *Kitty Hawk* to lift weights. A nightstick across the head had caused the bloody wound on the sailor who had run to Cloud's stateroom.

The six Marines who had been patrolling the hangar deck were blowing their whistles furiously as they fought the black sailors, now numbering about fifty after more joined the group from the mess deck fight. One Marine managed to get to a phone and call down to the Marine berthing area.

"Trouble on the hangar deck!" was all he had time to scream before fending off more attackers. That call alerted the twelve-man reaction force, who charged out of their compartment. When the reaction force arrived, led by First Sergeant Willie A. Binkley, they found the Marines and the sailors going toe to toe, the sailors using any makeshift weapons they could find in the hangar bay to counter the nightsticks, and there were plenty of them—tie down chains, wrenches, hammers, crow bars. The reaction force waded into the crowd, swinging nightsticks at anyone who wasn't wearing Marine green. In the brawl, one Marine, Corporal Robert L. Anderson, tried to come to the aid of another but was surrounded by sailors and beaten to the deck. As he struggled to get back on his feet, he tried to get a good look at the men's faces so he could apprehend them later. But there were too many fists flying in his direction, too many people moving around frantically, so Anderson took another tack. He crawled over to the man who was swinging a broken broomstick, a man he knew had landed at least one good punch on him, and lifted up the man's pants leg. Then he sank his teeth into the man's flesh as hard as he could and held on.

"He's biting me!" the man screamed. "He's biting me!"

Sailors nearby came to the man's aid and Anderson fell away, satisfied that he'd left a good mark on the man.

Soon the reaction force gained ground on the rioters. The show of force caused the melee to break up, the black sailors retreating to the aft portion of hangar bay 2 near the number 3 elevator, unchastened but temporarily beaten back. They were still screaming and threatening to kill the Marines, and they made no effort to leave the hangar bay. Instead, they formed a rough line across it, a show of strength and of their intention to do battle again. The Marines, on the opposite end of the hangar bay, also formed a scrimmage line, ready to advance. It was an old-fashioned showdown, with both sides waiting for their leaders to give the order to charge.

Townsend was making his way back to the bridge from the mess deck when he heard men shouting and got sketchy reports that there was a disturbance on the hangar deck. At first he thought the men might be referring to the fight he had just come from, that he was hearing old news. But as others ran by shouting about problems on the hangar deck, the captain figured he should investigate. He was near Cloud's office at the time, so he went by there to see if the XO knew anything. The room was empty, and there was blood on the floor.

Townsend hightailed it to the hangar bay, where he found the two groups facing off. *Not again. What the hell is going on here?* He also saw that the Marines had four black sailors detained already. Townsend stepped into the hangar bay between the two lines of men, shouting at them to knock it off. First Sergeant Binkley, in charge of the reaction force, quickly stepped to the captain's side to protect him.

Townsend spoke urgently to both groups.

"No more of this! This is the end!" he shouted, his anger evident. "You blacks disperse! And I'm going to put the Marines away right now!"

The black sailors started screaming at the captain, demanding to know why they couldn't gather in groups. Townsend told them he had never given such an order. The black sailors roared, taking the captain's statement as evidence that the Marines were just hassling them, and continued hurling insults, screaming that the Marines were nothing but the pigs of the Navy. Suddenly a stancheon, a heavy piece of metal railing from a work stand, came sailing through the air and narrowly missed the captain, hitting First Sergeant Binkley in the leg. The Marines instinctively moved forward to react, but Townsend cut them off.

"No! Stand back!" he told the Marines.

He then turned to the black sailors and tried to calm them. "There was no order to stop you being together. That is an error, a mistake on the part of the Marines. There is no intent on my part to ever have you broken up in groups of three. Now get about your business. We have solved the problems for the night."

The men weren't satisfied and they made no pretense of being respectful to the captain, screaming insults and accusing him of being just another honky trying to run them down. Trying to dispel the potential for a more violent confrontation, Townsend told First Sergeant Binkley to release the black sailors they had in custody and to take his Marines forward and away from the hangar bay. The Marines complied, reluctantly but immediately, double-timing it out of the cavernous room. They passed Cloud as he was making his way inside. Cloud stood at the doorway to the hangar bay and sized up the situation. The captain was surrounded by a crowd of about twenty black sailors, all angry and shouting and standing way too close to the boss. There was a lot of screaming and gesturing, profanities and name calling, complete disrespect for the captain. Another thirty or so black sailors were hanging back, but obviously agitated.

Cloud was concerned for the captain's safety. He thought Townsend looked in control, but just barely. If just one of the hotheads was crazy enough to throw a punch at the captain, that could lead to a full-fledged beat-down on Townsend, and that was a scary prospect. The Marines had been sent away, so it was just Townsend there with a bunch of angry men screaming in his face and jabbing accusatory fingers in his direction.

As Cloud approached, the black sailors soon started peppering him with insults too. Avinger and Rowe led the chorus of jeers.

"Oh yeah, here comes the XO now, the captain's house nigger!"

"I told you we couldn't trust that Uncle Tom!"

"Man, you ain't nothing but the white man's dog!"

The invectives stung, but Cloud understood where they were coming from. The blacks felt that either Cloud had betrayed them or he didn't really have any authority and the whites called all the shots. They had listened to the XO, and look what it got them: Marines bashing their heads in just for walking together.

Still on the periphery of the crowd, Cloud made eye contact with the captain, who was gamely trying to talk to the incensed sailors. Townsend wasn't so sure that he wanted the XO interfering. After what he'd seen on the mess deck, he didn't know what Cloud would do. Another black power salute? Yeah, that's just what he needed right now. So he waved the XO off, indicating that he could handle this situation. The XO wasn't at all sure about that, but he didn't have much time to worry about it. At 11:15 P.M., a sailor rushed up to Cloud and told him that there was big trouble in the sick bay.

"They're fighting down there, sir! It's real bad!"

In the sick bay? Why would they be fighting in the sick bay? Cloud took off running.

TOWNSEND SOON GOT THE men calmed down enough to follow his orders to disperse. At this point he just wanted them to break up and go separate ways, and he wanted them out of the hangar bay. As the men turned to leave, not satisfied and not calm but nonetheless complying with the captain's orders, Townsend took a moment to survey the scene, looking for any signs of sabotage, finding only the tools and equipment that the sailors had thrown in the confrontation with the Marines. Relieved, he proceeded out of the hangar bay with the intention of making his way back to the bridge.

Meanwhile, the officers standing watch didn't know what was going on with the captain or the disturbance he had gone to investigate. They were getting reports of violence in several parts of the ship now, and the lack of information was starting to trouble them. The captain and the XO were both belowdecks, in the middle of whatever was going on, and it was highly unusual to have the captain off the bridge when anything was out of order on the ship.

Townsend and Cloud were both trying to manage the riot mostly independently, because they had little ability to communicate with each other. Since neither man was on the bridge, it was nearly impossible for either one to keep up with where the other was at any given moment. They did not carry radios, relying instead on wall phones throughout the ship. No one knew who, if anyone, was coordinating the response to the riots. They couldn't keep track of what each other was doing, so it was impossible to present a unified face to the crew. If they had taken five minutes to discuss the situation calmly, if they had had a chance to put their pieces of the puzzle together, they might have found a more effective way to end the disturbance. And they might have avoided much of the distrust between them that the lack of communication was causing. Cloud was worried that Townsend either wouldn't do anything to stop the riot or would let Carlucci take charge, which would mean a lot of black sailors beaten down and then facing criminal charges. Townsend was worried that Cloud wasn't handling the black sailors correctly, that he was treating them as equals and encouraging them, which also could lead to forcing the Marines' hand. And the black power salutes . . . *good god!*

Both Townsend and Cloud wanted the uprising to end without having to use force to crush the black sailors, but still they saw the situation differently. Townsend viewed the problem as primarily a threat to the ship's operations, a specific effort to impair the functioning of the ship and not necessarily anything more grandiose. He wanted the discord put down quickly, but not in a violent, overly punitive way that would engender more hard feelings down the road. Besides, he felt genuine sympathy for those men who were getting a raw deal in the Navy, particularly the ones who didn't understand the contract they had signed. He was trying hard to balance the need for order with his reluctance to use violence against a group of disadvantaged black men. He kept thinking about all the scenes of civil disturbances that had wracked American cities in recent years. Police had used dogs and fire hoses against black protestors, and in the infamous prison riot in Attica, New York, just a year earlier, an armed response by the authorities resulted in the deaths of nine hostages and twenty-eight inmates, most of them black.

I don't want to be the man who does that to these black sailors. I could send the Marines in and be done with this, and nobody in the Navy would criticize me for it. But I don't want to do that to these men.

Cloud also wanted to avoid that outcome. On that point, the captain and the XO were in agreement. But Cloud felt he had a deeper understanding of the black sailors and knew that this already bad situation could get much, much worse. Most of the rioters probably had no specific goals about what they wanted to achieve beyond causing a ruckus and getting someone to hear their complaints. A few, though—the more extreme among them who were heavily invested in the black power, antiwar movement—might have more on their mind. That worried Cloud. It was hard to imagine sailors actually trying to seize control of a U.S. aircraft carrier, even more difficult to imagine them pulling it off, but it was his job as the XO to worry about such things, no matter how improbable.

As he made his way back to the bridge, Townsend kept hearing reports of violence elsewhere on the ship. Just as he would turn to check out a report in one area, another sailor would come racing by, screaming about something elsewhere. Sometimes it was white sailors running for their lives, some with bloody noses and busted lips, and other times it was black sailors screaming that the whites were killing them. *How much was real? How much was just men trying to stir something up?* Townsend had no way of knowing. At one point the captain encountered a black sailor he recognized as one of the ringleaders from the hangar bay dustup running down a passageway screaming "They're killing our brothers! They're killing our brothers!" The man seemed more angry than scared; clearly he was trying to get black sailors worked up, encouraging them to come out and join the fight.

Townsend stopped him and shouted, "Show me somebody being killed! Show me!"

The man had no answer and continued on his way like the town crier.

Townsend considered calling general quarters, the order that would send all 5,000 sailors racing to their combat positions. Generally that order broke up any violence. But he feared that calling GQ would disrupt the ship's operations and might even cause more violence, as black and white sailors encountered each other in passageways on their way to their positions. Townsend decided that the situation wasn't bad enough to call GQ—a decision that he would have to explain to his critics later.

By this point the riot was spreading throughout the ship as more of the black sailors heard that the uprising had begun. Black sailors told bewildered whites that they wouldn't live through the night, that the blacks were taking over the ship and taking it home to San Diego. Some sailors were beginning to realize that the violence on the *Kitty Hawk* may not have been entirely spontaneous.

The disorder and confusion of the night gave cover to those who had an agenda. While much of the violence was random, some of the more militant, organized black sailors took advantage of the opportunity to exact revenge on specific individuals. Some of the men on board knew exactly whom they wanted to go after. As the violence spread, one of the predetermined targets was twenty-year-old airman James W. Radford, the young mess cook who a few days earlier had refused to serve an out-of-uniform black sailor. He and the other sailor had nearly come to blows until another black sailor intervened, telling Radford's adversary that it was "not the time or place."

The black sailors had not forgotten. As they and some of their black brothers ran wild on the *Kitty Hawk,* they decided that now was the time, and this was the place. Radford was resting in his berthing area with several buddies, stretched out and largely unaware of the growing riot. He and his friends had heard talk about some fights and disturbances nearby, but they didn't know what was going on and didn't want to investigate. Suddenly a group of fifteen black sailors burst in, grabbed a white sailor out of his rack, and started beating him. The whites in the compartment went to his aid. By the time Radford got there, the black sailors had retreated, leaving the whites standing there in shock. *What the hell was that? Who were those guys?*

The man they beat wasn't hurt too badly, so Radford and his friends stayed where they were, wondering what would happen next. They didn't have to wait long. Radford had just settled back into his rack when another group burst in and started pulling sailors from their bunks. As Radford was trying to fend off a couple of guys, he saw another white sailor being beaten in the head with a pair of nunchakus, the wooden batons joined by a short length of chain that could inflict a brutal injury.

After beating the men severely, the black sailors left the compartment, and Radford tried to aid the man who had been attacked with the nunchakus. He was bleeding badly from head wounds. The other men, themselves bruised and bloody, picked him up and headed to the hatch to take him to the sick bay. As they stepped into the passageway, they encountered several white sailors who were also helping a wounded man, his arms draped around their shoulders.

"You can't go this way!" one man shouted. "They won't let you go through the mess deck to take guys to sick bay! You have to go up and over the hangar bay. We just came from there, and the chances of getting hit in the hangar bay are pretty good too."

Good god, they won't even let us take this man to sick bay, Radford thought. *This is like a full-scale war.*

A couple of the men took the severely injured man toward the hangar deck, the long way around to sick bay. The man was close to passing out and leaving a trail of blood everywhere. After seeing no more attackers headed their way, Radford stepped back into the berthing compartment. He and another white sailor sat down, not knowing what to do next. They were joined by a white master-at-arms who took refuge in their compartment but didn't seem eager to do anything about the violence.

The men looked up as they heard another group of raucous sailors coming down the passageway, but it looked like the group was going to just pass them by. A number of the black men had already passed when one saw Radford sitting on a couch.

"Hey, there's the man that gave Wilson the hassle the other day," he called to his buddies.

The group stopped and came to the hatch, staring at Radford, who had no idea what they were talking about.

"You're the honky who wouldn't serve a black man!" one of them shouted.

Oh geez . . . that? This is about that stupid thing with the guy out of uniform and I wouldn't serve him?

The blacks crowded into the compartment, pushing the whites around and paying special attention to Radford. It was time to make him pay for his crime. One of the leaders shouted for someone to go get Wilson, and a couple of men took off to find him. In the meantime, the leader commandeered a chair in the middle of the room and set himself up as the judge, telling Radford that he was going to be put on trial. He'd get a trial every bit as fair as what a black man would get back home, he said, and the rest of the room laughed. All except for the other two white men, who were trying not to draw any attention.

While they were waiting, some of the black sailors couldn't resist hassling Radford, pushing him around, getting in his face with insults, and finally punching him. Then a foam fog applicator, the same weapon that Pettus had seen used to beat the white sailor so badly, came flying down at him. It hit him hard in the arm once, then again squarely in the gut. He was left dazed and in a lot of pain. As it looked like he was about to get bashed in the face with the applicator, the "judge" stopped the assault.

"No! That is for Wilson to do."

The men stopped their attack and just held him there as they waited for Wilson to show up. When he did, the judge asked him to confirm that this was the man who refused to serve him in the mess deck. Radford was standing there, grimacing in pain and scared.

"Yeah, that's him," Wilson said.

The black sailors started shouting that it was time for Radford's beating, but the judge stopped them and called for quiet.

"All right, white boy, let's see what you got to say for yourself. Are you prejudiced?"

"What?" Radford mumbled.

"Are you prejudiced?"

Radford hesitated before saying anything. "You come in to do a job on me, so just go ahead and get it over with, whatever you're going to do. It doesn't matter what I say."

Another man in the crowd piped up, his voice oozing with a fake sincerity. "No, really. If you can come up with something that sounds good to us, we'll let you go. Why wouldn't you serve this black brother here? What have you got to say for yourself?"

Radford, unwilling to play their game, still didn't say anything. At this point, the white master-at-arms spoke up from where he had been trying to blend into the wall.

"Uh, can I just leave?"

The black sailors didn't care about him. One said, "You better leave quick, before we beat all those tattoos off you," so the master-at-arms ran away. Then they pushed the other white sailor out also. Radford was alone with the men seeking revenge.

The judge looked at Radford, waiting for his explanation, but he wasn't offering one.

"Hang him," the judge said calmly.

With that command, the crowd went wild. They pushed him over a table onto his back. He felt more punches and blows to his body, head, face, everywhere, as he was tossed about the room, off the table, onto the couch, all the while just trying to cover his head with his hands to block the worst of the blows. His efforts were futile. He felt the foam fog nozzle make solid contact with his head and the world started fading out. He felt blood all over him as he got lightheaded.

"He's got a knife!"

Radford couldn't tell who was shouting or who had a knife, but it didn't much matter. He couldn't defend himself anymore. He expected to feel the blade at any moment.

The man with a knife actually was a white sailor who had seen the attack from the corridor and brandished the knife but then ran off to save himself. That interruption brought the attack to an end, and the judge told the other men to throw Radford out. They tossed him out in the passageway and told him to find his own way to sick bay.

Radford lay there, bleeding and nearly unconscious, his cheekbone smashed, his jaw broken, his skull cracked open, a huge gash over one eye. His punishment for not serving a black sailor in the mess deck.

CHAPTER TEN

"IT'S REALLY HAPPENING"

Robert Keel had encountered one of the first groups of rampaging blacks earlier in the evening when he was in the aft mess deck before he was scheduled to go on duty, taking some time to write a letter home to his family.

He had ducked when the black man threw a bomb fin toward him and then he watched as the heavy metal skittered across a couple of tables, missing him. For a minute Keel had thought the other man was going to come after him, but then the black sailor took off to catch up with his buddies.

Keel hadn't known what to make of the incident, but it wasn't the first time he had seen seemingly random violence on the *Kitty Hawk*. Deciding not to report the assault as he didn't want to draw any more wrath from the black sailors, he had picked up his letter and proceeded toward his post as a communications technician in damage control, the central area where officers and crew monitored the ship's operation and managed emergencies. To get there, he had to pass through the hangar bay, where he encountered a large gathering of Marines, back on patrol after dispersing an earlier group of rioters there. Keel just kept his head down and continued on his way, but he couldn't help notice that the Marines seemed jumpy and on high alert. They all had their batons out, some slapping them in their palms as they looked around nervously, eyeing everyone with an unusual intensity.

What the hell is going on? Keel wondered as he hustled to his post, where he found a similarly tense atmosphere. Damage control central is the primary engineering watch station, where the engineering officer on duty stands watch, assisted by technicians like Keel. They were responsible for maintaining the ship's vital systems when the ship was under way, and they were especially important during any crisis aboard the carrier because they tracked reports of damage and oversaw the crew's efforts to repair or work around any problems. With monitors showing images from the flight deck and other vital areas, and instruments showing the status of every key operating system, the men in damage control knew about as much about what was going on in the ship as anybody did. If the bridge and the forward bridge were both destroyed, the ship could be run from damage control. As Keel entered, he found the engineering officer in his usual spot, in a chair up on a raised platform where he could see all the boards, gauges, and men. Keel's job was to act as the engineering officer's "talker," the crewman who relayed orders and other communications between the officer and the rest of the ship.

Keel sensed that this wasn't just an ordinary night in damage control, as the engineering officer seemed a little on edge. Putting that together with what he had seen in the mess deck and the hangar bay, Keel figured there was some racial disturbance on the *Kitty Hawk*. But he wasn't in any position to be asking questions. He couldn't just ask the boss what the hell was going on. His job was to stand there and relay communications by phone, and he'd find out soon enough if anything was seriously wrong. For a while, it seemed that maybe his suspicions were off target. Damage control didn't receive any reports of engineering problems. The monitors showed that the flight deck was secure, though Keel noticed that it was lighted brightly, which was unusual. He also thought he could see Marine patrols out on the flight deck, also unusual. But all the instruments showed that the *Kitty Hawk* was sailing to Yankee Station just fine, and there had been no announcements on the 1MC, the ship's public address system, from the captain or the XO about any disturbances, so Keel thought maybe there was no reason to worry.

But then reports started coming in to control about fights in different parts of the ship. There wasn't any substantive damage so far, so there was nothing for the engineering officer to handle yet. He was on alert, though, ready to respond to any sabotage. The bridge was keeping the engineering officer informed about the scope of the problem, and soon Keel understood that there was rioting in different parts of the ship, with serious concerns about sabotage and perhaps even black sailors trying to take control of the *Kitty Hawk*. The men on duty in damage control knew that Captain Townsend and XO Cloud had both gone to deal with the rioters, which Keel thought was a little odd.

If the rioters managed to disable any of the ship's critical operating systems, Keel and the other men in damage control would go into high gear. For the moment, all they could do was wait and watch. Then damage control got a call from the bridge. It wasn't an update on the situation; it was an unsettling question. Keel relayed the query to the engineering officer.

"Sir, the bridge wants to know if we've seen the captain."

The officer looked at Keel with surprise. "No, we haven't seen the captain."

Keel relayed the reply to the bridge. "Damage control has not seen the captain."

Okay, that was weird, Keel thought. Apparently the engineering officer thought it was weird too, though he would never say so. But Keel could tell just from the look on his face.

Keel continued standing watch. There was not much going on, just men monitoring all the dials and gauges, giving occasional reports to the engineering officer. After a while, there was another call from the bridge.

"Sir, the bridge is asking again if we've seen the captain."

Now the engineering officer really looked puzzled, and that was not comforting to Keel or the others who overheard the exchange.

"No," the officer replied slowly. "We have not seen the captain."

Keel passed on the message again. "Negative, damage control has not seen the captain."

Everyone was thinking the same thing, but no one could say it out loud. *Where the hell is the captain? And why can't the bridge find him? Just what the hell is going on?*

They all continued with their jobs, with just the minimal conversation necessary when everything is fine on the carrier. Except they were all worried that maybe everything wasn't really fine.

In a few minutes they heard the sound of the 1MC coming to life. On the 1MC circuit, the message would be heard in every nook and cranny of the huge ship. The voice was not one Keel immediately recognized; it wasn't Captain Townsend or XO Cloud.

"Attention. Will the captain please call the bridge?" the voice said. It was calm sounding, though Keel thought he heard a bit of tension. "Repeating. Will the captain please call the bridge?"

Okayyyyy, now this is getting really strange.

Again Keel stood in silence as the men in damage control wondered what was going on. *They can't find the captain? What the fuck?*

In just a few minutes, the same voice came on the 1MC again.

"Will the captain call the bridge? Will the captain call the bridge?"

Keel and the other men looked at each other, exchanging looks that said, *Man, this can't be good. Where the hell is the captain?*

A few minutes later the voice was back on the 1MC. This time it sounded much more harried, concerned, frustrated.

"The captain *will* call the bridge! Immediately!"

Holy shit, Keel thought. For the next hour or so, as Keel was finishing his watch, he and the rest of the men in damage control wondered what exactly was going on with the *Kitty Hawk.* The situation was unusual; most times they knew more about the ship's status than almost anyone else. But on this night they had heard only sketchy reports about violence in various parts of the ship, black sailors marauding, and the captain missing in action. Keel had plenty of time to stand there and work through all the scenarios in his mind, and he wondered if he was in the middle of a mutiny. Had they taken the captain? Could they really do that?

There's got to be another explanation. There's no way there could be enough men on the Hawk *who would participate in a mutiny.*

But if it's not a mutiny, what the hell is going on?

AT THE SAME TIME that Keel was on duty in damage control, young white men throughout the ship were being torn out of their bunks and beaten with chains, wrenches, pipes, and hammers. They had no idea why they were being attacked, and they wondered why the leaders on the *Kitty Hawk* weren't coming to their rescue. Groups of rioters roamed the ship, some more violent than others, all creating havoc and destroying property just for the hell of it. The ship's store, where sailors could buy snacks, personal supplies, and other small items, was thoroughly looted.

As John Travers scrambled away from his berthing area, where he had taken a few punches in the face, he could see that the rioters were gathering forces. Different pockets of men, a few here and a dozen there, were joining up and becoming a mob, the total always more dangerous than the sum of its parts. Travers stayed on the periphery of the group long enough to hear some of the men talking. Some had mentioned that they had started out in the forward mess deck, raising hell there before moving to the aft mess deck and joining up with the black men who were rioting there. Now they were planning to go back to their divisions and round up the black sailors they each knew. For the next four hours Travers stayed far enough away from the mob to avoid being attacked but usually close enough to tell which way it was going to move next.

Travers didn't know which way to go, but he kept trying to stay a step ahead of the rioting sailors. Looking for somewhere to hide, he made his way to a compartment that housed a group of electricians, the men he would be working with after finishing his stint as a mess cook. He found several white electricians and one black electrician. The men didn't pay much attention to his arrival because they were all discussing what to do with the black sailor, a man named Hooper. Travers just listened as Hooper told his white friends that he didn't want any part of what was going on, and he planned to stay where he was.

"But, man, if they find you here and you don't join them, they're gonna jump you," one of the white men said. Hooper nodded but didn't say anything. He knew that was true.

"We have to hide Hooper. We can't let them find him here," the men decided.

A couple of the men took Hooper to another compartment, a small work area where he could wait out the violence and seal the hatch from the inside. Hooper stayed there alone for hours. The electricians were so nervous that Travers didn't feel much safer with them, so he kept moving in search of a good hideout. He soon made his way up to the island, the structure that rises up from the flight deck and houses the bridge and other work areas. Radar 5, one of the radio rooms in which Travers hoped to work one day, was up there, but it was empty. That was fine with him; at this point, he just wanted to stay away from everyone. He didn't know what was going on with the *Kitty Hawk,* and for all he knew, neither did anyone else. *Why the hell aren't they putting this thing down? Where's the captain and the XO?* Travers was content to be anywhere that the mob wasn't. So he grabbed a life jacket from a locker nearby and put it on—falling off the flight deck is a constant concern on a carrier—then went out on an observation platform on the island, where he sat alone in the breeze for what seemed a long time, watching the waves and wondering what was going on. He had thought being alone would make him feel safe, but after a while it had the opposite effect. The not knowing, the wondering what was happening elsewhere, was worrying him.

Maybe this is stupid. If they come marching up those steps there, I'll have no place to go. They'll just throw me in the water and no one will ever know I'm gone.

It was one of the worst worries on a carrier—falling overboard. It was so easy. You could walk right off the ship in so many places if you weren't careful. One stumble could send you sailing over the edge. Maybe you'd bounce off the structures jutting out from the ship and break your head wide open, or maybe you'd fall several stories straight to the water, which would feel like concrete from that height. If you survived, the ship would keep sailing, passing by before you even had a chance to yell. You would be just a tiny bobbing figure in the vast blackness of the sea. If no one saw you fall, the ship would be long gone before anybody realized you were missing. Even if they launched a rescue right away, your chances were not good. Many sailors have lost their lives falling off of aircraft carriers.

Man, I don't want to go that way. I don't want them to throw me over.

So Travers decided to move again. He made his way down several decks and found himself near the sick bay, which was filling up with injured sailors. He walked in and saw a corpsman there who seemed to have more patients than he could handle. Travers offered, "Hey, I'll answer the phone for you," even though the phone wasn't ringing. It gave him an excuse to hang out in what he thought was a safe place.

CHRIS MASON, THE WHITE sailor from Alabama, was headed back to his berthing area after witnessing the wild scene in the aft mess deck.

As far as he knew, that was the only disturbance on the ship. But as he got closer to his berthing area, he started noticing that hatches were closed, some locked from inside. Normally the hatches were left propped open so that sailors could come and go easily and to improve ventilation. Mason started wondering what was going on. When he reached his own berthing compartment, he found the hatch closed and the handrail down, the entry securely closed from the inside. The sight made his heart jump, as if he had been left behind in an emergency. But what the hell was going on?

Mason started pounding on the hatch.

"Hey, open up! It's me, Mason! What the hell are y'all doing in there? Open this hatch!"

Soon the young man could hear the wheel spinning on the other side, then the hatch opened a few inches.

"Mason, is that you?" someone called.

"Yes! What the hell is going on?"

The door swung open wider and one of Mason's friends yelled at him to get inside. Mason didn't understand what was going on until he got inside and the hatch was secured tight again and he heard the men's stories, how they had been jumped for no reason, how groups of black sailors were running through the ship and pulling whites out of their bunks. They had been holed up in their compartment for a couple hours, they told him. Now things were starting to make more sense, and Mason told them what he had seen in the mess deck.

Though the men were putting the pieces together, no one had anything close to the full story. Each sailor knew only what he had personally seen or experienced or what he was told by others.

JOHN CALLAHAN HAD NO idea that the *Kitty Hawk* was in the middle of a full-fledged riot. The mess cook who was seeking conscientious objector status, who had seen so many racially based fights in the mess deck that he worried there might be some sort of blow-up or an attempt to seize control of the ship, had just finished a shift and was taking a shower near his berthing compartment. Scrubbing off the grease and grime and food smells was always the best part of the day. Suddenly he heard the shower curtain being pushed aside and turned around. There stood three black sailors, men Callahan knew and considered friends. The look in their eyes told him everything.

Oh my god. It's happening. It's really happening.

Callahan was so vulnerable, standing there naked with the water splashing his back. He had nowhere to run and no way to defend himself. The men dragged him out of the shower and threw him on the floor, then kicked him as hard as they could, screaming obscenities, telling him he was going to die. They kicked him over and over with their work boots, several blows landing hard on his head. Each kick to the head clouded his mind further. He felt himself losing consciousness as he lay there in a fetal position, naked and bleeding, moaning with each blow.

Why . . . why are they doing this? I know these guys.

Eventually Callahan passed out. When he woke up, he had no idea how long he had been unconscious. The pain in his head, particularly one ear, was excruciating, and his face was swollen, lips bloodied, most of his body beaten. Callahan tried to stand but couldn't. With his head throbbing and his whole body in agony, he managed to pull himself up on all fours and crawl out into the passageway outside the shower area. Seeing no one around, he crawled down the passageway, dazed. After what seemed miles but actually was only a few yards, Callahan realized he was in front of the brig. With muddied vision he could make out a Marine standing at his post. Callahan called out to him feebly, his voice encumbered by the blood in his mouth and his swollen, cut lips.

"Help me . . . I need help."

The Marine stayed where he was and told Callahan to go to sick bay.

"Sorry, man, I can't leave my post. I got orders to stay here."

Callahan didn't have the strength to argue. He continued his slow crawl down the passageway, not sure where he was or how to get to sick bay. He just crawled. Eventually he passed out again, lying in the passageway until someone found him. He woke up some time later in the sick bay.

TOM DYSART HAD BEEN standing watch alone on an electrical switchboard when the violence erupted on the *Kitty Hawk*. From his station, it was a straight shot down a passageway to the aft mess deck and then down to his berthing area, which was right below the mess deck. At the switchboard, Dysart couldn't tell what was going on elsewhere in the ship. Like the rest of the *Kitty Hawk* sailors, he had heard little over the 1MC—no official announcements or instructions to the crew, just someone looking for the captain. Occasionally he heard what sounded like yelling and scuffling, things being tossed around, but he couldn't leave his post to investigate. Then he got a phone call. It was a buddy calling him from another part of the ship.

"Tom, you're at the switchboard now?" His buddy sounded excited about something, maybe scared.

"Yes, of course I am. You just called me here."

"Stay where you are, man! Just close the hatch and don't let anybody in!"

"What the hell are you talking about? What's going on?"

"They're beating people up, just grabbing guys and beating the heck out of 'em."

"Who is? Who's beating people up?"

"A bunch of black guys. They're crazy. It's real bad, man. Just don't let anybody in!"

Dysart assured his buddy that he would be safe, then hung up and closed and locked the hatch to his work area. He didn't know what was going on, but from the fear in his friend's voice, he didn't want it to come in there with him. He stayed at his post, doing his job and wondering what the hell was going on out there. Not knowing was terrible; Dysart's mind raced. Was this really a riot onboard? Were black sailors trying to take over the ship? Sitting there by himself, and knowing how bad race relations had been up to this point, it wasn't hard to imagine the worst. After a while, when it was about time for his shift to end, Dysart heard someone pounding on the hatch. The sound made him jump and he feared they had finally come for him. But then he heard a familiar voice calling out for him to open the hatch, that it was okay.

Dysart opened the door and saw a friendly face, a black sailor from his division who just happened to be the biggest, burliest guy on the ship. He knew the man fairly well because they worked together, but they weren't close buddies.

"C'mon, man, I'll take you back to our compartment."

Dysart just looked at him for a moment and then he realized what the other man was offering: an escort through the dangerous areas. The two headed down the passageway. The other guy didn't say much and Dysart didn't feel comfortable asking him what was going on, so he just followed his bodyguard. As they got closer to the mess deck, they started encountering more black sailors, and Dysart could hear men screaming and throwing things. Several of the black sailors screamed obscenities at Dysart as soon as they saw him; some made a move to grab him. Dysart's bodyguard told them to get away, shoving aside those who didn't listen the first time. Dysart kept moving, shocked by the scene and immensely grateful for his escort. It didn't take much imagination to see what would have happened if he had walked out of his work area and headed to his berth on his own.

When they got through the mess deck and down to Dysart's compartment, the black sailor turned and walked off before Dysart had a chance to thank him. Dysart holed up in his berthing area with other men from his division, all of them sharing stories about what they had seen, how narrowly they had escaped being beaten, or how they hadn't been as lucky as Dysart.

White sailors weren't the only ones being assaulted on the *Kitty Hawk*. Seaman William E. Boone, a young black sailor who had been aboard since August 3, was still serving out his stint as a mess cook. On the evening of October 12, he was in a berthing compartment where he bunked with other mess cooks, four whites and one other black. They were watching television when a black sailor suddenly came running to the compartment and yelled for everyone to get out. "There's going to be trouble!" he shouted, before rushing away. The men didn't react right away and were still trying to figure out what the man was talking about when a gang of seven black sailors barged in, yelling at the two blacks to join them. Boone and the other man stood up reluctantly; evidently the crowd thought they were acting too slowly, so the intruders grabbed them and shoved them into the hallway. Then the mob pulled two white men off the couch and started punching them in the face. Boone just stood there in the hallway, trying to figure out what was going on and what to do. When he saw the black sailors move farther into the compartment and pull white sailors out of their bunks and beat them, Boone ran to the nearest phone and called for help from the master-at-arms. When help arrived and the black sailors scattered, Boone went to the master-at-arms office to make a statement about what he had seen. That's when he realized something was seriously wrong on the *Kitty Hawk*. The office was calling in every master-at-arms possible, on and off duty, to respond to fight calls. There were only a few dozen masters-at-arms available, and they couldn't offer much resistance to a violent mob. Unlike the well-trained and armed Marines, the masters-at-arms were only regular sailors assigned to security guard duty. They were unarmed and usually spent their time breaking up scuffles and writing out citations.

After staying there for a while, Boone returned to his compartment and found that another white friend had been beaten, attacked

while he was in the shower. The man didn't have many obvious injuries, but he was shaken up, nearly in tears from shock and fear.

"They kept hitting me in the chest," the man said quietly. "They
said I wouldn't bleed that way and then I couldn't pin anything on
them."

Boone could see the man was in pain, and they didn't know if any
of the assailants were still around, so he decided to help his friend go
to the nearby master-at-arms office to seek refuge and report the assault. As they were climbing a ladder to the next deck up, the white
sailor going first, a crowd of about twenty-five black men saw him and
attacked with some sort of club. The man managed to scramble up
the ladder and get away, but the mob pulled Boone down and started
beating him. With two men holding Boone's arms out, he was unable
to ward off the men punching his face and gut.

"What's wrong? Are you chicken to fight us?" one man yelled as
he punched and kicked at Boone.

The young mess cook took ten or fifteen blows to the face, leaving his nose broken and gushing blood. Finally the men released him,
and he moved toward the ladder to try to find help. Before he could
get up the ladder, one of his assailants grabbed his arm and delivered
a parting shot.

"Don't you tell nobody it was brothers that did this to you," he
said. "You tell anybody it was us and we'll kill you. We'll find you and
kill you."

GARLAND YOUNG AND THE other men in his berthing compartment
had slept through the early hours of the violence, unaware that anything was wrong. Things changed at 2 A.M., when about forty black
sailors burst in and started pulling men out of their bunks and beating
them. Young recognized one of them as a man who had been in his division earlier but was transferred because he was considered a troublemaker. Like everyone else in his division, Young couldn't get along

with the sailor no matter how hard he tried. The sailor claimed to be a Black Panther and was always talking about black pride. Young concluded that the guy had a chip on his shoulder and was trying to prove how black he was. He also was known for keeping an afro comb with the handle sharpened like a knife. Before Young could think of a way to defend himself, he was pulled out of his rack and thrown to the floor. Young scrambled to get away from the kicks and stomps of the rioters. He managed to get out of the compartment and, with a couple of his buddies, ran up one deck to a quiet area. There they stood in their skivvies, panting from the run, hearts racing, trying to figure out what the hell was going on and what they should do. After a few minutes they decided they had to go back. They didn't know where else to go, and once they could catch their breath, they decided they weren't going to let a bunch of thugs run them out of their own berthing area. They grabbed any weapons they could find before heading down. Young picked up a large breaker bar, essentially a ratchet with an extra-long handle to provide more leverage, and the group made their way back to the compartment, determined but anxious too. When they got to the hatch, they could see that the black sailors were still there, grouped on the far side across from the hatch where Young and his buddies stood. Also in the compartment were several whites who had been beaten and were now trying to stay down and avoid another attack. Young locked eyes with the Black Panther for a moment and then looked at the other man's hands. He was holding a straight razor.

"Come on, Young. I'm gonna cut some off of you," he snarled.

Young raised the breaker bar over his head and hurled it the other man. It missed, but that set off both groups, and they rushed to close the distance. As they were punching and kicking each other, one of the black sailors suddenly started yelling for his buddies to get out. They must have thought trouble was coming, because they rushed out, leaving Young and his friends alone. Then the white sailors quickly sealed the hatch, and Young started surveying the damage. The mob had opened the sailors' lockers, thrown all their belongings out, probably stolen some stuff, ransacked everything. But then Young noticed something curious. Two sailors were still asleep in their bunks. The mob hadn't attacked them, and they had slept through the whole thing.

STILL SHAKEN AND CONCERNED by the calls for the missing captain he had relayed in damage control, Keel wasn't sure what he would find when his shift ended at 11 P.M. and he left the relatively secure damage control area. As he made his way back to his berthing area, it didn't take him long to run into trouble. He saw roving gangs of black sailors, usually just a handful at a time, running through the ship, sometimes with weapons. They were causing a ruckus, but at first he managed to evade them by just stepping aside. Then he started seeing larger, angrier groups of men on the prowl, and he looked for a place to hide. He reached the first-class mess and found that a number of the white crew had holed up in there, so he joined them to wait out the trouble. The others in the compartment wanted to barricade the door, which opened inward and couldn't be sealed from the inside. At one point, a large, heavily muscled crewman from Guam walked by the room and laughed at how the white sailors were all huddled inside, discussing how to seal the door. The Guamanian sailor thought it was funny that they were so scared, when he could walk the passageways unopposed because, first, he wasn't white, and second, he was about 300 pounds of mostly muscle.

Finally Keel and the other white sailors closed the door and barricaded it, but it wasn't long before a crowd of black sailors rushed down the hall and tried to get in. The crowd was screaming and banging on the door, the many black hands on one side trying to push it open as just as many white hands on the other side tried to keep it closed. Keel grabbed a Purple-K fire extinguisher from the wall and stood one row back from the door. He pulled the pin and pointed the nozzle toward the widening crack in the door, ready to blast someone with the caustic powder. As the door opened wider, Keel made eye contact with one of the black sailors on the other side and shoved the Purple-K nozzle right toward his face. Seeing what he was about to get, the black sailor's eyes grew big and he fell back, allowing the men on Keel's side to push the door closed again.

The pounding and pushing continued for a few minutes, then the rioters gave up and moved on. Keel and the other men were charged with adrenaline now, fearful of another assault and not certain they could keep the door closed the next time. Soon they scattered out and took off on their own. Keel headed to his berthing area, leaving the fire extinguisher behind. He made it in without any more encounters with the rioters, but he told the men there what had happened to him, and he was wary, watching out for the next attack. When he heard the sound of trouble coming down the passageway toward their berthing area, Keel suggested they seal their hatch and wait out whatever was happening.

If they got the captain, this could be really bad, Keel thought. *We may be in some real serious trouble here.*

KEEL AND HIS white buddies were doing the same as men all over the ship: barricading themselves in small compartments and wondering what was going on. Were they on their own?

Boatswain's Mate Second Class James W. Brown, a white sailor from Carlsbad, New Mexico, was responsible for supervising thirty-eight men in his division, and he was with most of them in their berthing area when the violence broke out. One man had been going to take a shower when a crowd of black sailors knocked him back down the ladder he had just climbed, where he fell against the hatch to their berthing area. Like the rest of the crew, Brown and his men didn't know exactly what was going on, but it wasn't hard to figure out that some of the black sailors were causing disturbances. Brown had his men stay there with him, not wanting them to go out and get involved in the violence. One of the three black sailors who lived in the berthing area was there with Brown, and he didn't know where the other two were. He only hoped they weren't involved in any of the fighting.

Like Keel and his buddies, the men holed up and hoped the trouble didn't find them. But then one of Brown's men came running into the compartment, sweat pouring off his face and frantic with fear.

"They've got one of our guys up there! They're beating the hell out of him! We've got to save him!"

Then he turned around and ran back toward the other compartment where the man was being assaulted. Brown didn't want his men to follow, so he yelled at them to stay put and said he'd go after the other two men. Brown stepped out of the compartment but soon lost track of the other sailor and was in the passageway alone. He stopped running, not sure where the trapped man was, then turned to go back to his berthing area. Just then seven black sailors stepped out of a compartment and blocked his way. They were all armed with pipes, chains, broom handles, and other improvised weapons.

"Hey, here comes another honky," one of the men said. "Let's beat his ass."

Brown was terrified. He'd seen the brutal way these men, or their cohorts, had thrown his sailor down the ladder, and he understood that worse things were happening to other men on the ship. Now he was separated from friendly faces and surrounded by angry men with weapons.

"Look, I don't want any trouble with you guys. I just want to go back to my compartment."

One of the men was ready to pummel Brown. He raised a pipe up high and shouted, "Come on, let's do it!" But another of the black sailors put up his hand to stop him and said, "Wait. Wait, man, just wait." That sailor started arguing with the others, saying they didn't have to do it this way, that they could just let Brown go.

"Let's try it the way the XO told us," he told the rest of the group.

The other men weren't taking the suggestion well, yelling that the black sailor was a sellout, that he needed to get with the program and go on with what they needed to do. "Are you going to be with us or against us?" they shouted at him. Eventually the more levelheaded sailor gave up, assured the other black sailors that he was with them, and stopped arguing for Brown's release.

Brown knew he wouldn't stand a chance against these men, so he tried to talk his way out of a bad situation. In a quavering voice, he tried to assure the men that he was no threat to them, that he didn't know their names, didn't care anything about reporting them, and just wanted to get back to his compartment. He also urged them to save themselves.

"Guys, if you keep this up, you know this can't turn out well for you. They're going to catch you eventually," he said. "I mean, for god's sake, what are you trying to do? What are you trying to accomplish?"

One of the men stepped closer to Brown and shouted in his face.

"We are going to do what you white honkies can't do! We're going to get the ship home!"

Brown was aghast. *They really were trying to mutiny?*

"You're going to take the ship? How are you going to do that, man? *How?*" he yelled back, looking around at the men. "Do you have any idea how you are going to get the ship to go back?"

The men didn't have any reply. They looked at each other, tense and ready to spring, waiting for someone to respond or throw the first blow. After a moment, they started to turn away from Brown.

"Well, let's forget this guy," one said. "We don't need to fool around with him."

"Yeah, he's too fat to do anything with," said another. "Let's let him go."

With that, the black sailors moved on and left Brown standing there, shocked that he had talked his way out of a certain beating.

CHAPTER ELEVEN

"THIS IS MUTINY!"

At 11:15 P.M., Cloud was racing to the sick bay, the compartment that served as the carrier's emergency room and clinic, where there were reports of more violence. As he made his way there, a white corpsman named G. Kirk Allen was doing his best to treat the wounded while fending off fellow sailors intent on beating him, the other medics, and the wounded patients.

A native of Fort Wayne, Indiana, Allen had graduated high school in 1969 and left for boot camp with a couple of friends the next day, all three of them trying to avoid the draft into the jungles of Vietnam and earn eligibility for college funds under the GI bill. After training at Great Lakes Naval Training Center, Allen emerged as a corpsman and physical therapy technician, soon assigned to the *Kitty Hawk*. He wasn't so crazy about the idea of going to sea, but once he got to the ship, he settled in well and for the past six months he had become a valued part of the crew. Allen had noticed, however, that there was a definite tension among the races on the *Kitty Hawk*. Blacks and whites didn't mingle for the most part, and he sensed that there was trouble brewing. Like so many whites on board, Allen responded by keeping his head down and doing his job. On a carrier, especially one operating at high tempo in a combat zone, there was always plenty of work for corpsmen and the doctors on board. The sick bay, measuring about fifteen feet by thirty feet with a central supply room and a closet on opposite ends, regularly saw men who had suffered every type of injury, from a cut thumb to limbs caught in machinery and severe burns, not to mention the standard illnesses that crop up in any large group of people over a period of months. In addition to the sick bay, the *Kitty Hawk* had an operating suite and two nearby berthing areas that were used as hospital wards.

On October 12, Allen was among the legions of sailors on the *Kitty Hawk* who didn't know much of what was happening on the ship because they hadn't walked into any dangerous areas and there had been no ship-wide announcements about the trouble. He reported for duty at about 8:30 P.M., ready to work his scheduled shift and face whatever injuries and illnesses the night might bring. He had no idea what was coming.

As soon as he walked in, he could see fellow corpsman Mitch Philpott, who was white, busily checking a supply cabinet. He also noticed more people than usual in the sick bay, plus a couple department heads running around looking concerned. Philpott looked up when Allen walked in and said, "Hey, don't go anywhere. Get ready! All hell's breaking loose!"

"What? What's going on?" Allen asked. But his friend had already turned to do something else and didn't reply. The corpsman was left to wonder what was going on, and the usual aircraft carrier nightmares started flashing through his mind. *Has there been a crash on the flight deck? No, we're not doing night ops tonight. A fire? Probably not. I never heard a fire call. What does that leave? Are we under attack? Oh my god, did the enemy's MiGs get out to us?*

Allen was about to ask one of the department heads what was going on when the first casualties started arriving. Sailors began carrying in their wounded friends, two unconscious from blows to the head, another conscious but bloodied and bruised. The men delivering the patients looked like they had taken some blows themselves, but for the moment Allen and the five other corpsmen had three patients who looked like they could have serious injuries. The first priorities were to stop the bleeding, then to assess breathing and look for possible head injuries. He didn't have the time to ask what had happened. As Allen was bent over one patient, he heard a noise in the passageway outside, the sound of stomping feet, voices shouting in anger, metal banging on metal. He had his back to the door, so he looked up from his patient and turned just as a group of black sailors barged into the sick bay, shouting obscenities and waving tie-down chains, wrenches, pipes, and other weapons. The hatred and rage in their eyes shocked Allen.

These are our guys. What the hell are they doing?

One corpsman jumped in the supply closet and locked the door. Another jumped in the closet at the opposite end and hid there, holding the door closed from the inside, leaving Allen and three others there with the patients and about twenty very angry black sailors. The sick bay was practically shoulder to shoulder with sailors as the last of the group pushed their way in. For the first few moments, no blows were thrown; the black sailors just shouted and cursed, pushing the corpsmen around.

Sensing that the intruders were ramping up for an attack, Philpott shouted to the other corpsmen. "Get ready, boys! Here it comes!"

Just as the beating began, Allen saw a Marine run past the first hatch that led into the sick bay. He was a tall, lanky redhead from Idaho, clearly responding to a call for help. But as he passed the first sick bay hatch, he saw what was happening. When he got to the second hatch farther down the passageway, he stepped inside. The Marine's red hair stood out in the crowd. Allen, trying to defend his patient from the men who wanted to beat him again, could see the Marine release a two-and-a-half-foot green oxygen bottle from its restraints and grab it like a bat. Then he went after some black sailors who had a corpsman pinned. The Marine swung the oxygen bottle hard, the dull *thump* of contact sounding through the room even as men continued shouting and screaming obscenities. A couple of the attackers fell back, reeling from the blows, and then others realized what the Marine was doing and scrambled to get out of the way. That sight rallied the white corpsmen, who continued fighting back against overwhelming numbers.

"Come on, boys!" Philpott cried out. "We got 'em on the run!"

As the black sailors moved to get away from the oxygen bottle, which the Marine was still swinging back and forth in a wide arc, the corpsmen used the opportunity to push the men toward the hatches. They shoved and punched until they got many of the rioters out; the rest, who didn't want to be left behind, spilled into the passageway after them. The Marine followed, still carrying his oxygen bottle, and chased the crowd down the passageway and away from the sick bay.

The corpsmen were left panting, dazed and confused, with bloody lips and noses. None of them had suffered serious injuries, but their patients were worse off than when they arrived. The two men who had hid in the closet and supply room came out of hiding as the others were standing around wondering what the hell had just happened.

The violence reminded Allen of another race riot he had found himself in years earlier. During his senior year in high school, Allen and his friends had been at a popular hangout for the white kids called the Hullabaloo, when a group of black teenagers showed up. They refused to pay the cover price, made derogatory comments about just wanting to take the white girls, and then fists started flying. The white kids pushed the black kids back out into the parking lot and a free-for-all ensued, drawing the local police and the media. Allen had been surprised to see that the racial disturbances happening all over the country could make it to his neighborhood, but that was nothing compared to what was happening now on the *Kitty Hawk*. Halfway around the world, America's racial tension was getting Allen's ass kicked in the sick bay of an aircraft carrier, of all places.

For the next hour, the corpsmen and doctors cared for a steady stream of injured men, black and white, some brought on stretchers, some helped in by a friend, some just stumbling in on their own. The injuries ran the gamut from the superficial to the serious, from cut lips to crushed skulls.

About an hour after the first attack on the sick bay, another patient came in, and this time, all the corpsmen took notice. It was hard to miss that close-cropped red hair on the Marine with his feet hanging off the end of the exam table. It was the same man who had saved them by wielding the oxygen bottle so ferociously. Now he looked like the rioters had finally gotten the better of him. He was bloodied and badly bruised, his face beginning to swell. Concerned that he might have a skull fracture, the corpsmen took him to the nearby X-ray department. They placed him on a table to wait his turn while the technician tried to keep up with the number of men who needed to be checked. A black sailor waiting to be X-rayed noticed the Marine's arrival.

"You're the guy who hit me!" he shouted, pulling himself up on his elbows.

The Marine was groggy, but he turned his swollen, bloody face to look at the other man. Then he pulled himself up to a sitting position and stared at the man as intently as he could with just one eye still open.

"I thought I killed you," the Marine growled, clearly regretful that he hadn't.

For a moment the two men looked like they might go after each other again, but neither one was up to it. They both slumped back down and waited for their X rays.

MORE CORPSMEN AND PHYSICIANS had shown up soon after the first attack on the sick bay, so there were now a couple dozen working in the sick bay and the nearby hospital wards. Allen and the other medics couldn't believe what they were seeing. There had been no official announcement on the 1MC, no message from the bridge to explain, but they could tell from the injuries that men were beating the hell out of each other. The white men coming to the sick bay told them that it was a black-on-white riot, while the injured black sailors said the Marines had attacked them. When they got a chance to breathe between patients, Allen and the other corpsmen tried to figure it all out.

"How long is this thing going to last?" Allen asked, his white shirt stained with blood and wet with sweat. "How long can we keep up this pace? I mean, good god, how many people are involved in this?"

The others wondered the same thing, and they tried to piece together what they knew about the world outside their hatch, based on what they had seen and heard. They talked about where their patients had been attacked, which berthing areas and how so many injuries were coming out of the mess decks, where the least experienced, youngest crew members could be found. The night's violence didn't seem entirely random, not just a blowup here and there. The medics saw a method behind the madness.

"They knew what they were doing," Allen said to another corpsman. "This was organized. They had a plan in mind and executed it."

One of the corpsmen finally said what Allen and the others had been thinking.

"This is mutiny, boys!" he said. "This is mutiny! This is just absolute mutiny!"

They had all been thinking the same thing, but it was hard to believe. Sailors on the *Kitty Hawk* actually were mutinying. *It's true. That's what this is. A mutiny*, Allen thought. *Men get hanged for that.*

"My god, are they going to take over the ship?" Allen asked of no one in particular. "Why isn't someone stopping them?" No one had an answer.

The medics were tired but buzzing on adrenaline, every sense heightened as they cared for patients, moved them on to other treatment areas, and always, always, kept an eye on the hatches and waited for the next attack. *At least they'll have more of a fight on their hands next time,* Allen thought. *It's not just a few corpsmen here now.*

Word came that there was a man down in the nearby mess deck, and the corpsmen decided that someone should go get him. Allen volunteered, though he wasn't crazy about facing god-knows-what was going on out there, and headed down the passageway by himself. He was about thirty yards from the sick bay when he turned around a bend and suddenly, *whack!* he took three or four punches to the face. Allen went down on one knee, stunned, and looked up at his attackers. He was surprised and disappointed to see that one of the faces was a black sailor he knew, a corpsman "striker," meaning he wanted to become a medic one day and had spent a lot of time hanging out in the sick bay, getting to know the corpsmen and learning about their work. Now he was among the black sailors assaulting Allen in the passageway. The striker didn't actually hit Allen, but at one point they looked right at each other and Allen knew the other man recognized him. But he did nothing to help Allen.

Before any more punches were thrown, a black chief petty officer who worked in the sick bay happened on the scene and intervened. He had been on the way to sick bay to help and immediately sized up what was going on.

"What the hell do you think you're doing?" he shouted at the black sailors. "Can't you see that red cross on his arm? This is a corpsman! If you get beat up, who the hell do you think is going to take care of you?"

The men gave the chief some lip, calling him an Uncle Tom, a lackey for the white man, but they soon moved on. The chief helped Allen up and the two of them went back to the sick bay. Allen needed medical attention now, so two more corpsmen headed out to retrieve the man from the mess deck.

THE WOUNDED KEPT COMING. At one point a white sailor came in with multiple stab wounds, all of them small and not too deep, but enough to cause a lot of pain and bleeding. The man had been stabbed all over his arms and torso, little evenly spaced puncture wounds that Allen had never seen before. When Allen asked what had happened, the sailor said, "Forks. They're stabbing us with forks. Can you believe that shit?" Other men told of being slammed in lockers, having heavy hatches thrown on their heads and hands.

At another point in the evening Allen saw medics bring in an unconscious, naked young white man, bleeding from head wounds and severely bruised. It was John Callahan, the man who was beaten in the shower and left to crawl on his own to sick bay.

Travers, the sailor who offered to answer the phone in the sick bay to avoid worse violence, did what he could to help out. He didn't know much about first aid so mostly he tried to stay out of the way, especially when the patients started fighting. Many of the injured were still angry and combative as they were being treated, insulting the white corpsmen who were tending their wounds. Then they would jump off the table and run back to fight again.

During a lull in the action, Travers found himself looking down at a young white sailor on a stretcher, sporting the biggest shiner he had ever seen. The man's eye looked like a huge purple plum with eyelashes. Travers recognized him as the ship's cobbler. The *Kitty Hawk* was one of the last Navy ships to have someone dedicated to shoe repair, and this guy had been working alone at his little shoe repair station when a crowd of black sailors set upon him. The man had been taken by surprise and the rioters pushed his work cabinet over on top of him, a corpsman told Travers. The man was unconscious and the medics weren't tending to him, which worried Travers. He also noticed that a Marine, Corporal Robert L. Anderson, had been brought in, aided by a lieutenant. Anderson was sporting a pretty bad gash over his eyebrow, the product of his beating in the hangar bay. Though a little woozy, Anderson was still in fighting mode.

"If you see anybody come in here with a bite on him, let me know," he said to the corpsmen. "I did it and I'm looking for that guy."

NICHOLAS CARLUCCI, THE MARINE commander, was supervising his men in carrying out their primary goal of preventing sabotage, as the captain ordered. He was ready to send his men to any hot spots on the ship as soon as he got the order from the captain, but as midnight approached that order hadn't come, and previous encounters with the captain and the XO made it clear that they didn't want the Marines moving out in force. But as the night wore on and more people passed the word that the sick bay was under siege, individual Marines started to realize they were needed and they couldn't resist trying to help. After dutifully logging in his experience on the mess deck in which rioters tried to take his sidearm, Corporal Anthony Avina made his way to the sick bay. So did the white Lance Corporal Joseph A. Brock, who arrived with a black sailor who needed medical attention; the man had run into the wing of a jet while trying to get away after assaulting Brock, who already had been attacked with a hammer and a pipe.

Avina showed up first and found the sick bay was busy and hectic, the corpsmen trying to do their jobs in trying circumstances. Brock showed up soon after. He and Avina conferred and decided they would take up defensive positions in front of the two hatches to the sick bay, strong points that might help them fight off the rioting sailors even though they were certain to be outnumbered. They were tested almost immediately. About a dozen black sailors came charging down the passageway toward Avina, armed with chains, fire hose nozzles, four-by-fours; one even had a knife that looked to be at least fourteen inches long. At first Avina tried to talk to them, ordering them to stop, showing his baton and trying to "talk to them the way they talk," as he would later say, telling them to "Play it cool. Just play it cool." He had no choice but to try reasoning with them because he and Brock were seriously outnumbered. The black men stopped short of the Marine but jeered and taunted him. "Come on, hit me with your nightstick!" one yelled, then they attacked. Avina did his best to fend off the men with only his nightstick, knowing that he might make things worse by drawing his pistol. Besides, the Marines didn't carry weapons with a round chambered, so it would probably take him three seconds to draw the weapon, pull the lever back, and slide a round into the chamber. Maybe he'd get off one round before the mob took the weapon away.

The sailors mobbed him in the close quarters of the passageway and wrested Avina's baton away as he tried to protect his pistol. Brock tried to help but was also overwhelmed. Once the rioters got Avina's baton, they pushed him aside and rushed the sick bay, where the medics were ready to be attacked again.

"That's the one over there!" the black men shouted, and Avina realized they had come looking for someone in particular. This was the first time he saw that his fellow Marine Anderson was in the sick bay. The black sailors went right for Anderson and proceeded to beat him viciously, although the other Marines and corpsmen did what they could to defend him and Anderson himself put up a good fight, swinging a green oxygen bottle at a black sailor who was threatening him with a broomstick. Before he could make contact with the oxygen bottle, another sailor hit Anderson from behind with a four-by-four and he went down, where he was pummeled by at least two more men. After he took several more blows, another black sailor grabbed him under the arms and lifted him to his feet, then shoved him toward the hatch.

"Get out of here!" the man shouted at Anderson. "Just go!"

Anderson stumbled down the passageway on his own, away from the sick bay, but he was stopped soon by a corpsman who ushered him into another compartment used for aviation medicine, the specialized medical care provided to the ship's fliers. There he was treated for his injuries.

The crowd went elsewhere, leaving the corpsmen and the two Marine defenders to regroup. Soon two more Marines joined Avina and Brock in defending the two hatches. The Marines were tired, bloodied, and overwhelmed, but they also were determined to protect the sick bay.

"Just guard that door and don't let anybody through!" Avina called to Brock and his partner. "Nobody but medical personnel gets through!"

The defenders didn't have to wait long. Brock saw a large mob of black sailors waving weapons. *Oh my god, they look like a lynch mob.* Brock looked back at Avina.

"They are taking over! We can't stop them!" Brock shouted. Then he took off for the nearest guard shack, where he could call for more manpower. He got through to the Marine compartment and told them more help was needed in sick bay. Then he dropped the phone and raced back to his position. By the time he returned, Brock saw that most of the mob had headed in another direction, leaving only a few stragglers to curse the Marines and make halfhearted attempts at breaking through to the sick bay. The Marines would carry on like this for hours, fighting off assaults on the medics and the wounded.

CLOUD, STILL DESPERATE TO stop the violence from escalating, praying that he could ratchet the animosity down before either the blacks or the whites, the rioters or the Marines, did something irreversible, was on his way to the sick bay about 11:20 P.M. when he passed by his office, the scene of the previous meeting with the ringleaders. He noticed that three black sailors were there, all armed with chains and pipes. The XO stopped and asked them what they were doing, and they told him they were looking for First Sergeant Binkley, the Marine who had led the reaction force to the hangar deck. They considered him most responsible for the beatings that had taken place; besides, they hadn't liked him even before tonight. Cloud knew who Binkley was, and he knew that—rightly or wrongly—many of the black sailors regarded him as the "Bull Connor" of the Marines on the *Kitty Hawk,* a reference to the Birmingham, Alabama, official notorious for using fire hoses and police dogs on black protestors.

"What do you want with Binkley?" the XO asked.

"We're going to kill him," one of the men said. Just like that. Very matter-of-factly: We're going to kill him.

Good god, when is this going to end? Cloud thought. He told the men they weren't going to do any such thing, ordering them to get to his office and wait for him. The men grumbled but complied, and Cloud called the ship's legal office. When someone answered, the XO gave him clear orders.

"Get somebody out there and find First Sergeant Binkley! Find him right now and bring him to my office. Personally escort him to my office! Do you understand?"

The sailor on the other end acknowledged and Cloud hung up. *If they're out for Binkley, then I need to keep him nearby. If he's with me, maybe I can keep him from being assaulted.*

Then Cloud tried to talk some sense into the three assassin wannabes. He didn't have much of a chance before a chief aviation ordnanceman, Charles M. Johnson, showed up with a young black sailor in tow. Johnson was the lead criminal investigator on the *Kitty Hawk* and worked with Cloud on disciplinary matters. The black sailor had been detained by a Marine for being with a violent group and he was crying hysterically, seemingly terrified. The Marine had given the detainee over to Johnson and the legal officer was hoping Cloud could do something with him. Cloud saw that the handcuffs on the man were so tight that they were drawing blood. The XO ordered the chief to release the cuffs. Johnson was trying to do that but couldn't find the right key: he had something more important on his mind. But then Binkley showed up, escorted by Captain Carlucci. As soon as the black sailors saw Binkley, they leapt toward him and started screaming obscenities, threatening to kill him right there.

Binkley and Carlucci held back. Cloud tried to settle the men: three wanting to kill Binkley on the spot, two Marines restraining themselves from fighting back, a chief eager to say something, and a hysterical sailor handcuffed and sobbing on the floor. Cloud ordered Binkley to sit down at one end of the office and told Johnson to stand in front of him. Then he ordered the angry black sailors to the opposite side of the room.

"Stop it! Just calm down! Nobody's going to kill anybody here!" Cloud told them.

When Cloud paused to take a breath, the legal officer spoke up. He had been stopped on the way to the XO's stateroom by a young corpsman with tears in his eyes, begging for help in the sick bay. Johnson blurted out the urgent message as soon as he saw an opening.

"XO, they are killing people down in the sick bay!" he said. "Will you come down there and see if you can quiet down the situation?"

Only then did Cloud realize how shaken the chief looked. Johnson was flustered for several reasons. In addition to the frightening message from the corpsman, he had been assaulted himself that day, surrounded by a sea of black faces and threatened with death. After that he had seen more assaults. He also felt guilty because he realized now that he should have told the XO about some scuttlebutt and ominous reports he'd heard around the ship over the previous twenty-four hours. On at least three different occasions, white sailors had reported to Johnson that black men had told them, "You are not going to sleep tonight." He also got a report from a department head that a black sailor had stepped into a berthing compartment full of white sailors and screamed, "You fucked the niggers, you fucked the Indians, you fucked the Chicanos for 300 years, and tonight you are going to pay for it!" When an officer told him to settle down and go to bed, the black sailor had responded, "I answer to a higher authority."

Johnson realized that if he had passed on that information, the captain and XO might have been able to prevent the violence. Instead, the ship was going crazy. Johnson felt partly responsible for not preventing it.

"They are killing people! Come see what you can do about it!" he pleaded.

Cloud had already heard one report of trouble in the sick bay and now Johnson's report made that situation seem even more urgent, so once again he would have to leave one hot spot for a worse situation elsewhere. He ordered the legal officer to keep the black sailors there in his office. Then he turned to Binkley.

"You're coming with me," he said, looking intently in the Marine's eyes. "You stay with me at all times. You are *never* to leave my side for any reason? Do you understand?"

"Yes, sir," the Marine responded. He had no idea if he was under arrest, being protected, or asked to bodyguard the XO.

The black sailors left in the XO's stateroom with Johnson looked at him and realized he couldn't hold them there, so they pushed past him and ran out. Johnson managed to hang on to the handcuffed prisoner, and he got the right handcuff key from a passing Marine. Johnson took the man along as he chased after the other sailors. After making a couple of turns, Johnson found himself before a large group of angry black sailors who started heaping abuse on the only white face around. Fearing another beating, Johnson handed the handcuff key to a black first-class petty officer standing nearby.

"Get these handcuffs off this man," he told him. "We don't need him in this crowd showing what the Marines did to him with these handcuffs on his wrists."

Then Johnson quietly backed away from the crowd and ran for his life.

CLOUD APPROACHED THE SICK BAY about 11:30 P.M. and could hear the commotion as he got closer. At the open hatchway that led down to the sick bay, four chief petty officers were standing around. When Cloud approached and saw the scene, he realized that he shouldn't take Binkley into that mess. He'd only be a hot target for the black sailors. So he told Binkley to stay with the chiefs and ordered them not to let the Marine leave.

Cloud hurried down the ladder and to the sick bay, astounded and appalled at what he was seeing. *In the sick bay?*

The few Marines defending the sick bay were just pushing back another assault by a crowd of black sailors, and the XO's appearance seemed to have a calming effect. The black sailors stopped shoving forward, and Cloud was able to enter. He could see that this was only a lull in the chaos. The sick bay was full of injured sailors, black and white, corpsmen and doctors busily moving from one table to another, and the whole place looked like a hurricane had come through. Supplies were scattered everywhere, gear was torn off the walls, blood was sprayed around; it was a total mess. But the violence stopped when he arrived. That was a good sign. *Maybe I'm making some progress here.* Cloud started looking for a doctor, someone in charge who could give him a report, but his attention was diverted to a man coming down the passageway from the aft portion of the ship, shouting. As the white sailor got closer, Cloud and the others in the sick bay could hear what he was yelling.

"They got the captain! They got the captain!"

The man ran on by, and everyone in the sick bay paused what they were doing for a second to look around the room at each other. *They got the captain? This is really a mutiny?*

Cloud raced into the passageway, heading aft, in the direction the man had come from. The last time he had seen the captain, Townsend was in the hangar bay surrounded by angry black sailors. Cloud was regretting leaving the captain alone with them like that. *What have they done?* he thought. *This is crazy.*

Cloud raced through the ship. As he passed by the personnel office, he came upon a chief who looked terrified. He locked eyes with the XO and said, "They got the captain! They killed the captain! Oh my god!"

Cloud couldn't believe what he was hearing. *They've killed the captain! These crazy fools are taking over the ship! They've killed Townsend!* Cloud's heart was pounding and his mind was racing. He'd never been more stressed or scared in his life. No mission over the jungles, no antiaircraft fire had ever heightened his senses like this. *The captain of a United States aircraft carrier has been killed by his own men? How can that be? What should I do?*

Cloud's mind blazed through all the scenarios, all the options, all his training. They don't really teach commanders what to do in this situation, but Cloud was determined to seize control back from the rioters, to stop this bloody insurrection before it went any further. Cloud believed that this whole crisis was instigated by a confrontation between the Marines and the black sailors, so he once again thought that separating the two groups was a top priority. Whatever the reason for the riot, whatever criminal charges might have to be brought later, right now the task was to stop the violent confrontations. And if the captain had been killed—*My god, could that really be true?*—then he was now in command of the *Kitty Hawk*. Clearly, he had to act.

From where he stood, Cloud realized he could make it to damage control central in a hurry. It was almost straight down a few levels, and damage control had access to the 1MC circuit that could deliver a shipwide message. He raced down the ladders and bolted into the damage control compartment, startling the engineering officer and the sailors standing watch there. At 11:35 P.M. Cloud grabbed the microphone for the 1MC and began talking to the crew.

"This is the executive officer speaking. May I have the attention of every *Kitty Hawk* crew member? This is an emergency," Cloud said, in a shaky voice that alarmed the sailors who had had little information during the riots. This sounded like the executive officer was in a panic. "Do not listen to what anybody else tells you. I want you to do exactly as I tell you. *I ask you, I implore you, I order you,* to stop what you are doing! All black brothers proceed immediately to the after mess deck. Every member of the United States Marine Corps proceed to the forecastle immediately. This is an emergency!"

Cloud's goal was to separate the black sailors and the Marines. He thought most of the rioters were already in the aft area, and he figured they would be willing to return to the mess deck, the scene of their earlier successful negotiations. Sending the Marines to the forecastle would put them some distance from the black sailors and minimize the confrontations. This stopgap measure would slow the riot and give him a chance to talk to the black sailors again. Cloud had to stop these constant blowups, these repeated confrontations that happened after he and the captain thought they had everything under control.

Cloud's address over the 1MC did not have the calming effect he intended. Even though rioting had been going on for more than three hours at this point, many men on the ship were so isolated that they had not even known there was a problem, and suddenly the XO came on the horn sounding like he was scared to death and begging his "black brothers" to get away from the Marines. Those who were already in hiding or had been assaulted took no solace in hearing that the *Kitty Hawk*'s upper command was rattled and telling the Marines to retreat. To the rioting black sailors, the XO's address was proof that they were making headway, that they had the *Kitty Hawk* command on the run and that the Marines were being told to stand down.

Keel thought it sounded like the XO was in a panic. So did Mason. So did Young. They all found Cloud's announcement to be unnerving. They were troubled by what seemed a lack of control by the ship's top officers. The whole military structure is premised on the guys at the bottom of the ladder being able to trust that their leaders will look out for them as long as they follow orders and do their jobs. The white sailors, for the most part, were not fighting back and trusted that the top brass would take care of the situation, that they would be protected. The XO's announcement and the lack of any other good information made them doubt whether that was true. The paucity of information and orders created a vacuum for the sailors, and into that vacuum were swept all the fears and anxieties of young men left on their own.

Why is this thing being allowed to continue for so long? Mason wondered. *And where the hell is the captain?*

Young tried to piece together what the XO's message meant. Clearly Cloud was taking over command of the ship. He was a black man. Black sailors were taking over the ship, and then the black XO comes on the horn to say he's got the ship. What was the crew supposed to think?

This is it. They've killed the captain, Young thought. *The white guys are going to have to jump overboard before the Navy nukes this carrier. There's no way they're going to let this carrier get anywhere near a Navy base with these guys in control.*

After the announcement, many of the white sailors just dug in, staying in their compartments to see what would happen next, wondering when the next mob would attack. Young went to the fire station in his berthing area and took the canvas hose off the reel. He opened the valve all the way so that the high-pressure hose was fully charged, then took the heavy metal nozzle end back to his bunk. He lay down, wrapped his arms around the charged hose, and turned on his side so he could watch the hatch. If anyone came through, Young was willing to blow them off their damn feet.

CHAPTER TWELVE

"CAPTAIN, I AM SCARED TO DEATH"

T he captain, meanwhile, was in hangar bay 2, searching for any signs of sabotage—still his primary concern. He was perfectly safe, uninjured, and pretty much by himself. He had contacted the bridge since the frantic calls for him to check in, but there was still a complete lack of communication between him and Cloud.

The crowd of angry blacks had moved on, and it was just Townsend with a few sailors going about their jobs and others passing through. Townsend was reassured by the fact that the hangar bay had not suffered much actual damage, and there did not appear to be any effort to sabotage the multimillion-dollar planes parked there. He was starting to make his way through the hangar bay to exit when he heard the 1MC come to life. When his XO's voice boomed and echoed through the huge hangar bay, Townsend stopped and just stood there, listening, hardly able to believe what he was hearing.

"Do not listen to what anybody else tells you," Cloud called out in a shaky voice. "I want you to do exactly as I tell you. *I ask you, I implore you, I order you,* to stop what you are doing! All black brothers proceed immediately to the after mess deck. Every member of the United States Marine Corps proceed to the forecastle immediately. This is an emergency!"

What the . . .? Good god, what is the XO doing?

How could his XO make such an inflammatory address to the crew? *What the hell is he trying to do, get the whole ship whipped into a frenzy?*

Townsend was bothered as much by the XO's tone as by his words. He was dumbfounded by the message. And appalled.

Why is the XO taking over the ship? he wondered. But then he thought back to what he had seen earlier, with Cloud appeasing the rioters and giving black power salutes, calling them "brothers." *I guess I was right to be worried about what I saw. His actions up to this point amounted to pretty much trying to take over the ship anyway.*

Townsend was furious, and concerned that Cloud's announcement would worsen the immediate trouble and further degrade his own authority. He couldn't let this continue a minute more. He raced to the end of the hangar bay, out the hatch, and toward damage control, where he could get on the 1MC himself. His immediate concern was to countermand Cloud's order. As far as he knew, the Marines already had been told to stay in their berthing area, and he didn't want them piling out to comply with Cloud's order. Surely that would just cause the Marines to run into groups of black sailors again, and Townsend knew that would spark more violence. He wanted the Marines to stay in quarters, damn it, where he could control them. Why the hell was Cloud trying to roust them?

The captain thought the executive officer was overreacting. And he kept worrying that Cloud really was on the side of the black rioters. *Does my XO really want this riot to end? Or is he just encouraging it because he feels an allegiance to the black sailors?* But that couldn't really be true, could it? No matter what the motivation, Townsend thought his XO was handling this all wrong.

If the man is going to panic like that and just make things worse, maybe he should go to his quarters and let somebody else handle the problem.

Townsend made it to damage control in no time, sped along by the fury that was coursing through him and his fear that Cloud's announcement was about to put a match to the *Kitty Hawk* powder keg. As he came around a corner toward damage control, he ran into Charles M. Johnson, the white legal officer who had been in Cloud's stateroom with the black sailor in handcuffs. Johnson had escaped from the crowd of angry black sailors by leaving his prisoner with them, then he made his way back to the legal office, which was near damage control. He had encountered other groups of marauding black sailors along the way, armed with broken broomsticks and dogging wrenches, but he managed not to get beaten again. He was relieved to see the captain was safe. Recognizing Johnson as a chief who worked closely with the XO, Townsend curtly asked where Cloud had made the 1MC announcement from. Johnson said that damage control was the best guess.

Townsend found Cloud exiting damage control. The XO was still deeply concerned with how to stop the riot from escalating, his mind racing with possibilities and trying to figure out how to find the captain. He thought he might be in charge of the carrier, an incredible obligation to have land in your lap. Cloud was intending to head toward the aft mess deck to meet with the black sailors again. Townsend and Cloud paused and looked at each other, but with very different expressions. Cloud was relieved to see the captain, happy that he was uninjured and still in command.

"Captain, I got word you had been hurt, maybe worse," Cloud told him.

"I'm not," Townsend responded tersely. He didn't say anything else but shot a look that told Cloud everything he needed to know about what the captain was thinking.

Townsend was full of anger for the man he thought was trying to take over the ship, the officer who was sounding like he didn't want this disturbance to end. As Townsend stood there, he seriously considered firing Cloud on the spot, telling him to go to his quarters and wait for disciplinary action. But the captain held off, thinking it better to remain calm and not escalate the situation. God only knew how news that he had fired the black XO would be received by the crew.

Cloud told the captain where he was heading. Townsend hesitated, on the verge of delivering a dressing down the likes of which have rarely been heard. Instead, he gritted his teeth and said, "If anybody ever writes a book about this ship, this is going to be the most fucked-up chapter!"

He meant it as a way to defuse the tension, opting for levity instead of an angry outburst, but Townsend knew that this was not a shining moment for the *Kitty Hawk*.

Cloud muttered his agreement and Townsend continued on into damage control. The engineering officer and the sailors working there were relieved to see him, that the reports of his death had been greatly exaggerated. Townsend had no time for pleasantries or status updates. Instead, he strode directly to the 1MC microphone, as Cloud had done a few minutes earlier.

"This is the captain. Disregard what the XO just said," Townsend announced, the annoyance clear in his voice. "The XO's words were premature and based on erroneous information he received. He thought the situation was more serious than it really is. Do *not* go to places. Blacks are not to proceed to the after mess deck. Marines are not to go to the forecastle. That's the last thing we want to do, to segregate into two separate camps. I do not want any gatherings of anyone.

"Everybody go about your normal business. Cool it, everyone. Break up peacefully and proceed back to your spaces. The Marines will not use any weapons and will leave you alone. There will be no weapons used unless I call for it on the box.

"Those of you who have grievances I will meet with you right now on the forecastle. The rest of you I want to cool it. Knock off this senseless behavior before more of your shipmates are seriously injured. I know everybody is hot under the collar. I know you are disappointed at not going home as planned. So am I. But we've got to live with it, so cool it.

"I'm okay and the XO is all right. I repeat, I'm heading for the forecastle now and will meet with anyone and try to work out your grievances. But for God's sake, the rest of you cool it and go back to your spaces."

As Townsend was making his announcement, Cloud waited in the passageway outside damage control with Johnson and two Marines. The XO wasn't pleased to hear Townsend countermand his order and, in the process, make him look foolish to the crew. More important, though, he still thought it was right to send the Marines and black sailors to opposite ends of the ship. It was the captain's call to countermand that order, but Cloud disagreed.

Townsend stayed in damage control long enough to receive reports on the ship's status. The engineering officer reported that from a mechanical and operational standpoint, the *Kitty Hawk* was doing just fine. There was no serious damage or sabotage anywhere. Most of the violence seemed to be confined to the second deck, so Townsend left, intending to take a look there. As he stepped out, Johnson, Cloud, and the Marines all looked at him expectantly.

After hearing both addresses from the ship's leaders, and after his own frightening experiences that day, Johnson's emotions were close to the surface.

"Captain, I am scared to death," he blurted out.

Johnson meant that he was scared for the ship, that he feared something truly terrible was building among the crew. He was worried that Townsend and Cloud were no longer in control of the *Kitty Hawk* crew. But as soon as he said the words, he realized that they sounded whiny and that the captain probably thought he meant he was scared for his own safety. It hadn't come out right, and Johnson regretted giving the captain the impression that he was buckling in a crisis. He already regretted not telling the XO about the threats he had heard before the riot started, and now he had told the captain he was scared. He started to say more, to try to explain what he really meant, but the captain cut him off.

"Chief, I want you to stop in the legal office and I will speak to you," Townsend told him, sounding calm and paternal, as if he were trying to reassure Johnson. The captain was doing his best to project a composed demeanor. *This damn panic is their worst enemy,* he thought.

Chastened by Townsend's countermanding his orders and realizing that the captain interpreted his announcement as a challenge to his authority, Cloud too tried to explain himself.

"Captain, I didn't know where you were, and the last time I saw you, you were with that group that looked pretty hostile. Then I got word that you had been killed or injured, so I had to act."

"I understand that," Townsend said, but Cloud could tell he was still angry. The captain stared intently at his second-in-command. Then he said, "You jumped the gun, XO."

"Captain, this thing is getting out of hand," Cloud said, moving past his own defense and trying to convey a sense of urgency. "A great number of our crew do not believe me, do not believe you, and they don't believe our sincerity, primarily because we told them they would be all right and they're not. After that first meeting on the mess deck we told them there would be no problem with the Marines, and look what happened."

Townsend gritted his teeth and let out a deep breath. "*You* got this thing off track with the way you were talking to them up there. It's your job to stop this mess, and you were up there being conciliatory and placating those men. I saw what you did."

Cloud knew that Townsend was talking about his efforts to bond with the black crewmen and convince them that he understood their plight. And he realized the captain must have seen his black power salute. Cloud could see a distrust and wariness in the captain's eyes that wasn't there before, and he could understand it. From the captain's perspective, Cloud had to admit, things looked suspicious.

"Captain, I'm not trying to placate anybody or polarize the crew between black and white," he said. "I assure you that's not my intent. We've got to put this thing down or else it's going to blow up even more."

Cloud realized he wasn't making any progress with Townsend. At that moment, about twenty black sailors came rushing down the passageway, screaming "Get them!" and "Kill them!" To Cloud, it looked like the crowd was just trying to stir up trouble and find a good target for some abuse. Both he and the captain moved to stop the men. Among the group was Terry Avinger, the troubled young man who kept swinging wildly from troublemaker to reformed optimist. He was one of the angriest black men on the *Kitty Hawk* now. Townsend saw Avinger and felt a mix of anger and disappointment, realizing that his efforts to rehabilitate the young man had been for naught.

Cloud stepped into their path and raised up his hands, shouting "Stop!" The mob didn't slow. Instead, those in the front ran right through the XO, knocking him to the deck. Townsend took off after the group with the two Marines close behind. After a few steps, Townsend stopped and turned to look back at Johnson.

"Go to your quarters!" he barked.

Cloud scrambled to his feet and held up his hands to slow down five black sailors, including Avinger, at the tail end of the crowd, making them pause long enough to hear him out.

"You men are doing it the wrong way!" he cried. "Give me your weapons and get on with it!"

A couple of the men handed over their weapons but others refused, then all moved on to catch up with the group. Avinger lingered long enough to talk to Cloud, moving closer to the XO's face and speaking plainly. Calmly, but defiantly.

"You know your way won't work," he said. "You told us the Marines would not hurt us, would not bother us, and they were out there beating us up just like they had been told. You are no better than the others. We don't believe you. You are a liar. You are just as bad as all the rest."

Avinger pushed past the XO, but Cloud grabbed him by the arm and tried to restrain him. If he could just talk to Avinger, he could convince the man to stop what he was doing. The sailor would not be held and broke away.

"Stop!" Cloud shouted. "I order you to come with me!"

Avinger never stopped but turned his head to shout back at the XO.

"I am not going to obey you! You're just as bad as all the rest."

Dejected but still determined, Cloud followed Avinger, both men running to catch up with the now-departing mob. The XO considered trying to physically detain Avinger but figured the mob might just turn on him. In the confusion of trying to catch up with the crowd, the captain and the XO became separated again. Having lost the mob they were chasing, Cloud continued to look for trouble spots as he moved aft. Black sailors were continuing to beat white sailors in passageways, pulling them out of bunks and work areas. As Cloud intervened, trying to pull sailors apart and wrestle their weapons away, the sound of Townsend's voice on the 1MC still echoed in his mind.

The public exchange between the XO and the captain left most of the crew on the *Kitty Hawk* even more worried and confused. First they hear calls from the bridge looking for the captain, then the XO's message gets them concerned that the ship is going to hell in a hurry. And then the captain comes on right after and slaps down his own XO. Many of the sailors wondered which was worse: a ship in serious trouble but led by two competent officers working in concert, or a ship in some kind of trouble but without any unified command at the top. This type of uncertainty, this confused chain of command, was exactly the opposite of how they'd been taught the ship should operate in a crisis. Like pack animals that don't care so much which dog is the leader so much as that they're being led by *somebody,* the crew was discomfited to hear such a public display of disagreement. *Is anybody really looking out for us? Is anybody really in charge?*

Cloud was stinging from the public rebuke. He realized the captain's misgivings, but now he was caught between his white boss and his black sailors, with neither completely trusting him. Cloud hadn't been aboard the *Kitty Hawk* long enough for the black sailors to develop any faith in him, and his position as XO prompted a certain amount of skepticism from blacks who distrusted authority figures. Some of the events of the evening had not helped shore up his credibility with them. The captain, however, had started the day with complete faith in his XO, a faith that was shaken when he saw Cloud raise his fist in a black power salute and then try to take over the ship with his crazy announcement. Cloud, realizing that he was operating pretty much without the captain's support, could have gone back to his quarters and let things play out under Townsend's command. The captain probably wouldn't mind, he figured. He didn't know that Townsend had nearly ordered him to do that anyway. But the XO was too much of a team player and felt obligated to do his job. Hurt feelings or regrets about his actions that night were not going to get him down. (By now he was recognizing that his urgent address on the 1MC might have been wrong—not his strategy in separating the crew, but perhaps his haste in believing the reports of Townsend's death.) Cloud still thought he was the one who really saw the big picture— what caused the violence and where it still could lead—and he was still desperately trying to prevent a disaster. Maybe the captain thought he could just tell everyone to knock it off and that would be enough, but Cloud had seen enough violence that night to convince him otherwise.

Moving through the ship on a different route, Townsend also found pockets of black sailors roaming the ship, some armed and some just pounding on hatches, ripping gear off the walls and jumping on any white sailors they encountered. He went to the sick bay to check on trouble there and used his authority to quell another assault on medics and patients. The medical staff and injured men there were somewhat reassured by the captain's presence, but they also wondered why he was there instead of on the bridge, running the ship. Seeing the captain personally intervening to stop the violence only made them wonder more about exactly what was going on. Mutiny?

Townsend also encountered more black sailors running around screaming "They are killing our brothers!" Some were hysterical, and some were clearly just trying to stir up more resistance. As he had done earlier, Townsend demanded, "Show me!" and no one could. Townsend broke up any fights he ran into, demanding that the sailors stand down and hand over their weapons, which they always did. He could see, however, that often the men picked up other weapons as soon as he stepped away. Townsend never encountered a single crew member who refused to hand over a weapon when ordered and, unlike Cloud, he was never personally assaulted, despite spending much of the evening in the midst of the riot. (The iron stancheon thrown his way earlier in the hangar bay didn't count, Townsend felt. Some of the others who were there would disagree.) Due to the lack of direct, one-on-one defiance to him, Townsend concluded that, despite everything he had seen among the crew and his own XO's questionable actions, this was no mutiny. The situation wasn't good, but the *Kitty Hawk* crew could not be in mutiny if the captain was able to wade right into the middle of rioting sailors and not be taken down.

Cloud feared that Townsend might be pushing his luck. Earlier reports of the captain being injured or killed had sounded entirely plausible, and he was not sure that the violence was on the wane.

Many of the sailors who were aware of the violence and the extent of the danger, particularly the department heads and mid-level officers, waited for orders on how to respond, but those orders never came. In the end, many of the white sailors who were terrorized that night felt they were let down by the way the *Kitty Hawk* leaders did not immediately and decisively end the riot.

WHILE CLOUD WAS FOCUSED on the men of the *Kitty Hawk*, trying to understand what was going on with the different factions and how to best handle the fighting, Townsend's attention was drawn more to the ship's operations and in this respect, the captain and the XO were carrying out their duties just as would be expected in the Navy: The XO was trying to keep his finger on the pulse of the disturbance and understand its complexities, and the captain was trying to make sure the *Kitty Hawk* remained operational. Townsend feared sabotage more than rebellion, and for good reason. The armed services, and the Navy in particular, had seen plenty of sabotage in recent months, and the Navy command had specifically warned Townsend to be on the alert. And some saboteurs might not mind if their interference took Navy lives. Townsend didn't know that, in fact, Chris Mason, the white sailor from Alabama, had heard rumors that black sailors were talking about trying to sabotage bombs on board to create a massive blaze like those that crippled the carriers *Forrestal* and *Oriskany* in recent years. Hundreds of men died on those ships when accidental fires set off bombs, some as large as 1,000 pounds.

The bombs and planes were vulnerable to saboteurs. Many crew members knew just what safety devices on the bombs to circumvent to make them dangerous while still on the *Kitty Hawk*, and everyone knew that it didn't take much to disable the planes, whose jet engines could be destroyed by something as small as a loose screw sucked into the spinning blades. Townsend wasn't the only officer on board who realized the danger of sabotage. Others were taking measures to ward off any destructive acts.

A petty officer ordered Marvin Davidson, a young bomb assemblyman from South Bend, Washington, to move his squadron's bombs from the hangar deck back to the bomb magazine—a locked storage facility—for added safety. Davidson, a white man, had not been attacked but had heard reports of fighting, like many sailors on the *Kitty Hawk*. The petty officer explained that there were fears of sabotage and that it was up to the squadron to make sure no one messed with their bombs, so the sailor scrambled up seven ladders from his berthing area to the hangar deck. He was opening the final hatch to the hangar deck when several hands snatched him up and dragged him through the opening. It happened so quickly that at first Davidson couldn't see who was grabbing him, and he could hardly make out anything the men were shouting at him. All he heard was lots of cursing, then he felt blows commence as soon as he was thrown down on the deck. The black sailors beat and kicked him for what seemed a long time, then suddenly someone pushed his way into the scrum and started tearing the assailants away, yelling at them to knock it off and get away. The black sailors fell back and the rescuer picked Davidson up off the deck.

The young sailor tried to focus and see who had just saved his bacon. *Wait a minute, is that . . .is that the captain?* Davidson was still a little dazed from the beating, still confused about what was going on. *Yeah, that's the captain.* Townsend was still standing there looking at him as the men who assaulted him ran off.

"Are you okay, sailor?" the captain asked.

"Yeah," Davidson said, wiping the blood from his face and trying to recover his senses.

"Are you sure?" Townsend asked. "Would you like to go to sick bay?"

"No," Davidson said. "I've got bombs to move."

Davidson wiped more of the blood from his face and limped off to secure his bombs. Townsend was reassured to see that young men still protected the *Kitty Hawk*.

There were good men on this ship, black and white, and Townsend knew it. Maybe if he could get some of them involved, they could influence the hotheads. With that thought in mind, Townsend went searching for men he could trust.

CHAPTER THIRTEEN

"HE IS A BROTHER!"

Shortly after midnight, Robert Keel and his buddies were hunkered down in their berthing compartment and prepared for the next fight. The hatch was sealed tightly, but they could hear men running past on the other side, and the announcements on the 1MC by the XO and the captain had only left them more worried than ever. Keel and his buddies didn't know exactly what was wrong on the *Kitty Hawk* or how bad it was, but the young men's minds raced with fear and anticipation. With little real knowledge, almost no hard information other than what they were told by those who had witnessed some of the violence themselves, the sailors filled the void with worries about what was going on out there, on the other side of that sealed hatch. Would the rioters come for them and manage to break in? Were they taking over the ship? Did they try to take the captain? Were they doing the right thing by just sitting there, or should they go out and fight?

The captain's message had not reassured them much and the men agreed that it was time to arm themselves. They weren't going to just sit there and wait for something to happen. They had to be ready when trouble came, and they might have to go out there and help regain control of the *Kitty Hawk.*

"They caught us by surprise, but come morning, we're taking this ship back," one sailor said. "We're not going to let them take this ship and do this to us."

The rest of the sailors agreed, and the men set about finding or making weapons. It was a relief to have something to do instead of just worrying. Keel looked around and, because their berthing compartment was in the ship's forward IC area with its abundance of electrical supplies, he quickly found a length of multiconductor armored cable, about an inch and three-quarters thick, solid and heavy but with a good flex. He took a two-and-a-half-foot length of the cable and used electrical tape to attach a large steel nut to the end of it, creating a flexible cudgel that he could use to clear a path in front of him. His buddies came up with a similar array of cables, wrenches, chains, and tools they could use to defend their space and mount a counterattack.

Armed but still hobbled by their lack of information, the men didn't know when to make their move. Waiting till morning seemed like a good idea, but no one slept. They sat and worried more, talked some, tried to distract each other with mindless talk.

They were all startled by a rap on the hatch, which caused them to look at it and then each other. The pounded was repeated. One man stood up and went to the hatch, hesitating before doing anything. A voice on other side called "Open up! It's the captain!"

Someone nodded to the man standing at the hatch, agreeing that he should open it. The sailor slowly opened the hatch and, sure enough, there was the captain.

Keel had the same thought that was going through most of their minds:

The captain? What the fuck is the captain doing here? This can't be good.

At least they knew the captain was still okay. Townsend was calm and asked to speak with one of the sailors in the compartment, a black man he knew was popular and influential among the other black sailors. Townsend had found him by asking around until sailors pointed him to the right berthing area. The black sailor was clutching a wrench, just as scared as the rest of men in the compartment. The man stepped forward to talk to Townsend.

"Will you come talk to these men and try to stop this?" the captain asked.

Like Keel, the black sailor had already seen the rioters in action, and he didn't want any part of it.

"No sir, Captain," he said, his tone respectful but firm. "You made this mess. You fix it."

PERRY PETTUS HAD MADE his way back to his berthing compartment after witnessing the assault on the white sailor. He didn't want any part of that kind of viciousness, but he still held on to the anger and resentment from his earlier mistreatment. He sat and stewed about it, hearing the sounds of fights and disturbances nearby, until one group of black sailors came rushing by his compartment just after midnight and he decided to tag along. They were on the hunt again, snatching white sailors out of their bunks, tearing through their belongings, generally creating a mess. Pettus hung in the back of the crowd, not wanting to be part of the violence, but he roamed the ship again and, like many other black sailors, ended up on the forecastle, where the captain had said he would meet with anyone, not just black sailors, who had a grievance. The captain wasn't there yet, and fortunately the Marines had followed the captain's orders to disregard the XO's earlier instruction for *them* to head to the forecastle. So black sailors milled about on their own, waiting for someone to hear their complaints. The crowd was a mix of the most determined agitators like Avinger and the less extreme sailors like Pettus. Some of the men were trying to whip up the crowd, yelling for them to get ready for a fight. Black power salutes were made in unison as the group seized control of the forward deck.

After failing to convince the black sailor in Keel's group to help negotiate with the rioters, Townsend made his way back to the sick bay to check on the situation there. Cloud, meanwhile, was making his way to the forecastle to meet with the black rebels. With the ship in turmoil, scores of men injured, and the possibility of worse violence looming, the XO was desperate to end the crisis. With every passing minute, he felt a growing need to act, to do something to stop this insurrection.

When Cloud reached the forecastle about 12:15 A.M. on October 13, about 150 black sailors were gathered there, mostly young sailors but a few petty officers too. They were crowded into an enclosed area at the very front of the ship that held machinery for raising and lowering the carrier's huge anchor chains. Cloud was discouraged to see that senior petty officers were involved. Many of the men were bare-chested in the overheated space. The crowd was raucous and being pumped up more by the ringleaders. Nearly all of them were armed. As they saw the executive officer walk up, the crowd turned on him, screaming "Kill, kill! Kill the motherfucker! Let's tear this ship apart!" There was a traitor in their midst.

Pettus, on the periphery of the crowd, joined in the shouting but was growing more uncomfortable by the minute. The men seemed to be whipping themselves up for something explosive. Realizing he might not be hard core enough for this crowd, Pettus was beginning to fear for his own safety. There was a lot of jostling and pushing.

Cloud did his best to make himself heard over the crowd, imploring them to calm down and listen to him, but the men grew ever more menacing. As Cloud tried to make his way forward to where the ringleaders were whipping up the mob, he knew exactly how defenseless he was. His black skin was the only thing saving his life at that moment. If a white man had walked into that crowd, if the *captain* had walked in, this crowd would have thrown him overboard.

"There's the fucking traitor! There's the Uncle Tom!" men screamed in Cloud's face. "He's no better than the rest! We ought to kill him! We ought to throw him over the side."

Cloud continued pushing his way through the crowd. No one threw a punch at the XO, but he was pushed around and there were repeated calls for violence.

"Kill him! Beat him up!" men kept shouting, but those closest to Cloud seemed reluctant to throw the first punch at the senior officer.

Cloud finally reached the front of the room where the group's leaders were. He tried to call for the men's attention, but they were in no mood to hear from the XO again, not after what happened last time. Cloud kept trying to shout for them to listen, to just give him a minute, but he had to endure more jeering and threats. The vitriol was unlike anything he had seen so far. These men were on the precipice of doing something truly terrible. Cloud knew he had to do something drastic to get the men's attention.

Surrounded by the raging mob, convinced that he had lost all credibility with them and might die at any moment, the XO raised his fist high in a black power salute. He hoped the gesture would show the black sailors that he was on their side, that he was there to help.

Cloud stood there with his clenched fist held high, waiting for a reaction, but nothing changed. They weren't buying it this time. The men continued screaming for him to be killed, calling him names, pushing him around.

Finally, seeing Cloud's raised fist, one of the ringleaders decided to give him another chance. The man stood high on the ship's anchor chain, raised his hand, and called for quiet.

"Listen to him! Listen to what the man has to say! The least you can do is listen to what he has to say!" he shouted.

Eventually the crowd began to quiet down. They begrudgingly gave Cloud the floor, and he knew this was his last shot. He had to reestablish his credibility, at least the small amount he had had before the men felt betrayed by the confrontation with the Marines on the hangar deck.

"My black brothers . . ." he began. The crowd muttered its disapproval, and several men shouted that he wasn't black at all. A couple of the ringleaders shouted for them to be quiet and let him speak.

"We have to find a better way to solve our problems," he continued. The crowd was letting him talk, but Cloud knew their patience wouldn't last long. "You've got to stop this violence. Now, I know you admire both Malcolm X and Martin Luther King, Jr. They both died for their causes, but the methods of the two men greatly contrasted with one another, didn't they? Now in the final analysis, even though both men met death by violent means, I think the black community in America today can say that Martin Luther King, Jr., was certainly the most effective of the two. He was more successful because he followed the peaceful lead of Gandhi."

The crowd was still restless, but they were listening.

"Those are the men who are the backbone of the black movement and the black principles in the United States today," Cloud said, the emotion unmistakable in his voice. "Look at the tactics of Gandhi in India. If you follow the practices of Gandhi, and of Martin Luther King, Jr., you can live today and tomorrow and the next day in pride and respect. But if you continue to use the tactics that you are using here tonight, the only thing you can guarantee is your death and the further worsening of the situation that you are trying to correct."

Cloud looked over the men. He could see that he was getting through to some of them. But others still resisted, shouting "Don't believe him! He's just like whitey!" There were plenty in the crowd who were bigger fans of Malcolm X than King, Cloud knew, and he wasn't giving up on them.

"I hear you, brothers! But don't doubt my sincerity as a black man sympathetic to your problems. Yes, I'm a Navy officer and I want to see this situation rectified within the legal framework of our society. I'm your XO, but underneath this uniform I am a black man just like you."

He was winning some of the men over, but others were trying to pull them back, yelling that Cloud was just lying to them, that he was an Uncle Tom, he couldn't be trusted. Cloud knew this was a pivotal point. *What am I going to do? How can I convince them?* After a long pause, he addressed the crowd again.

"If you doubt for one moment that I understand your problems, if you doubt for one moment that I am a sincere black man . . ." His voice trailed off. He looked over the crowd, making eye contact with several men. He could see the contempt in their eyes, the way they looked at him with disgust and skepticism.

With a sudden burst of resolve, Cloud reached down to a man standing in front of him and took his weapon, a heavy piece of steel about two feet long. With the weapon in hand, Cloud tore off his uniform shirt and tossed it away. He stood bare-chested before the crowd and thumped his chest hard with a fist as he looked at the other men fiercely. Fury and determination in his voice, he raised the weapon high and shouted.

"The first man in this crowd that for one moment does not believe my sincerity, I hold this weapon and I bare my back for you to take this weapon and beat me into submission right here!"

Pettus couldn't believe what he was seeing. The other men were dumbstruck, even Avinger and the other hard-core black militants. Men instantly fell silent. Not a word was spoken. Not a single sound rose from the crowd. For the first time in a long while, Cloud could hear the hum of the carrier's engines and the soft *whoosh* of the waves on the hull.

Cloud stood there for a long moment, the weapon held high, his heart racing and lungs heaving, wondering if one of the sailors would suddenly charge. He knew that if one man attacked, the whole crowd was likely to follow and he would die an agonizing death, right there on the deck of the *Kitty Hawk,* at the hands of his own men.

But the crowd remained silent, the men glancing around at each other, wondering what to do next. They still looked angry, but Cloud sensed that they were wavering, that he might have convinced them.

My god, you have to believe me . . .

Then one man in the crowd yelled "He is a brother!" And, slowly, it spread through the crowd. The other men took up the chant, all of them, shouting "He is a brother! He is a brother! He is a brother!" One of the ringleaders, the man Cloud thought might be the first to take him up on his offer to beat him, approached and calmly said, "Let's do it your way."

With the crowd still chanting "He is a brother! He is a brother!" Cloud raised his fist in a black power salute, full of pride and relief.

The men returned the salute as they continued chanting their support for Cloud, and one by one sailors began coming up to the XO and throwing their weapons at his feet. Cloud told the crowd he didn't want their weapons and ordered them thrown over the side. Men by the dozens went to the railing and heaved their pipes, wrenches, chains, and knives into the sea.

"We're with you all the way," one of the sailors told him. "Let's do it your way."

Cloud was immensely relieved that he had ended the rebellion. It was 1:30 A.M. He put his shirt back on and mingled with the men for nearly an hour, talking to anyone who had a grievance and assuring them that they could also take their concerns to the captain, by way of the human relations staff. After he had spoken with everyone who seemed to want to say something to him, he got the group's attention again and told them to return peacefully to their quarters or their assigned duties. With another raised fist salute and a shout of "Black power!" the crowd, relaxed now, began to disperse. Cloud could even see some of the men laughing and cutting up, a far cry from an hour earlier, when he thought these same men might rip him to shreds.

As Cloud was about to leave the forecastle, a white master-at-arms came to him and looked concerned.

"XO, there's an injured man in a compartment over here and we can't get him out," the man told Cloud. "He's near death, but every time we try to go in and get him, the blacks fight us."

Several of the black sailors, including a couple of the riot's ring-leaders, overheard the master-at-arms. Confident now that he had the crowd on his side, Cloud told the two ringleaders to go with him to the communications office, where the injured man was trapped, a short distance away. Four more black sailors joined them. On the way they passed the black sailors who had been fighting to keep the res-cuers from the injured man, but seeing the ringleaders walking with the XO, they stood aside. Cloud and the other black sailors entered the compartment, where they found nearly a dozen white sailors holed up, trying in turns to get the injured man out and protecting him when the rioters tried to break in. They were relieved to see the XO enter the compartment with confidence, obviously in charge of the black sailors with him.

The white sailors stepped aside. What Cloud saw saddened and repulsed him. Radioman Third Class Lynwood Patrick—the white sailor whose beating had so sickened Perry Pettus that he turned away from violence, the one Pettus had thought looked like a scared child playing dress-up—was lying unconscious on a canvas stretcher soaked with blood. Patrick's skull was caved in, and he had deep lac-erations on his forehead and defensive wounds on his hands.

Without waiting for Cloud's orders, two white sailors and two black sailors stepped over to the stretcher. The four men each took a handle and gently lifted Patrick. They silently carried the most seri-ously injured victim of the *Kitty Hawk* mutiny through the crowded compartment and out into the passageway, all sailors, both black and white, standing aside to let them pass. The stretcher bearers were given free access through the passages, down the escalator, all the way to the sick bay.

After more than five hours, the worst of the violence on the *Kitty Hawk* was over.

CHAPTER FOURTEEN

"BY A HIGHER AUTHORITY"

G. Kirk Allen, the corpsman, was still working in sick bay when the stretcher bearers arrived with Lynwood Patrick. The obvious head wound and the amount of blood instantly got everyone's attention. Blood was still leaking from the man's head, and the dark masses of congealing blood told them that the young sailor had been injured some time ago. Unfortunately, he was waking up. It would have been a blessing to stay unconscious. He was crying out in pain, begging someone to make it stop hurting.

"Looks like a cranial skull fracture," one of the corpsmen said. A doctor hurried over to the exam table and, after a quick look, ordered the corpsmen to take Patrick to the operating room.

The doctor was in the OR with Radioman Patrick for only a few minutes before he came back out.

"We've got to medevac him off," he said to Allen and the other corpsmen nearby. "He's got a bad skull fracture. We can't treat it here."

Anything bad enough to require medevac from the carrier, which offered the best medical care in the fleet short of an actual hospital ship, was serious indeed. The corpsmen all looked at each other with concern.

"We're medevacing guys *into* Vietnam?" Allen said to another corpsman. "This is really serious."

The medics continued tending to Patrick and the other injured men. There were no more attacks on the sick bay, no more mobs of sailors trying to force their way in and assault the injured along with their caregivers. After a day full of tension and several hours of rioting, the corpsmen hoped the black sailors were ready to stand down and stop the violence.

The corpsmen were right. Following Cloud's speech in the forecastle, many of the black sailors dispersed. Some returned to their berthing areas or their assigned work stations, while others hung out in the common areas, talking over the events of the day. Others remained in the forecastle with Cloud, but they were peaceful. There were no more reports of violence other than the occasional shove in a passageway or a random punch thrown by some sailor who was still feeling angry.

About 3:30 A.M., Townsend made his way to the forecastle and met with many of the black sailors. At this point, Townsend knew only that Cloud had managed to settle the rowdy crowd. He knew little about how Cloud had managed to do that. The sailors had plenty of complaints, and both the captain and the XO were willing to listen as long as the threat of violence was no longer an issue.

With the black sailors brought under control by Cloud's extraordinary speech, however, the captain and the XO both worried about the possibility of a retaliatory strike from the white sailors. They had been largely passive up to this point, reluctant to fight back even as they were being attacked. But Cloud and Townsend knew how the minds of young men worked, and they knew that the white *Kitty Hawk* sailors probably were pretty steamed up. The captain and the XO were both determined to head off any retaliation from the white crew.

It wasn't long before they got word that some white sailors had been preparing weapons and were planning a counterattack. Keel and his buddies were ready, having had plenty of time to fashion their weapons and steel themselves for what they thought had to be done. After many hours of being holed up, Keel and his buddies opened the hatch, took a look around, and determined that the worst of the violence seemed to be over. They didn't feel trapped anymore; now they felt chagrined and were determined not to be hunted down on their own ship again. They had no way of knowing whether this was just a lull in the violence or if the mutiny was over, but they were ready to fight if there was going to be a next time. And it wasn't just Keel's friends. Plenty of other whites were feeling the same thing, ready to show that they wouldn't cower on the *Kitty Hawk* a second time. Keel saw one confrontation in a passageway between an angry white sailor and a black man trying to pass by. The white sailor exchanged insults with the black sailor, and then the white man passed on the rumor that was floating around.

"We're ready for you this time," he said. "If you want do this, you and your buddies meet us at 0700 on the aft mess deck and we'll do it."

That kind of challenge was flying around all over the ship, and soon someone went to Cloud in the forecastle and told him a mob of white sailors appeared on the verge of violence. At 5 A.M. Cloud made his way to a berthing area adjacent to the forecastle and found about 150 white sailors who were growing increasingly enraged at the events of the past 12 hours. They were pissed off about the attacks, and some of them showed their wounds from being ripped out of their bunks and beaten. The rowdy bunch made it clear to the XO that they were entirely dissatisfied with the way he and the captain had let the violence go on for so long. This crowd of white sailors was nearly as rough on Cloud as the black sailors had been four hours earlier.

"You're nothing but a nigger!" one white sailor shouted. "You're just like all the rest of them! How can you exercise any authority on this ship?"

Cloud took the insults calmly and waited for the sailor to finish screaming. When he was done, Cloud spoke.

"By a higher authority I was appointed as executive officer of this ship," Cloud yelled, not even bothering to try to hide the passion in his voice. He wasn't going to let this thing boil over again. "You men, as part of the *Kitty Hawk* along with the blacks, are crew members of one ship. You *will* obey the orders and edicts of the commanding officer. If you don't do any better than the blacks did earlier, you will be criticized just as severely, and you will lose any respect you have at this point."

Cloud implored the crowd of whites to seek redress for their grievances through the proper channels and not to seek revenge. With the men still refusing his order to put down their weapons, the XO changed tactics and took a hard line. After everything that had happened, he was in no mood to mess around. Relying on a threat of punishment instead of the pleas for brotherhood that he used earlier with the black sailors, the XO explained how the situation was going to play out.

"The choice, simply stated, is yours. Either you will do it the legal way and stay correct and proper, or you can take up your weapons as you are threatening to do right now and every one of you will be subject to a long prison term away from your wives, families, and loved ones. Now, what do you want to do?"

The XO stood there waiting for a response, but even the biggest loudmouths in the bunch didn't have anything more to say. He ordered the men to stay where they were and to put their weapons down. There shouldn't be any more violence, he told them, but leave all the lights on just in case. The men grumbled and complained some, but Cloud was confident they weren't going to look for trouble.

He turned and left, back to the forecastle to talk with the captain about how they were going to get breakfast underway.

It was nearly dawn, and the *Kitty Hawk* still had work to do.

THE CREW MEDEVACED THREE crewmen off the *Kitty Hawk* in the early hours of October 13: Patrick with the cranial fracture, another with a pancreatic laceration, and one more with internal injuries. A total of fifty-two men were treated in the sick bay, and many more did not seek care for relatively minor injuries. Townsend visited the sick bay that morning, after the crisis was over, to thank the medics for their hard work. He spoke to the men as a group, thanking them for performing well in an extraordinary situation.

Flight ops resumed as scheduled at 7:58 A.M. Townsend was immensely relieved, and proud, to see that his ship had weathered the crisis and never missed a beat. The events of the previous 24 hours had been challenging and difficult, but the *Kitty Hawk* came through and was ready for business as usual. Cloud also saw the importance of resuming flight operations that morning, on schedule, and many of the crew felt reassured by the sound of steam shots coursing through the pipes deep in the ship and the *thump* of aircraft landing on the flight deck. The tension was still thick, the animosity among some sailors just barely contained, but resumption of flight activities told the sailors that the *Kitty Hawk* had survived.

As the crew cleaned up after the riot and got on with the business of bombing Vietnam, many were still wondering just what the hell had happened. Most had been told nothing of an official nature. Though the violence had ended, no one was quite sure that it wouldn't resume without warning. The men were uneasy as they went about their duties, wondering what happened last night and what would happen next.

Townsend and Cloud were both too busy with the day's business, and too exhausted from being up all night, to debrief each other in any detail. It would be some time before they compared notes and understood some of the particulars of what had happened on October 12, what led up to it, and how their missteps and miscommunications sometimes made the problems worse. Townsend remained steadfast that he and most of the crew handled the crisis as best they could, but he was still coming to terms with how his XO had handled himself during the uprising. Clearly he had been instrumental in ending the riot, Townsend thought, but what he did was so . . . "unorthodox" would be the formal way to describe it. As he mulled over the day's events, Townsend couldn't get over the image of his XO raising his fist in a black power salute.

Eventually, Townsend took Cloud aside for a private talk. The captain had plenty of praise for Cloud in some areas, particularly his rescue of Radioman Patrick after the showdown on the forecastle. But he also made it clear that he was surprised by Cloud's demonstrations of brotherhood with the rioting sailors and what he saw as a panicky response when the men needed to see a calm, cool officer in control.

"Look, you were very helpful in getting people under control," the captain told Cloud. "But you used some very bad techniques, totally unacceptable techniques. That message on the 1MC nearly took this thing in another direction. That was a bad move."

Cloud acknowledged the captain and didn't try to argue the point.

"I know everything you did was in sincere good faith and goodwill, but some of it was just totally unacceptable," Townsend told him. "We can't have that on this ship."

Cloud thought that Townsend had made his point and they were finished, as both men needed to get back to work. But then Townsend looked him in the eye and spoke gravely.

"Cloud, hear this. That black power salute and all that talk about being a brother . . . If you ever do anything like that again, any more black power salutes or anything like that, you're off the boat. I can't work with you."

Cloud took the criticism without complaint, neither surprised nor willing to debate his actions at that moment. But he also felt hurt that the captain did not give him enough credit for what he did to stop the violence. He wondered if Townsend realized that he had risked his life to calm the rioting sailors.

Many of the crew on board, men like Pettus who had been witness to the most violent, pivotal moments of the prior night, had no doubt about Cloud's contribution. From the moment he left the forecastle early that morning, Pettus was certain that the XO had saved lives, possibly even Pettus's own life, with his dramatic speech calling for a peaceful resolution. The XO's invitation to men full of rage, challenging them to beat him down if they didn't believe he was truly a black man with their best interests at heart, was the bravest thing Pettus had ever seen. And it would remain so for many years to come.

Townsend had not been in that crowd, he had not seen the way those black sailors looked at Cloud with a virulent hate that could have turned homicidal in an instant, and so on October 13 he did not fully appreciate what his XO had done to save the *Kitty Hawk*. For weeks and months after the event, the captain continued to feel that he had had a good handle on the situation. His XO, however, felt that the uprising had been something different, something bigger, more complex, something scarier than just a fistfight among young sailors. He believed that he had been smack in the middle of the whole thing all night long, seeing firsthand the very worst of it all and understanding the gravity of the situation better than the captain, grasping the terrible potential of what could have happened. Townsend reassured himself and his officers that, though this had been an exceptionally violent disturbance, it was nothing more than that; it certainly was *not* a mutiny. But as the captain of a high-profile American warship, Townsend had a vested interest in parsing the definition of the word "mutiny," and not everyone agreed with his description. Many of his crew members, especially those who were in the middle of the worst violence and heard the rebels' plans to take the ship home, had no qualms about calling what happened a mutiny—albeit a disorganized and unsuccessful one.

Definitions aside, there was no denying what happened on the USS *Kitty Hawk* on October 12 and 13, 1972. Call it a mutiny or call it an isolated incident of violence, the end result would be the same for Marland Townsend and Ben Cloud. As they oversaw flight ops and maintained order on the ship that day, the same thought kept running through their minds. Both men realized that they would be held responsible for the *Kitty Hawk* riot.

There will be hell to pay for this, they thought.

CHAPTER FIFTEEN

"PLAIN CRIMINALS?"

P lanes flying off the *Kitty Hawk* the morning after the riot had been a welcome sight for Townsend and Cloud, and it reassured Townsend that the violence had been perpetrated by a relatively small group of black sailors. The captain knew most of the crew was still with him, that he could trust them to follow orders and do their jobs.

But the days after the riot were not routine. Townsend understood that the rebellious faction on board could not be underestimated. He had the ship locked down, effectively putting the men under martial law. No unnecessary gatherings, lights on throughout the ship to discourage skulking in dark passageways, the whole carrier operating under the "condition zebra" that required leaving many hatches and passageways closed off. Normally intended to stop the spread of fire, smoke, and water in an emergency, in these days after the riot condition zebra prevented easy travel by groups. Townsend also ordered increased patrols by officers and masters-at-arms, and, most of all, zero tolerance for any kind of violence. Townsend's goal was to stop any minor disturbances as quickly as possible so that the violent sailors couldn't gain the momentum they had on October 12 and 13. The captain knew he had to keep a tight lid on the crew if they were to finish their assignment on Yankee Station. There was no way his ship was going to be pulled off line because the crew was out of order. The violence was over, but the angry crew members were still aboard the *Kitty Hawk* and they hadn't gotten much happier in the immediate aftermath of the violence.

The crew directed much of their continuing anger at Townsend. For several days, the captain's cabin phone rang periodically; when he picked it up, the voice on the other end would blurt out obscenities and threats.

"We're going to get you! You're dead!" Then the phone would go silent. There was no way to trace who made the call, and though Townsend didn't fear for his life, he did find the calls disturbing. Others on board, such as Marines Avina and Binkley, also were threatened regularly because they were seen as having committed egregious acts against the black sailors during the riots. Though the serious violence had ended early on October 13 and the lock-down prevented large groups from gathering, many of the crew still witnessed sporadic attacks and were constantly on guard.

The violence had opened Townsend's eyes to some of the long-standing problems on the *Kitty Hawk* and pushed him to make changes that he had been reluctant to order right after coming aboard. The self-imposed segregation on the carrier had to end. In the week after the riot, Townsend ordered his division officers to stop the segregated berthing. No longer would there be any all-black areas. Some compartments remained all white simply because there weren't enough minority sailors to mix in there. Townsend also ordered that a senior enlisted man must remain in the berthing area between 10 P.M. and 6 A.M. to discourage any misbehavior by the lower-ranking sailors.

Townsend did not change the policy that required nearly all new sailors on the *Kitty Hawk* to serve a stint as mess cook. He still believed in the egalitarian goal of having everyone serve their fellow crew members.

On October 13, Townsend transferred Terry Avinger and two other sailors off the ship. Within days they were in the brig in San Diego. The man that Marine Corporal Robert L. Anderson had bitten during the hangar bay melee did seek care in the sick bay, and the bite mark was sufficient to have him detained and later charged. Upon hearing Townsend's report of the disturbance via the ship's secure radio transmission, the commander in chief of the Pacific (CINC-PAC) dispatched three legal teams to the *Kitty Hawk* to investigate the incident, identify those responsible, and prepare charges against them. The Navy teams identified twenty-nine sailors who actively participated in the violence and refusal of orders. CINCPAC urged Townsend to conduct courts-martial on the ship, meting out justice then and there. Anyone found guilty could then be removed from the ship to serve their sentences. Townsend knew why CINCPAC wanted him to go ahead and try the men there: *They just want to keep it all quiet back home, to suppress it and avoid publicity. But if I court-martial these men here, there's no way they'll be able to get an adequate defense, and these are serious charges. Some of these guys, God didn't give them much to work with. And now if we just find them guilty and give them dishonorable discharges, we can ruin them for life. They need really good civil attorneys.*

Onboard courts-martial weren't unheard of, and Townsend himself would have benefited from conducting the trials on board the carrier and dispensing justice quickly and quietly. The more attention the incident got, the worse consequences the captain would face. It was in his own best interest to placate the Navy and save his own hide by court-martialing the men on board. Yet having them court-martialed at sea, with only Navy defense attorneys to depend on, didn't suit Townsend. He wanted to see the men tried and punished as necessary, but he wasn't interested in railroading them through just to bring the whole thing to a quick and quiet end. Also, the captain worried about what would happen on his ship if he put the men on trial. Would their buddies flip out and riot again? Would a second riot maybe be even worse? No, Townsend wasn't going to let CINCPAC push him into this.

Townsend told CINCPAC that he would detain the men until they could be tried back home. Surely the *Kitty Hawk* would be called back to San Diego soon. He was right. The orders finally came, and the *Kitty Hawk* left Yankee Station on October 31, eight days after the United States ended all bombing above the 20th parallel in a goodwill gesture meant to aid the peace negotiations in Paris. The carrier reached San Diego on November 28, ending one of the longest aircraft carrier deployments in U.S. Navy history.

Once the carrier returned to San Diego, the Navy continued with its investigation of the worst rioting on a Navy ship in modern history. In San Diego, twenty-nine sailors, all but three of them black, were charged with crimes stemming from the riots. After some legal wrangling back and forth and the assistance of the National Association for the Advancement of Colored People (NAACP), many charges were dropped or reduced. In the coming months, nineteen of the sailors would be found guilty of at least one charge.

In the end, the charges against Terry Avinger were dropped for lack of a speedy trial. However, he was court-martialed on separate charges related to a disturbance at the North Island naval station in San Diego where he was being held. Found guilty of those charges, he was sentenced to two months of confinement, a reduction in grade, and a forfeiture of $400 in pay.

The Navy kept the situation under wraps for the most part, with scant information released to the media. Major newspapers and other media reported right away on the disturbance, but details were scarce and the root causes were not yet understood. The riot on the *Kitty Hawk* was followed on November 3 by a sit-down strike by black sailors on the carrier *Constellation,* which was conducting exercises off the coast of California at the time. The sailors said they wanted to show solidarity with their black brothers on the *Kitty Hawk* and also to air their own grievances. Though there was little violence in the *Constellation* incident, the strikers openly defied the captain and threatened to throw him overboard. In some ways, their rebellion was more clearly mutinous than that on the *Kitty Hawk,* even though no one was seriously injured. The *Constellation* incident also received much more media attention than did the *Kitty Hawk* riot, in part because the relatively peaceful nature of the strike paralleled nicely with civil rights protests back home and allowed reporters to portray the black sailors as heroes rather than violent criminals.

With two cases of open rebellion and dozens of other instances of disobedience and sabotage, the Navy's discipline problem caught the attention of Congress. Within a month of the riot, the U.S. House of Representatives Committee on Armed Services called for special hearings on the troubled waters of the Navy and formed the Special Subcommittee on Disciplinary Problems in the U.S. Navy. Chaired by Representative Floyd V. Hicks, a Democrat from Washington State, the subcommittee began its work on November 20, in the Rayburn House Office Building in Washington, DC. Its two other members were Representative Alexander Pirnie, a Republican from New York, and Representative W. C. (Dan) Daniel, a Democrat from Virginia. The congressmen wielded great power over the Navy through their positions on the Armed Services Committee, which controlled the purse strings for all matters military and had the power to dictate policy.

Hicks started the session by reading the House Armed Services Committee's mandate to the subcommittee:

"The subcommittee is directed to inquire into the apparent breakdown of discipline in the U.S. Navy and, in particular, into alleged racial and disciplinary problems which occurred recently on the aircraft carriers USS *Kitty Hawk* and USS *Constellation.*"

In his opening statement, Hicks clarified the goal of the subcommittee's hearings.

"We cannot overlook the possibility that there may exist at this time an environment of—for lack of a better word—permissiveness, wherein all that is needed is a catalyst. Perhaps perceptions of racial relations in the cases provided that spark." Clearly the Armed Services Committee did not like hearing reports of sailors refusing orders and interfering with the operation of ships at sea. Was the problem a lack of discipline, a too-soft approach by the officers in charge?

The congressmen subpoenaed a long list of Navy leaders and witnesses, starting at the very top with Admiral Elmo Zumwalt, Jr., chief of naval operations. The *Constellation* officers had to explain the nonviolent sit-down strike by black sailors, and then Townsend, Cloud, Carlucci, and scores of others from the *Kitty Hawk* had to testify about the riot. The congressmen grilled the witnesses, demanding to know from all the top officers how such events could occur on Navy ships. The testimony was devastating, with many sailors attesting to the poor discipline on the ships and the way the riot on the *Kitty Hawk* was allowed to continue for hours, the ship in turmoil for even longer.

Some of the most hard-nosed comments came from a surprising source: the chaplain of the *Kitty Hawk*. Lieutenant Commander Robert J. Riley was a man of God, but he had no sympathy for the black sailors who had rioted. He cut them no slack, insisting to the committee that the rioters knew exactly what they were doing. Riley, a picturesque figure with an elaborate mustache and goatee, told the committee that he thought the black crew had planned the whole incident, saying that the attacks "went along too smoothly that night, their running around. They had something working."

Riley expressed sympathy for the much-maligned masters-at-arms, who didn't do much to quell the violence and sometimes just hid or ran away. Riley pointed out that they had to go up to angry men wielding wrenches and fog foam nozzles, "and you don't even have a stick. You have a little red hat and a badge."

When the questions concerned Townsend's response, Riley made it clear he did not approve.

"I don't know, and I still don't understand, why we didn't go to general quarters that night, or why the Marines weren't brought back out again," he told the subcommittee. "I think the captain, I know he honestly believes what he did that night was correct. He felt he could go around and pacify this thing.

"In my talks to him I said, 'Captain, I don't see how. You can't talk to a militant or to people worked up that way. I am an Irishman and in my family I have some IRA members. There is nothing thicker than a thick Mick when he is on the move. You don't argue with them. They just walk away from you or run right over you.

"'That is one of the things we have to understand here, dealing with people like that. It would be nice to talk with these guys, but not when they are screaming and yelling and swinging things. Sometimes we have to use force.'"

Chief Aviation Ordnanceman Charles M. Johnson, who worked closely with Cloud as a legal officer and missed the opportunity to warn his superiors about the impending violence, told the subcommittee that while he had no evidence, "I have the feeling it was an organized thing."

"It is hard to recognize it as a spontaneous solidarity?" Pirnie asked.

"I don't believe it was, sir," Johnson said. "It happened too many places at the same time."

Johnson also told the congressmen that he thought there was "outside interference" that aided the rebellion, implying the involvement of black militant or antiwar groups outside the Navy.

The congressmen also heard from twenty-year-old seaman Charles A. Beck from Cape Girardeau, Missouri, who had been seriously injured on the *Kitty Hawk.* He told his story of being attacked twice. He broke away from his assailants the first time but then he was attacked again, along with other white sailors, by a group of about twenty-five black sailors who said the whites were going to be put on trial for their crimes against the black man. Beck fought back when cornered and then tried to run, but he was caught and severely beaten with chains and dogging wrenches. The attackers split Beck's head open "on the aft part," as he described the back of his head, and gave him a concussion and numerous facial cuts. As he slumped to the deck, bleeding profusely, one of the attackers stabbed him in the buttocks with a knife. Beck recounted how he was about to pass out from blood loss and the beatings when the crowd stopped the assault and just walked away, leaving him lying there.

Representative Daniel asked Beck if he had any opinion as to whether the attacks were premeditated or spontaneous.

"I would characterize it as premeditated radicalism," Beck responded. "They tried to terrorize the ship. They completely wanted— I believe that is what they wanted. They tried to terrorize me and they did. They got their job done. I was terrorized at the time it was happening. I was scared for my life the second time I was getting beat."

The question of premeditation was important to the subcommittee and to the Navy. A bunch of sailors suddenly going nuts and running amok was bad enough, but a planned effort to disrupt operations or take over the ship was considered far more serious. The subcommittee put Admiral B. A. Clarey, commander in chief of the U.S. Pacific Fleet (CINPAC), on the hot seat, having to explain the actions of his officers in charge of both the *Constellation* and the *Kitty Hawk*. The subcommittee chairman, Hicks, told the admiral that he considered the *Constellation* incident more serious than the *Kitty Hawk*'s because even though it was nonviolent, it clearly was a premeditated, organized resistance by the crew.

"This, it seems to me, was deliberate mutiny on the *Constellation*. What happened aboard the *Kitty Hawk*, I don't know that we have reached any conclusion," Hicks said. "I have not reached any conclusion as to whether that was a planned situation or not. But I have no doubt in my mind about the *Constellation*."

"Yes sir, certainly that was collective subordination in my view," Clarey said.

"Well, that might be a nicer way of saying mutiny," Hicks replied. "They didn't exactly try to take over the ship, but they decided that it was going to be run the way they wanted it run. The captain could come down from the bridge when they told him to come down from the bridge."

Hicks then referred to how the black sailors from the *Kitty Hawk* who were then still facing charges had refused to testify before the subcommittee unless they could come together, with their counsel and with assistance from outside groups. Hicks said he had almost acceded to their demands but then was advised not to appease the men; if he did, he would be acting the same way the captains of the aircraft carriers had.

"It was just a continuation of the same thing. They had the bit in their teeth and they were going to do it the way the riots are [conducted] on the outside," Hicks said.

When it came time for Townsend to face the subcommittee, the congressmen had a good feel for what they thought went wrong on his ship. They criticized the captain for not maintaining a clear chain of command, for not calling general quarters to end the violence, and for being too willing to negotiate with the rioters. Some committee members tried to paint a picture of a captain more interested in appeasing the men trying to take over his ship, too eager to talk with them or just hope they would settle down on their own, when he should have brought his fist down and ended the violence with force, quickly and decisively.

Townsend was calm and cool as he was being questioned, exactly as anyone who had worked with him would have expected. He didn't like being second-guessed by politicians who had no idea what it was like being responsible for the welfare of 5,000 men in a war zone, but he wasn't going to be ruffled by their glib aspersions about his abilities as a leader or their outright accusations that he had made bad decisions. Townsend took the opportunity to tell the committee that he knew the riot had its roots in many Navy policies and procedures that could be changed. For starters, recruiters should stop lying to inductees about what they would face in the Navy, he said.

But Townsend also was blunt in his assessment of the men responsible for the violence on the *Kitty Hawk*. Because the hearings were held in executive session, meaning no reporters or spectators were allowed, Townsend and the congressmen did not feel much need to sugarcoat their opinions.

In response to a question about what resources were available to crew members who had grievances, Townsend explained that before the riot, there already were avenues for seeking redress, but "I maintain, sir, this particular case is caused by a group of just plain—I think I can say this since we are in executive session—just plain thugs who simply didn't use the system."

"Plain criminals?" Daniel asked.

"They never used this system at all, that is the important thing. These people were not at all interested in any kind of system that would be set up to work for them. But the good young blacks, people we should be able to depend on and the people we can get on our side and wean away from their background with the solidarity being presented to us by other blacks, will respond to this system."

The subcommittee also questioned Townsend on why he never called general quarters. Wouldn't that have stopped the riot?

"I felt it unsafe to do that. I felt we would have had people killed if we went to GQ. I still hold to that."

Townsend also had to defend his decision to leave the bridge, saying it was necessary for him to see what was going on in the far recesses of the ship. He also had to explain policies such as those that allowed segregated berthing and required duty as mess cooks as well as his response to earlier incidents of violence or misbehavior. Throughout his testimony, Townsend was self-assured but willing to accept the idea that he could have made some better decisions. Not all of the comments were critical, and Pirnie sometimes came to Townsend's defense. The big question for the *Kitty Hawk* captain was what he would do differently next time. What about sending in the Marines?

"The Marines were never called out by me in this incident. They were on the scene and armed, without the direct order of the CO, XO, or the Marine CO. That was one of the things that caused the problems in the after mess deck," Townsend said. He avoided answering whether he would send them in for a similar situation. Townsend explained that his masters-at-arms were now better trained and more focused on responding to such incidents. At the first sign of any disturbance by a group of sailors, a master-at-arms is to call his superior and report it, which will result in more masters-at-arms being dispatched right away, Townsend explained.

"We will at that time, in the early stages, the very earliest possible stages, go to GQ," Townsend said, conceding to the committee what they wanted to hear. "I have worked out plans for flooding the space with khaki, showing a lot of chiefs and officers' attention, and have written even an instruction to that effect."

Then Townsend went on—unprompted by any follow-up question—to make a startling statement about the response plan he had just outlined.

"But to be honest, it is flawed against a determined uprising. If this is displayed several times, they will kill the key people and you will lose control of the ship. That is not beyond the realm of possibility, in my opinion, in these days."

Clearly the events of October 12 and 13 had made an impression on Townsend. He didn't want to call this event a mutiny, and he thanked God that no one had been killed, but he was warning the congressmen that a far worse outcome was possible.

Next it was Cloud's turn to face the committee. As they had been with the captain, the committee members were cordial but direct in their questioning, first giving Cloud a chance to explain his background and how he came to be XO of the *Kitty Hawk.* The committee members complimented Cloud on an outstanding career up to that point but then moved on. What did he find when he reported for duty on the *Kitty Hawk?* Cloud explained that he was mostly pleased with what he found, and he recognized immediately that the ship had a good system in place, the human resources staff, to address grievances from minorities. But he also told the committee that the crew was wary of Townsend, finding him more aloof and strict than the previous captain. Many of the black crew also hadn't liked the old captain much either, accusing him of promoting racial inequities. They had hoped that Townsend would change that when he took over, but the black crew was disappointed that Townsend had not addressed their problems, Cloud said. So did they welcome a new black XO with open arms? he was asked. Not exactly. Cloud explained that the black crew was highly suspicious of any black man who climbed the ranks in the Navy. He told the committee members that "among the black community on the ship there is this open and vehement, in many cases, distrust of anyone that is older and more senior and who has more experience. Because here again, 'they got that way by practicing Tomism' or something else which would closely—"

"Practicing what?" Pirnie asked.

"Uncle Tomism."

"Well, is that term going to apply to everybody who is successful?"

"It generally does."

"Isn't that a fundamental weakness in our endeavor to try and create an equal society?"

"Yes, sir. I believe it is. Let me say this: I think it is generally presumed by the young blacks that we are talking about here, the eighteen- to twenty-two-year-olds, that anybody that is black and that is successful got that way basically by compromising their principles of blackness, if I may use that term."

Cloud went on to say that he considered himself a successful black man who was "very, very proud of my heritage," and he did not think he had compromised his black heritage in order to get where he was. But he knew from the start that the black crew of the *Kitty Hawk* saw him as "a token success" who was put in the XO position only to show black sailors that the Navy does not discriminate. Some sailors saw his appointment to XO as "tokenism in its truest form," he said.

"Who is telling them that?" Pirnie asked. "He wouldn't think it otherwise."

"It is his mother and father in the community he comes from," Cloud said. "It comes from the ghetto, from the street."

Correcting that attitude would be key to preventing a recurrence of the *Kitty Hawk* violence, Cloud told the committee, and its members agreed with him. Cloud also echoed some of the same calls for improvement that the committee had heard from Townsend—being more honest in recruiting efforts and avoiding the induction of men who were simply incapable of advancing beyond the lowest ranks of the Navy.

Then the committee moved on to what they really wanted to hear from Cloud: why he had done what he did. Cloud recounted the entire event as he recalled it, providing details about his involvement with the various incidents throughout the ship and his understanding, after the fact, of why the violence lasted so long. He often reiterated that his decisions and his actions were driven in part by what he understood of the black crew's impression of him. He knew that he was starting from a point of skepticism and distrust; therefore, he had to find ways to get the rioting sailors to trust him. The committee members listened patiently, but the nature of their questions clearly implied that some thought Cloud had been more interested in appeasing the rioters than in stopping them. However, even those who were skeptical of his actions were caught up by Cloud's testimony as he sat and talked nearly without interruption, telling the dramatic story of the *Kitty Hawk* riot. The committee members knew the basic story and were waiting for Cloud to explain himself, especially as he got to the part of the story in which he tore off his shirt and challenged the crew to beat him if they did not believe he was a true black man. They had read the reports of this extraordinary speech and the black power salutes, and more than a few felt Cloud needed to explain himself. The XO could only try to justify his actions for those who clearly disapproved of how both he and Townsend had responded to the crisis.

Cloud did his best to explain, but he wasn't backing down from what he had done.

"Later on, sir, as the evening wore on . . . there were serious doubts as to my credibility, as to what I had said, as to whether or not I could effectively convey the wishes and desires of the command . . . It was a situation which I recognized at that time deserved drastic and nonmilitary means to quiet."

After telling the committee about his dramatic speech on the forecastle, Cloud explained why he had taken such a brazen step. He said he had realized that "drastic non-military means of controlling this crowd were necessary." He also explained that he knew he had lost all credibility with the black rioters when the Marines confronted them after he told them they would not be harmed.

"The methods that I used admittedly were unorthodox, and I will admit unmilitary," he told the committee members who would pass judgment on him. "But I felt, and as I feel right now, sir, they were absolutely necessary to prevent loss of life and extreme destruction to the *Kitty Hawk*. And in retrospect I must say that looking back on that situation, the tempo and tenor of the situation at that time, and knowing what would be at stake, I would do it again."

Cloud knew exactly what was at stake, and he didn't shy away from owning his actions in the early morning hours of October 13, 1972.

"And if for the sake of my career, it was deemed that my conduct at that time was drastically nonmilitary, and not in keeping with the tenets of what is expected of me as a naval officer, then I am willing to sacrifice this career, full well knowing that what I did then in my own mind prevented death and destruction on the *Kitty Hawk*."

EPILOGUE

After the subcommittee completed its hearing, Chairman Hicks announced that they had found no instances of racial discrimination that could have justified either the *Kitty Hawk* riot or the *Constellation* strike. Hicks said, "[T]he riot on *Kitty Hawk* consisted of unprovoked assaults by a very few men, most of whom were below-average mental capacity, most of whom had been aboard for less than one year, and all of whom were black." The subcommittee concluded that "permissiveness exists in the Navy today" and that the permissiveness contributed to the problems on both carriers.

The "Command History" of the *Kitty Hawk* for 1972, an official summary of deployments and notable events for the ship over the course of a year, was filed with the Chief of Naval Operations on February 27, 1973. The report describes the riot succinctly: "A brief but well publicized disturbance occurred onboard on the night of 12 October but operation of the ship was not affected."

Though both Townsend and especially Cloud could be credited with ending a mutiny and race riot with minimal bloodshed and disruption of the carrier's effort in the war, the Navy did not see it that way. They were in control of the *Kitty Hawk* during what some would call one of the most embarrassing and shameful chapters in Navy history, and they would pay the price. Townsend became the first Vietnam War carrier commander to be passed up for admiral—a development that, considering his outstanding record, can be explained only by his being at the helm during the *Kitty Hawk* riot. Townsend says the riot was "a career buster for me." The Pentagon removed him from his position as captain of the *Kitty Hawk* almost immediately and transferred him to a desk job in Washington, DC, where he stayed until his retirement a few years later. A long and accomplished career in the Navy came to a quiet, disappointing end. Townsend then began the second stage of his life as mayor of a California city and a successful businessman. He regrets the way his Navy career ended, but he says he is over any wounded feelings and has enjoyed his post-Navy life. Many of Townsend's colleagues and those who served with him agree that the Navy lost a good officer when they let him go.

Cloud's star also took a tumble, but he stayed on as XO of the *Kitty Hawk* for more than a year after the riot, going to sea on another deployment with a new captain. His career would never be the same, however. The riot still hung heavy over him and cast a pall over his personnel jacket. He was deeply disappointed when, in 1974, the Navy transferred him to Prairie View A&M University, a predominantly black university in Texas, to run its ROTC program—honorable work for a Navy officer but clearly a big step down for the XO of a carrier. The message was clear. After several years there, he was transferred to Naples, Italy, where he commanded the Naval Support Activity, and then he was sent to his final assignment as an aviation detailer in Washington, DC, in which he watched over the careers of all Navy captains going into aviation. Cloud retired in 1984 with the rank of captain. There is no denying that the riot on the *Kitty Hawk* changed the course of his life. Instead of a long career as a senior Navy officer and perhaps command of an aircraft carrier, his Navy career ended on shore.

Although their time serving together on the *Kitty Hawk* was brief, Townsend and Cloud share a unique bond—a bond formed not on the night of October 12 and 13, 1972, but in the months and years afterward when they could look back and better understand what happened on the ship. They butted heads at the time and attacked the problem from different directions, but each man now has a better understanding of what his counterpart was trying to do and why some decisions were made. They still disagree on tactics, with each man saying he was, for the most part, correct in handling the situation as he did, but they say they have no ill will toward each other.

Cloud describes Townsend as a gifted and talented officer, "a hell of a leader" who had all the attributes of someone who should have become a flag officer. He admits to some hurt feelings over the fact that, even after so many years, Townsend has never expressed directly to him an appreciation for what the XO did to stop the riot. Townsend does state readily that his views on Cloud's actions have changed significantly over the years. He was on the record in 1972 as sharply criticizing his XO's methods, but now he is much more conciliatory. Where he first saw a renegade officer who was badly mishandling a crisis, Townsend now looks back and sees a good officer using unorthodox but ultimately successful techniques to help put down a rebellion.

"I admire Ben very, very much. He's a fine officer," Townsend told this author. "He did what he felt was right at the time and I continue to support him. The ship would not have been able to do what it did without the cooperation of both of us working together. Unfortunately, he had been aboard ship for a very short period of time when this happened and the expectations of the black sailors were beyond anything Ben could do anything about. He's a very fine officer and I consider him a good friend."

Townsend acknowledges that both he and Cloud could have acted differently during the crisis. In particular, Townsend says he wishes he had seen the trouble coming and prevented the violence.

"Did I make mistakes? Yes. I won't say I'm not guilty of that, but I'm proud of my crew and that ship," Townsend says. "Ben and I had to resolve some differences but in the end I think we both did a fine job. No one was killed, there was no real damage to the ship, no sorties interrupted. I would hope that I would have been a little bit wiser in seeing this thing coming on the *Kitty Hawk* but I didn't. The fact that we still met our sorties at eight o'clock in the morning just as we were supposed to is a testament to the fact that the crew was behind us, not against us."

TOWNSEND'S AND CLOUD'S CAREERS were the most directly affected by the *Kitty Hawk* riot, but they were not alone in seeing their lives pivot on October 12, 1972; the riot changed the lives of many men.

Robert Keel, who went on to a successful career in business, feels strongly that what happened on the *Kitty Hawk* was a mutiny. The way he sees it, the fact that the rioters never made it to the bridge and didn't seize control of the carrier doesn't mean they didn't want to or that they wouldn't have if Cloud hadn't stopped them.

"I don't know of anyone except the Navy who does not think this was a mutiny," Keel says. "Is it really a mutiny if a handful of people with no hope whatsoever of taking over the ship rebel against authority? Is that really a mutiny? I guess that is semantics and history will decide, I'm sure, that there has never been a mutiny in the United States Navy and there will never be a mutiny in the United States Navy."

That does seem to be the more or less official Navy position. Navy records and historical accounts produced under the auspices of the Navy never refer to the *Kitty Hawk* incident as a mutiny. They adhere to the same interpretation put forth by Townsend and Cloud: what happened was a disturbance, a violent uprising that was serious in both scope and potential for escalation, but not a mutiny because the rebels did not make any serious effort to take control of the bridge or seize the captain. The Navy also points out that the disturbance was relatively small, saying that if an aircraft carrier is like a city at sea, the riot took place only on a few city blocks. Keel and many other sailors who were there react with anger and indignation at such comments and say the Navy is just covering for itself by downplaying the severity of the incident. Keel is particularly incensed by the claim that the riot was small. "It was small only because the ship was so huge. You had hundreds of sailors terrorizing thousands of others. The idea that this was some small thing is just a lie."

In the years after his Navy service, Garland Young was troubled at least as much by his memories of the riot's aftermath as by the violence itself. He was called to testify during the prosecution of sailors after the riot but received death threats from the Black Panthers, and once he took the stand he was accused by defense attorneys of being a racist. After being disturbed by the experience for many years, Young applied for disability benefits with the Department of Veterans Affairs, citing depression stemming from posttraumatic stress disorder (PTSD) caused by the *Kitty Hawk* experience. Young's request was denied, and he says he received a letter explaining the main reason: Young had called the *Kitty Hawk* riot a "mutiny" in his application. "'There has never been and there never will be a mutiny on an American man of war,'" Young recalls the rejection letter stating.

Like many others, Young still thinks he survived a mutiny. "In my opinion, any time you try to take control of a ship and change its course from one place to another, that's a mutiny," Young says. In 1999, he received full disability benefits for a combination of PTSD and other health issues.

Many other sailors on board the *Kitty Hawk* that day still live with the memories of what they went through, terrible images and fears made all the worse because the Navy hardly acknowledged what happened to them. Robert Keel and John Travers, Perry Pettus, Chris Mason, and Garland Young still struggle to understand what happened to them and to make sense of it all. Travers still has nightmares about the rioters finding him up above the flight deck, where he had escaped from a mob, and throwing him overboard. He feels himself being thrown off the ship and landing in the dark waters, then watching the *Kitty Hawk* sail on. Perry Pettus still thinks often about seeing the man beaten with the fog foam nozzle and still feels guilt for his role in inciting the crowd. John Callahan, the sailor who was attacked in the shower, ended up getting conscientious objector status and was discharged soon after the riot. His terrifying experience was one reason he became a counselor specializing in the treatment of people who have suffered emotional and physical trauma. He says his experience in being attacked on the *Kitty Hawk* helps him understand his patients. G. Kirk Allen, the corpsman who treated wounded men in the sick bay while fighting off attackers, says images from that night are permanently fixed in his mind. "They will never go away, the rage on those guys' faces as they broke in and the absolute hatred that was bearing down on us," Allen says.

The ringleaders of the riot, including Terry Avinger, went on to more trouble and criminal activity after being discharged from the Navy, but some managed to straighten out their lives as they got older. After charges against Avinger related to the *Kitty Hawk* were dropped and he was court-martialed for a different assault charge, he was discharged in 1973. For several years, his life continued to swing wildly from promising to disappointing, just as it had before and during his time on the *Kitty Hawk*. He got his high school diploma after leaving the Navy, but he also began taking drugs, then spent time in jail, where he took college classes. He continued his studies after leaving jail, but before long he was serving a two-year sentence for drug trafficking. In 1984 Avinger finally found his footing for good and began what would be nineteen months of drug rehabilitation. After more education and an increasingly solid job history, he became an employee assistance counselor for Amtrak. Avinger is, by all accounts, an upstanding citizen whose goal now is to help those facing the same struggles that led him astray earlier and to show his grandchildren that it is never too late to do the right thing. Looking back on that period of his life with the perspective that comes with maturity and with his training in mental health, Avinger says he recognizes that his behavior was driven by unresolved grief issues related to the deaths of his brother and father. "That grief led to my behavioral responses, my aggressive behavior, my having a noncaring attitude about life in general," he says. "I was angry at God, and with some of the racial issues going on at the time, I was able to transfer my anger at God into racial hatred."

A hopeful sign of progress against the inequities that spurred his anger as a young man came when Avinger's own daughter attended Girard College, the kindergarten-through-twelfth-grade private institution whose segregation had so enraged him when he was younger and living in the Philadelphia neighborhood.

A CEASE-FIRE TOOK EFFECT in Vietnam on January 23, 1973. The *Kitty Hawk* was deployed in the western Pacific again in November 1973.

The *Kitty Hawk* riot was a turning point for race relations in the Navy. The incident revealed the simmering discontent among black sailors and showed that some of their anger was justified because of how they were recruited and how they were treated in the Navy. It also revealed that a significant portion of the problems stemmed from cultural misunderstandings—the white establishment of the old Navy just didn't get why some black sailors reacted negatively to what others saw as routine unpleasantness, such as mess deck duty.

Though that awareness came as the result of violence and criminal activity, the Navy finally recognized that it had to change how it dealt with black sailors. In the years to come, the Navy made many improvements in policies and procedures: Test standards were raised again to avoid sailors enlisting and then finding they were unqualified for advancement; criminal record limitations were tightened to eliminate the "thugs," such as some of those involved in the *Kitty Hawk* riot; recruiters were prohibited from overpromising about career potential and living conditions; voluntary racial segregation on ships was prohibited; and the Navy made sure minority sailors were given a formal system through which to complain and seek redress for grievances. The *Kitty Hawk* riot provided momentum for Admiral Elmo Zumwalt's fledgling effort to improve race relations. Within two years, the Navy provided a racial awareness seminar to more than 70 percent of all naval personnel. By 1977 the number of blacks in the Navy—both enlisted men and officers—was rising steadily, partly as a result of affirmative action programs. Sailors in today's Navy, of all races, benefit from many of the lessons learned in the *Kitty Hawk* incident.

Though the riot drew some media attention, it was quickly forgotten by most people. The Navy does not deny the story, but it has downplayed its scope and significance. The result is that few Americans know that it happened or realize how close the country came to seeing its own citizens killing one another on a ship that was supposed to be an example of America's best.

Fewer still know how a singular act of courage by a black executive officer prevented greater bloodshed. In his actions and words, Ben Cloud showed that there is more than one way for a military leader to sacrifice himself for his men and his country.

BIBLIOGRAPHY

INTERVIEWS AND CORRESPONDENCE WITH AUTHOR

Allen, G. Kirk
Avinger, Terry
Callahan, John
Cloud, Benjamin
Dysart, Tom
Keel, Robert
Mason, Chris
Pettus, Perry
Townsend, Marland
Travers, John
Young, Garland

PERIODICALS

"Black Pleads Guilty in Kitty Hawk Case." *The New York Times,* March 8, 1973, p. 31.

"Carrier Airman Convicted in Race Rioting in October." *The New York Times,* February 21, 1973, p. 26.

Communist Party, USA. "The Vietnam War and the Revolt of Black GIs." *Revolutionary Worker,* February 26, 1995.

"Congressional Investigators Ask Marines to Explain Role in Racial Trouble Aboard the Carrier Kitty Hawk." *The New York Times,* December 7, 1972, p. 24.

"Conviction of Black Overturned By Navy." *The New York Times,* February 28, 1973, p. 44.

"Court-Martial Opens for First of 21 Blacks on Carrier." *The New York Times,* December 30, 1972, p. 2.

"Hicks Seen Ideal Head for Kitty Hawk Probe." *The Washington Post,* December 4, 1972, p. A2.

"Hill Panel Criticizes Navy 'Permissiveness.'" *The Washington Post,* January 24, 1973, p. A3.

"House Inquiry Links Navy's Racial Strife to Laxity." *The New York Times,* January 24, 1973, p. 11.

"House Panel Ends Study of Disorders on Ships in Pacific." *The New York Times,* December 13, 1972, p. 17.

"Kitty Hawk Back at Home Port; Sailors Describe Racial Conflict." *The New York Times,* November 29, 1972, p. 24.

"Kitty Hawk Cases Frustrate Navy." *The New York Times,* March 16, 1973, p.11.

"Kitty Hawk Crewman Pleads Guilty on Charges of Rioting." *The New York Times,* February 6, 1973, p. 20.

"Kitty Hawk Crew Describes Racial Battle Aboard Ship." *The Washington Post,* November 24, 1972, p. A3.

"Kitty Hawk Officer Denies Orders Conflicted During Riot." *The Washington Post,* December 7, 1972, p. A3.

"Kitty Hawk Officer Traces Riot to Marine Dispersal of Blacks." *The New York Times,* January 26, 1973, p. 6.

"Kitty Hawk Sailor Enters Guilty Plea." *The New York Times,* January 6, 1973, p. 23.

"Kitty Hawk Sailor Guilty on One Count." *The New York Times,* January 3, 1973, p. 79.

"Kitty Hawk Trial Delay Requested." *The Washington Post,* November 6, 1972, p. A8.

"Last Kitty Hawk Case Completed." *The Washington Post,* April 10, 1973, p. A2.

"Last Trial Is Held in Kitty Hawk Case." *The New York Times,* April 11, 1973, p. 11.

"NAACP Says It Has Proof White Kitty Hawk Sailor Lied." *The Washington Post,* February 24, 1973, p. A10.

"Navy Withdraws Charge." *The New York Times,* January 12, 1973, p. 66.

"The New Captain, Another Queeg?" *Kitty Litter* (San Francisco, CA), Vol. 1, Issue 7 (August 1972).

"Prejudice and Perjury Charged in Investigation of Carrier Riot." *The New York Times,* February 24, 1973, p. 58.

"Sailor Tells Inquiry Blacks Beat White." *The New York Times,* December 27, 1972, p. 14.

"Sailors Cleared in Riot Charge." *The Washington Post,* January 13, 1973, p. B8.

"Sailors Describe Racial Battling." *The New York Times,* November 24, 1972, p. 17.

Socialist Worker Online. *Rebellion in the Ranks: The Solders' Revolt in Vietnam.* Accessed at www.socialistworker.org/2005-2/553/553_06_SoldiersRevolt.shtml.

"Storm Warnings." *Time,* December 11, 1972. Accessed at www.time.com/time/magazine/article/0,9171,878095,00.html.

"21 Black Sailors, Accused in Kitty Hawk Riot, Refuse to Appear Before Congressional Inquiry Unit." *The New York Times,* December 8, 1972, p. 19.

Vietnam Veterans Against the War Anti-Imperialist. *The Vietnam War and the Revolt of Black GIs.* Accessed at www/vvawai.org/sw/sw31/pgs_25–34/black_gis_revolt.html.

"Witness in Kitty Hawk Hearing Charges That Whites Beat Black Officer in Rioting on Carrier." *The New York Times,* December 26, 1972, p. 16.

BOOKS

Cortright, David, and Zinn, Howard. *Soldiers in Revolt: GI Resistance during the Vietnam War.* Chicago: Haymarket Books, 2005.

Guttridge, Leonard F. *Mutiny: A History of Naval Insurrection*. New York: Berkley Trade, 2002.

Sherwood, John Darrell. *Black Sailor, White Navy: Racial Unrest in the Fleet during the Vietnam War Era*. New York: New York University Press, 2007.

Woodman, Richard. *A Brief History of Mutiny: Furious, Savage and Bloody: 400 Years of Rebellion*. New York: Carroll & Graf Publishers, 2005.

OFFICIAL HEARINGS AND PUBLICATIONS

Commanding Officer, USS *Kitty Hawk*. "Command History, 1972." February 27, 1973.

Committee on Armed Services, House of Representatives, 92nd Congress, 2nd Session. *Hearings Before the Special Subcommittee on Disciplinary Problems in the U.S. Navy*. Washington, DC: United States Government Printing Office, 1973.

Department of Defense. *Project 100,000: Characteristics and Performance of "New Standards Men."* Washington, DC: Office of the Assistant Secretary of Defense, Manpower and Reserve Affairs, 1968.

Fey, Peter. *The Effects of Leadership on Carrier Air Wing Sixteen's Loss Rates During Operation Rolling Thunder, 1965–1968*. Fort Leavenworth, KS: U.S. Army Command General Staff College, 2006.

Haak, Frank S. *Investigative Report of November 18, 1972: Formal One-Officer Investigation to Inquire into the Circumstances Surrounding an Incident of Racial Violence which Occurred on Board USS KITTY HAWK (CVA 63) on the Night of 12 October 1972*. Washington, DC: United States Navy, 1972.

Mayo, George D. *Fleet Performance of Project 100,000 Personnel in the Aviation Structural Mechanic S (Structures) Rating*. San Diego: Naval Personnel Research Activity, 1969.

Reuter, W., ed. *1972 Westpac Cruise, USS* Kitty Hawk *CVA63* [cruise book]. San Diego: Pischel Yearbooks, 1972.

Sellman, Wayne. Statement on Post-Service Experiences of Project 100,000 [P/100000] Vets. Hearings Before the Subcommittee on Oversight and Investigations House Committee on Vets' Affairs, February 28, 1990.

USS *Kitty Hawk*. Media Kit. San Diego, 2008.

USS *Kitty Hawk*. Ship's log, 1972. Washington, DC: United States Navy, 1972.

NOTES

CHAPTER ONE

The material in this chapter is based on the recollections of Robert Keel. Most of the personal stories featured in the book are based on the recollections of the person being discussed, as told to the author, and usually confirmed by other records or consistent with known facts. Material not cited in these notes as coming from another source came from personal interviews with the subject.

CHAPTER TWO

Townsend's background is based on his account to the author.

p. 9. Townsend was beginning to doubt: John Darrell Sherwood, *Black Sailor, White Navy* (New York: New York University Press, 2007), pp. 69–70.

CHAPTER THREE

p. 17. "The methods that I used": Committee on Armed Services, House of Representatives, 92nd Congress, 2nd Ses., *Hearings Before the Special Subcommittee on Disciplinary Problems in the U.S. Navy* (Washington, DC: United States Government Printing Office, 1973), p. 583.

Cloud's background is based on his account to the author.

CHAPTER FOUR

p. 42. His college degree earned him: Sherwood, *Black Sailor, White Navy*, p. 66.

p. 43. Townsend was under the impression: Committee on Armed Services, House of Representatives, *Hearings*, p. 1133.

CHAPTER FIVE

p. 47. Military applicants had been screened since 1950: Wayne Sellman, Statement on Post-Service Experiences of Project 100,000 [P/100000] Vets, Hearings Before the Subcommittee on Oversight and Investigations House Committee on Vets' Affairs, February 28, 1990.

p. 48. Just over half of all project sailors: Department of Defense, *Project 100,000: Characteristics and Performance of "New Standards Men"* (Washington, DC: Office of the Assistant Secretary of Defense, Manpower and Reserve Affairs, 1968), p. 12.

p. 49. A 1969 assessment of their performance: George D. Mayo, *Fleet Performance of Project 100,000 Personnel in the Aviation Structural Mechanic S (Structures) Rating* (San Diego: Naval Personnel Research Activity, 1969), p. 29.

p. 49. "These data provide no evidence": Sellman, Statement on Post-Service Experiences.

p. 50. "using the nigger against the gook": Communist Party, USA, "The Vietnam War and the Revolt of Black GIs," *Revolutionary Worker*, February 26, 1995, p. 1.

p. 57. That kind of attitude led to a scathing attack: "The New Captain, Another Queeg?" *Kitty Litter*, Vol. 1, Issue 7 (August 1972).

p. 59. At first, resistance within military ranks: David Cortright and Howard Zinn, *Soldiers in Revolt: GI Resistance during the Vietnam War* (Chicago: Haymarket Books, 2005), p. 107.

p. 59. "Either quit the Army now": Communist Party, USA, "Vietnam War," p. 3.

p. 60. One poll found that 76 percent of black servicemen: Ibid.

p. 60. A publication of the Revolutionary Communist Party: Ibid.

p. 60. One of the most prominent uprisings was at Fort Bragg: Ibid., p. 70.

p. 60. A great many of the incidents: Ibid., p. 71.

p. 61. A particularly bad uprising took place: Ibid., pp. 73–74.

p. 61. In the Navy, until 1971: Ibid., p. 107.

p. 62. The Navy would record a total: Ibid., p. 912.

p. 62. Townsend had received classified messages: Committee on Armed Services, House of Representatives, *Hearings*, p. 525.

p. 64. The men often complained about the captain's mast: The captain's mast is named so because in earlier times the captain held the proceeding at the mizzenmast of a three-masted ship, the middle one that traditionally separated the officers' and crew's quarters.

p. 65. On June 8, 1972, Avinger: Sherwood, *Black Sailor, White Navy*, p. 72.

p. 69. Twenty-year-old James W. Radford: Committee on Armed Services, House of Representatives, *Hearings*, pp. 1003–1004.

p. 70. A white mess cook refused: "Storm Warnings," *Time*, December 11, 1972. Accessed at: www.time.com/time/magazine/article/0,9171,878095,00.html.

p. 72. formally organized command structure: Perry Pettus insists that no such organized structure existed among black sailors, that it was only imagined by whites on the *Kitty Hawk*. Marland Townsend and many officials who investigated following the riot disagree, saying that the command structure definitely existed, even though the less-involved black sailors might not have known it.

p. 73. One dap, known as Kill the Beast: This description of the anti-white dap is provided by Pettus.

p. 74. There were those who took all the symbolism: Committee on Armed Services, House of Representatives, *Hearings*, p. 787. Chief Aviation Ordnancemen Charles M. Johnson, who worked closely with XO Cloud as a legal officer on disciplinary matters with the crew, told the committee that he thought the number of seriously militant black sailors was small but that they pressured many more to show allegiance and participate in the riots on October 12. Black sailors were ridiculed and ostracized, or worse, if they did not show allegiance to the black cause on the *Kitty Hawk*, he told the committee. During the riot, Johnson said, he looked at a crowd of about 100 rampaging in the mess deck and guessed that only 10 or 20 of them had joined the group willingly.

CHAPTER SIX

p. 79. "Men of the *Kitty Hawk*": The actual words spoken by the captain were not recorded, but this is the way Garland Young recalls them. In particular, he recalls that the men thought the captain's choice of words and tone were insensitive for such a discouraging announcement.

p. 80. In July, a white sailor had jammed: Sherwood, *Black Sailor, White Navy,* p. 79.

p. 80. So, as he had done for the previous: Committee on Armed Services, House of Representatives, *Hearings,* p. 496.

p. 81. And these were very experienced women: Garland Young recalls that the black sailors on the *Kitty Hawk,* including a good friend of his, were upset because most of the prostitutes in Olongapo would not accept black customers. Not only were the black sailors offended by the discrimination, but they also were left sexually frustrated, he says. Young surmises that the inability for young black men to obtain the same relief that the white sailors enjoyed was one more factor contributing to the high tension on board.

p. 81. At the height of the war: Sherwood, *Black Sailor, White Navy,* p. 80.

p. 85. a black *Kitty Hawk* sailor, Airman Dwight W. Hornton: Ibid.

p. 86. a white shore patrolman from the oiler: Ibid.

p. 88. The investigator forced his way into the head: Ibid., p. 81.

CHAPTER SEVEN

p. 93. had the two Marines who had been posted: Committee on Armed Services, House of Representatives, *Hearings,* p. 604.

p. 95. Word was going around of how a white sailor: Ibid., pp. 603–604. Carlucci testified that, after investigation, the white sailor's version of the story was different, but apparently there had been some dispute between the two and some interaction with Filipino nationals. The Filipinos would not cooperate with the investigation, so Carlucci dropped it. The white sailor, however, had to live with the Marines for protection over the next several days.

p. 99. Townsend had the men sit: Townsend does not recall the incident described by Pettus, but he says it is consistent with how he would have reacted that day to news that Marines had handcuffed black sailors for being in groups of more than two. Pettus is certain that he and his friends were taken to the captain and that the captain apologized for their treatment.

p. 100. Another spat broke out: Sherwood, *Black Sailor, White Navy,* p. 83.

CHAPTER EIGHT

p. 108. Airman Rowe had been charged: Frank S. Haak, *Investigative Report of November 18, 1972: Formal One-Officer Investigation to Inquire into the Circumstances Surrounding an Incident of Racial Violence which Occurred on Board USS* KITTY HAWK *(CVA 63) on the Night of 12 October 1972* (Washington, DC: United States Navy, 1972), p. 77.

p. 111. A black gunnery sergeant named Robert L. Sellers: Committee on Armed Services, House of Representatives, *Hearings,* p. 601.

p. 112. watching the 1969 movie *Paint Your Wagon:* Ibid., p. 570.

p. 113. A legal officer who had been watching the movie: Sherwood, *Black Sailor, White Navy,* p. 84.

p. 115. That's how Carlucci found them: Committee on Armed Services, House of Representatives, *Hearings,* p. 601.

p. 116. Corporal Avina, a San Antonio, Texas, native: Ibid., p. 721.

p. 117. His hand was firmly planted on the holster: Ibid., p. 721. There is some dispute as to whether Avina was trying to draw his weapon or simply secure it during the scuffle. In the heat of the moment, and also thereafter, many black sailors insisted that Avina had tried to draw his weapon and that that is what set off the scuffle at the hatch. Avina testified that he was only trying to secure the loaded weapon after he felt someone pulling on his shoulder strap. He was not trying to draw it to use against the rioters but only to gain control of the gun once the scuffle began, he said. The sequence of events strongly suggests that there would have been no reason for Avina to choose that moment, as he was leaving and before the scuffle began, to draw his pistol.

p. 119. *I'm being put to the test:* Committee on Armed Services, House of Representatives, *Hearings,* p. 573. In testifying before the committee, Cloud recounted what he was thinking at the time, along with what he said to the crew and how he came to understand that his authenticity as a black man was being tested.

p. 120. *I'm going to either have to throw the XO out:* Ibid., p. 526.

p. 122. *If he gives any more black power salutes:* Ibid., p. 520.

CHAPTER NINE

p. 123. reviewed the procedures on responding to civil disobedience: Sherwood, *Black Sailor, White Navy,* p. 87.

p. 124. Carlucci suggested that Townsend and the XO: Ibid.

p. 124. "We're going to have three-man patrols": Committee on Armed Services, House of Representatives, *Hearings,* p. 602. Carlucci's orders are presented as he recalled them during his testimony to the committee.

p. 126. "They're at it again": Ibid., p. 575.

p. 128. sank his teeth into the man's flesh: Ibid., p. 805.

p. 129. "No more of this! This is the end!": Ibid., p. 533.

p. 130. "That is an error, a mistake on the part of the Marines": Ibid.

p. 130. Townsend told First Sergeant Binkley: Ibid., p. 603.

p. 130. He thought Townsend looked in control: Ibid., p. 576.

p. 134. "They're killing our brothers!": Ibid., p. 519.

p. 135. Radford was resting in his berthing area: Ibid., p. 1,003.

p. 136. "Hey, there's the man that gave Wilson the hassle": Ibid. The testimony in the report was altered to remove the names of those sailors who were facing criminal charges; the report has Radford referring to "Sailor 14" instead of using the man's name. "Wilson" is a pseudonym for this sailor.

CHAPTER TEN

p. 143. The ship's store, where sailors could buy: Some *Kitty Hawk* veterans report that when the ship's officers and Navy investigators were collecting evidence following the riot, they found "negatives" from Polaroid cameras that had been stolen from the ship's store. The rioters reportedly stole the cameras and film and used them to take pictures of each other ransacking the store, discarding the portion of the film that was peeled off to develop the photograph. These "negatives" supposedly showed some of the rioters and could have been used as evidence against them. The author's attempt to access this material and other investigative records resulted in a letter from the Department of the Navy stating that "the entire record is missing and presumed lost."

p. 147. The Marine stayed where he was: Because Callahan is now a mental health professional who works with people who have experienced traumatic incidents, he readily acknowledges that such people sometimes recall in vivid detail things that did not actually happen. He says he recalls this incident with the Marine quite clearly, but because it is hard to imagine that the Marine rendered no aid at all, he sometimes wonders if it really happened.

p. 150. Seaman William E. Boone: Committee on Armed Services, House of Representatives, *Hearings,* pp. 933–945. This account of Boone's experience is taken from his testimony to the committee.

Boone was facing criminal charges stemming from the riot, which he told the committee were unfounded because he was a victim, not a rioter. He was represented by counsel during his testimony. The outcome of his criminal charges is unknown.

p. 154. Boatswain's Mate Second Class James W. Brown: Ibid., pp. 682–683.

p. 156. "We are going to do what you white honkies can't do!": Ibid., p. 683.

CHAPTER ELEVEN

p. 164. He also noticed that a Marine: Committee on Armed Services, House of Representatives, *Hearings,* p. 802.

p. 165. About a dozen black sailors came charging down: Ibid., p. 722.

p. 166. Anderson himself put up a good fight: Ibid., p. 802.

p. 167. Brock saw a large mob: Ibid., p. 733.

p. 168. "We're going to kill him": Ibid., p. 576.

p. 169. "You are not going to sleep tonight": Ibid., p. 777.

p. 169. "You fucked the niggers": Ibid., p. 787.

p. 171. So he told Binkley to stay with the chiefs: Ibid., p. 577.

p. 171. "They got the captain!": Ibid., p. 578. Cloud took the statements seriously. In Cloud's testimony to the committee, he said: "Armed with the information that I had, and the reasonableness of the situation existing as I saw it, namely, the captain being in an environment completely surrounded by a group of hostile blacks, I thought it was very, very possible that he could have been injured and it could have been very, very possible that he could have been killed at that point."

p. 172. "This is the executive officer speaking": Haak, *Investigative Report,* pp. 30, 578. The XO's statement is reproduced as found in the Navy report, which is taken from onboard recordings of the 1MC announcements. In Cloud's testimony to the committee, he said, "My plea over the 1MC was very impassionate," and it is clear from the context of his statement that he meant without emotion. But the sailors who heard it uniformly report a different impression, saying Cloud sounded panicky and scared. Cloud says his announcement was justified by information he had at the time and that any senior officer would have done the same thing, "being concerned, as he would have been, for the safety and integrity of the ship."

CHAPTER TWELVE

p. 176. *Why is the XO taking over the ship?:* Committee on Armed Services, House of Representatives, *Hearings,* p. 534. These thoughts are taken directly from Townsend's testimony to the committee in which he described hearing Cloud's message and his immediate reaction to it. Townsend went on to tell the committee, directly after those comments, that he soon realized the XO had the best intentions: "He was, I must stress, trying to do his job the best he could. He had been aboard for less than eight weeks, had limited command experience, and had limited shipboard experience at that. But he is a damn good man and working to the best of his ability." In the heat of the moment, however, Townsend reacted very negatively to Cloud's actions.

p. 177. Townsend was full of anger: Ibid., p. 534. It bears repeating that this was Townsend's thinking at the time, in the middle of the crisis, but he soon softened his impressions of Cloud's actions that day.

p. 178. he seriously considered firing Cloud on the spot: Townsend confirmed to the author that he considered dismissing Cloud on the spot. He soon changed his assessment of the XO's actions and was satisfied he was correct in not firing him.

p. 178. "If anybody ever writes a book about this ship": Committee on Armed Services, House of Representatives, *Hearings,* p. 534. Townsend also recounted this comment to the author. A December 11,

1972, article in *Time* magazine claimed the comment was made over the 1MC as Townsend was countermanding Cloud's orders to the crew, but that is inaccurate. Townsend made the comment directly to Cloud.

p. 178. "This is the captain": Haak, *Investigative Report,* p. 31. The captain's words are rendered exactly as found in the Navy report, which is taken from onboard recordings of the 1MC announcements.

p. 179. "Captain, I am scared to death": Committee on Armed Services, House of Representatives, *Hearings,* p. 785.

p. 180. Chastened by Townsend's countermanding his orders: Ibid. The conversation between Cloud and Townsend is based on his recollection of it to the committee. The words are not exact quotes but reflect the content and tone of what was said by the two men, according to Cloud's testimony.

p. 181. Cloud stepped into their path: Ibid., p. 581. In his testimony to the committee, Cloud tried to put a soft spin on the incident. He said he was "knocked down to the ground, but it was a collision which was just as much my responsibility as it was theirs. It was not an assault."

p. 182. "You know your way won't work." Ibid. This passage is taken from the exact words that Cloud used to recount the confrontation to the committee. He told the committee that he recognized the sailor as Avinger.

p. 183. By now he was recognizing that his urgent address: Ibid., p. 579. In his testimony to the committee, Cloud explained that he thought the announcement was the right strategy at that moment but soon started to wonder if he had acted in haste. He said that, even at the time of his testimony, he still thought it was the right strategy to try to isolate the black sailors in the aft mess deck but that "had I been armed with the information that the commanding officer was in good health, there is no doubt in my mind that I would not have made that announcement."

p. 186. A petty officer ordered Marvin Davidson: Sherwood, *Black Sailor, White Navy,* p. 96.

CHAPTER THIRTEEN

p. 191. "You made this mess. You fix it." This account is provided by Robert Keel. Townsend does not recall this specific incident in detail, but he confirms that he was in a forward berthing area and at one point was searching for a black sailor he knew was respected by the crew. Garland Young recalls a very similar incident happening in his berthing area, when the captain stopped by to ask a black sailor to come help negotiate with the rioters. That black sailor also turned down the captain.

p. 192. When Cloud reached the forecastle: Committee on Armed Services, House of Representatives, *Hearings,* p. 583. The passage in which Cloud makes his dramatic speech to the black sailors is taken from his own testimony to the committee, in which he recounted in detail the mood, his actions, and his words to the crowd. Details also have been confirmed to the author by Cloud and sailors who were there. Cloud told this author he was emotional and "impassioned" in giving the speech.

p. 197. The white sailors stepped aside: Haak, *Investigative Report,* exhibit 168. Pettus did not know the identity of the man he saw beaten with the fog nozzle, and he was not present when Patrick was rescued, so there is no way to know with certainty that it was the same man. But there is strong reason to believe that Patrick was indeed the man Perry Pettus saw attacked with the fog nozzle. The official medical report on Patrick states that he was attacked in his bunk, but Patrick was not found in a berthing area, as one might expect if he were attacked there, but in the communications office near the forecastle, where he apparently was taken for refuge from the mob. All the records agree that Patrick was the most seriously injured man on the *Kitty Hawk.* Pettus remembers the beating he saw involving blows to the head that would be consistent with the injuries Patrick suffered. The author was unable to contact Patrick for confirmation.

CHAPTER FOURTEEN

p. 201. Cloud made his way to a berthing area: Committee on Armed Services, House of Representatives, *Hearings,* p. 587.

p. 204. "Look, you were very helpful": Ibid., p. 520. This conversation is taken from Townsend's testimony to the committee, in which he recounted the conversation with Cloud, and from Townsend's interviews with the author.

CHAPTER FIFTEEN

p. 210. Found guilty of those charges: Sherwood, *Black Sailor, White Navy,* p. 98.

p. 211. Though there was little violence: Ibid., p. 150.

p. 211. "The subcommittee is directed to inquire": Committee on Armed Services, House of Representatives, *Hearings,* p. 1.

p. 212. "We cannot overlook the possibility": Ibid., p. 2.

p. 212. the attacks "went along too smoothly": Ibid., p. 646.

p. 213. "I have the feeling it was an organized thing." Ibid., p. 776.

p. 213. also heard from twenty-year-old seaman Charles A. Beck: Ibid., p. 996.

p. 214. "This, it seems to me, was deliberate mutiny": Ibid., p. 889.

p. 216. "just plain thugs": Ibid., p. 506.

p. 216. "I felt it unsafe to do that": Ibid., p. 519.

p. 217. "The Marines were never called out": Ibid., p. 526.

p. 217. "plans for flooding the space with khaki": Ibid., p. 527.

p. 218. "among the black community on the ship": Ibid., p. 554.

p. 219. "tokenism in its truest form": Ibid., p. 555.

p. 220. "The methods that I used": Ibid., p. 583.

p. 221. "And if for the sake of my career": Ibid., p. 575.

EPILOGUE

p. 223 "[T]he riot on the *Kitty Hawk*": "Hill Panel Criticizes Navy 'Permissiveness,'" *The Washington Post,* January 24, 1973, p. A3.

p. 223. "permissiveness exists in the Navy today": "House Inquiry Links Navy's Racial Strife to Laxity," *The New York Times,* January 24, 1973, p. 11.

p. 223. The "Command History" of the *Kitty Hawk:* Commanding Officer, USS *Kitty Hawk,* "Command History, 1972," February 27, 1973, p. 4.

p. 226. The Navy also points out: Sherwood, *Black Sailor, White Navy,* p. 99. The author, Sherwood, is citing testimony to the subcommittee by Cloud but seems to agree with the assessment. Sherwood is an official historian with the U.S. Naval Historical Center.

p. 230 Within two years, the Navy: Ibid., p. 192.

p. 230. By 1977 the number of blacks in the Navy: Ibid.

INDEX